T5-AXN-092

# THE MANAGEMENT OF HEADQUARTERS–SUBSIDIARY RELATIONSHIPS IN MULTINATIONAL CORPORATIONS

To
Ruben Rausing


This book is dedicated to Dr Ruben Rausing at his
85th birthday June 17, 1980. Dr Rausing is a honory
doctor at the Stockholm School of Economics 1959,
industrialist and entrepreneur, founder of Tetra Pak,
initiator of the Institute of International Business
in 1975 and a very generous contributor to the institute.

# THE MANAGEMENT OF HEADQUARTERS-SUBSIDIARY RELATIONSHIPS IN MULTINATIONAL CORPORATIONS

*edited by*
Lars Otterbeck

**St. Martin's Press    New York**

658.04
M266

ISBN 0-312-51233-3

M.R

Library of Congress Cataloging in Publication Data

Main entry under title:

The Management of headquarters.

1.    International business enterprises   -
Management - Addresses,  essays, lectures.
2.    Subsidiary corporations - Management -
Addresses, essays, lectures.  I. Otterbeck,
Lars, 1942 -
HD62.4.M36   1981      658. 1'8      81-9129
ISBN 0-312-51233-3                    AACR2

v

# Contents

# Appendices, Figures and Tables in the Chapters

# 1  Lars Otterbeck:

# Introduction and Overview

How are multinational corporations actually managed?
What goes on inside the corporation between the home
country firm (parent company or headquarter) and the
local firm (subsidiary or affiliated company)? What
autonomy does Siemens, IBM, or Ericsson leave its
subsidiaries? How are strategies formed in Brown
Boveri, Bristol Myers, or ICI? What control systems
are used in SKF, IVECO, or Mitsubishi? These are
the questions that are addressed and answered in
the articles of this book.

## Background

During the 1970's a steady stream of books and articles dealing with various aspects of the multinational
corporation has appeared. The articles in this book
add to our understanding of the MNC by reporting on
new research that analyzes the relationships within
the MNC. These relationships are often triggered by
external circumstances but without a good understanding of what actually goes on inside the system one
cannot foresee or understand how the MNC will respond
to external influence.

## Biases in Past Research

It seems as if what has been written about MNCs and
what is usually taught in classrooms has several
biases.

Bias 1. The focus is American. It is true that US
corporations still dominate the world of international business, but to a diminishing extent. The pio-
neers in research on the MNC were Americans (illu-
strating the first stage in the product life cycle
concept à la Vernon). The market power of leading
business schools, leading journals and printing

houses and the ready acceptance of the rest of the
world of obviously powerful theoretical explanations
have led to a continued dominance of the American
focus. This focus implies that text books tend to
assume that MNCs are among other things

- very, very large
- industrial corporations
- with a large sophisticated home market
- whose international operations are relatively
  small (seldom more than 50 %) and of recent origin
  (less than 60 years).

These companies also operate under strict antitrust
regulations. Their management style is very competitive. Direct confrontation is all right. One speaks
a language which almost everybody in the business
world understands.

Bias 2. Economic theory can explain companies' external behavior. The doctrines that are most adhered
to were formulated before the MNC became an actor on
the international scene. But entities that internally
administer flows of goods, capital, information and
people across borders may behave very differently
from what the theory prescribes about relations between independent actors.

Bias 3. The writer, teacher or analyst typically
takes a partisan role in the emotional field that
MNCs seem to develop. They are either inherently
bad - and must be controlled, restricted or forbidden - or inherently good - and must be left for
themselves or maybe supported. Since MNCs are often
perceived as powerful, outsiders such as noncommitted
academic writers often tend to take an adversary
role.

Bias 4. MNCs can be understood by looking at their
formal structure, their products and their financial
situation. Difficulties in getting access to more
sensitive data probably account for this bias.

## A Re-Direction of Research

This book tries to steer clear of biases like those
mentioned, at times by introducing counter-balances
biases.

In our development of management programs and academic courses in international business, where the stu-
dents usually come from European countries and work
or will work in European companies, it has been
evident that people do not easily fell comfortable
with material which does not appeal to their common

sense. Since there is no Theory of International Business (and God help us, there never will be) one needs to balance the material so that economic theory dominates where appropriate, organization theory where it helps, antropology where it fits, etc. In such efforts I have found a lack of material in how the internal functioning of the MNC system is managed.

This may be illustrated with an incidence from a conference we organized where a very high ranking U.N. official refused to believe that a large MNC after having been repeatedly disappointed with its long range planning attempts had stopped making such plans and was merely muddling through. The U.N. official, well trained in economics and believing firmly that businessmen were rational, could not accpet that large economic units were so careless as not to plan, and, "besides how can one control an entity which cannot even control itself"?

Ever since the Institute of International Business at the Stockholm School of Economics was formed in 1975, we have tried to direct our research efforts so as to come close to the realities of international business. In these efforts we have been greatly helped by the very open and supportive attitude of most Swedish firms and by the School's excellent reputation as an institution where serious and valid research is done.

The largest research project so far conducted at the Institute is called Managing the Relations between Headquarters and Foreign Operations in Multinationals. This project was started in 1976 and was designed in collaboration with researchers also from other countries (see articles by Hedlund, Leksell, Negandhi, Otterbeck and Welge in this book). As this project was coming to its fulfillment we thought it might be fruitful to gather researchers from all over the world with an interest in the internal functioning of transnationals.

The symposium was held on June 1-4, 1980. No fewer than 33 researchers from 14 countries participated actively in very constructive discussions. 30 papers were presented of which those most relevant to the core of the present subject are included here.

In the editing of the papers I have tried to preserve the flavour of each paper so that the reader may get a feeling for the cultural biases in them. In a field so rich of cultural misperceptions it is important to remember that also the thoughtful observer/analyst has his own biases.

Not only national culture but also research tradition strongly affects the way the analyst observes reality and the way he interprets it. Like so many other examples of gatherings of social scientists we shall find here that the methodology used to analyze a given phenomenon can vary a great deal.

## The Articles

In the first paper SINGH gives an expose of parent-affiliate relations in MNCs as they relate to developing countries. This paper highlights several of the important considerations relevant for MNC managers and government officials in any type of country. There is no doubt that host countries will demand that the local subsidiary not be left at the discretion of a foreign parent, that an increasing amount of R&D, production etc. is done locally and that training for locals be more common. The issue is one of balancing the subsidiary's integration in a global corporate network with its integration in a national economic and social system. The questions of ownership, control and transfer of tangible and intangible resources become important considerations.

## Autonomy of affiliates

One important research area regarding the relations between parent company and foreign subsidiary of affiliated companies is how decision making power is allocated between the units. It has often been assumed that it would be in the interest of the company to centralize decision making power to the highest extent possible whereas the host country was assumed to demand as large a degree of autonomy for the local affiliate. Such a crude and simplified notion seems rather naive in the light of the findings reported here. Forces such as economics of global standardization and rationalization, responsiveness to local markets, financial coordination, motivation of local employees etc. all suggest that the matter may be more complex. Also one might assume that there are differences between industries, between companies of different home country origins and also differences that bear upon the tradition and growth history of the company. It may not even be a question of a zero-sum game where the parent and the affiliate in some way share a given amount of power. Maybe some companies have found effective ways of handling the relationships that do not easily lend themselves to an interpretation on a one dimensional scale. We may recall the concepts of ethnocentric, polycentric and regiocentric companies introduced by Permutter (1965) or the open vs. close relationships by Brooke & Remmers (1970) as alternative concepts.

HEDLUND reports on an in-depth study on six Swedish multinationals and 24 of their foreign subsidiaries and affiliated companies. Here a "critical incidence" method is applied to validate the overall findings from interviews. Also a sample from US and Japanese companies is used for comparison. Hedlund finds the subsidiaries of Swedish firms to be very autonomous (with differences among functions and between types of firms) and, closely related to this finding, they are also managed in an informal and personalized manner.

Autonomy may be interesting per se, but whether there is a level of autonomy that is associated with a high degree of effectiveness would be important to know when designing the structure of a MNC system. In a study of German chemical firms WELGE proposes that indeed high autonomy or "low coordination intensity is ... correlated with above average economic and social effectiveness". This finding is very thought provoking. According to popularly held views, chemical firms should derive very tangible advantages from large scale operations and global coordination. In addition, the stereotype of an (effective) German firm would hardly be a loose uncoordinated, decentralized one. There seems to be no doubt as to the reliability of Welge's findings. But, like any other study in the social sciences the question of causality, if there is any and if so, in what direction cannot be proved by data but rather suggested by interpretation.

NEGANDHI and BALIGA, in their report on American, German and Japanese firms, find centralization to be gaining in strength again, particularly for US and German firms. The authors voice a fear that the drive for global rationalization may have gone too far.

## Administrative processes

Large MNCs seem to be among the most complex of organizations. Not only do they operate on several markets, they also typically have a number of products. They are staffed with people of different training, nationality and who speak different languages. The infrastructure and the environment may differ from one subsidiary to the next. Laws and traditions differ, etc.

The section on administrative processes in MNCs offers new insights from very penetrating studies made by researchers with a wide cultural background (i.e. who have different cultural biases). The companies studied are headquartered in the United States, Germany, Sweden, France, Japan and other countries. And their subsidiaries are "everywhere".

BARTLETT and KAGONO take on the by now almost classi-
cal sequence of organizational forms for MNCs that
came out of the Harvard Multinational Enterprise
Study, led by Vernon.

In textbooks we learn that MNCs go through stages
of organizational structures, starting with a functional orientation. Then an export department is
added; this department becomes an international
division; meanwhile the rest of the corporation may
be given a product division structure; then perhaps
reional divisions (if narrow product line) or world-
wide product divisions (abandoning the international
division) and finally, in the ultimate stage, MATRIX.

Bartlett's article illustrates a fundamental methodological problem. By looking beyond organizational
structures he has found many more devices that MNCs
use in order to respond to the multifocussed demands
from their environments. The five US food companies
he studied have all retained a fairly simple structure with an international division and rather than
going through dramatic structural changes they have
adopted other means to allow for a "flexible multi-
demensional decision making process". The point, or
the normative implication, here is: don't make things
more complicated than they need be. Who said that
matrices are effective? They appeal to researchers,
because they are complex.

Kagono shows that Bartlett's findings are neither
unique to the US environment, nor a product of
Bartlett's research methodology. He also demon-
strates a higher performance for companies with
simpler structures! Using very formalized, structured
methods on a large sample of large Japanese firms,
Kagono tests a set of hypotheses, derived from research during the last decade or so. The author
expects to find the functional form of organization
to be more suited to firms facing more certain and
less complex environments and the multidimensional
form for complex and uncertain environments. Divisions are also expected to be given higher autonomy
as the complexity of their task environments increases. The power should shift from production to
marketing and then to R&D and finally more complex
integrative devices should be introduced.

The results are well-founded and striking. The author
concludes that "a simple structure with a single primary focus may work better than a sophisticated
structure with dual focus of corporate-wide level
even in a highly uncertain and complex environment".

Without preempting our discussion in the final chapter we might ask two questions at this stage:

1. Do the Japanese have a culturally inherited skill in working "in the matrix mode" without adopting a matrix structure?

2. Are some strategies simply too complex for a single firm, i.e. is there a trade-off between strategic complexity and organizational complexity?

The last question leads us to the article by DOZ & PRAHALAD which study in considerable depth strategies, structures and processes in a few large MNCs headquartered in the United States and Europe. Doz & Prahalad use an unorthodox method of research. They collect a wealth of data on the MNCs they study and on their industries and environments, seemingly without any clear framework in mind. They then try to establish some pattern in what constitutes effective or ineffective processes. This method, indidentally, is not totally unlike the one used by Hedlund, Leksell & Otterbeck.

In their contribution, PRAHALAD & DOZ discuss what the parent needs to be able to exercise legitimate control over its subsidiaries. When products are new or unique, subsidiaries are dependent upon HQ and control is easy to achieve. As products mature and subsidiaries grow, such control, called "substantive" in the article, becomes increasingly difficult to achieve. HQs have to increasingly rely on administrative control, or more direct and overt methods. In maturing industries also host governments tend to demand, and with some force, that subsidiaries be more autonomous (cf Singh). Larger mature subsidiaries may have managements that strive for independence and try to expand the subsidiary's activities outside the scope of the parent'.

Joint ventures are more common in mature industries. Here there is a partner to take account of (joint ventures will be more thoroughly dealt with later). The conditions make it very difficult for the maturing MNC to exercise effective strategic control over its joint ventures. Conclusion? Stay in early-life-cycle business? But to stay in such businesses requires frequent strategic shifts which demands control ... Or, following Welge, it does not matter if HQ loses control; in fact it might be advantageous for the individual MNC.

In the following paper in this section LEKSELL reports on the administrative processes in six Swedish

high technology but fairly mature MNCs. The important
contribution of this paper is to show the wide range
of mechanisms that are used for coordinating the
company. The sheer complexity of the personalized
ways of managing, (through visits, telephone conversations and career policies) casts in doubt any
attempt to capture the relations in simple one-
dimensional scales.

Finally LINDGREN and SPÅNGBERG report on typical
patterns of taking control after a MNC has acquired
a foreign company.

## Ownership and transfer policies

The issue of ownership has been raised in several of
the papers, starting already in Singh's. Host countries more and more demand local ownership. Very
tight coordination (centralization) regarded as
necessary by some MNCs for global rationalization,
is often assumed to require 100 % ownership by the
MNC. The first few papers in this section deal explicitly with the aspect of headquarter-subsidiary relations that have a bearing upon the degree to which
the parent owns or should own "its" foreign affiliate.

HOLTON prefers to phrase his paper in a strictly
normative manner. He is mainly concerned with the
process of entering into joint ventures. Based upon
the author's experience and first-hand observations
on joint ventures, particularly in developing countries, he concludes that the business plan is the critical element for a successful joint venture. The
process of drawing up such a plan requires that the
partners carefully think through their future relation in all its aspects.

Once joint ventures have been entered into they have
to be managed. OTTERBECK's paper reports on the same
six Swedish multinational that were the empirical
foundation for Hedlund's and Leksell's papers. These
are firms that have wholly owned subsidiaries and
joint ventures among their foreign affiliates.
Striking similarities are found in the way these
MNCs actually go about the day to day management of
wholly owned and partially owned "subsidiaries". Until these findings are challenged we might ask our-
selves whether MNCs are not, on the whole, too
afraid of sharing ownership, i.e. whether 100 %
ownership is neccessary. Bearing in mind Prahalad's
& Doz's view that for a MNC to be able to exercise
substantive control it needs something more than just
ownership, we might also ask whether ownership is
ever sufficient.

The final step in decreased ownership share seems to be foreign operations under a management contract with no equity, or only a very minor share, on the part of the MNC. BROOKE and HOLLY in their paper discuss such forms for international business activity. The authors report on early experiences by British firms in contractural agreements and lay the groundwork for a new study which is to tell us whether such firms are effective in transferring technology.

## Public Affairs

While the internal mangement of MNCs has been in focus throughout this book, we must not forget that the internal activities bear upon the firms relation to and adaptation to its environment.

In the last paper presented here BLAKE reports on a survey of what roles headquarters and subsidiaries have in managing the public affairs function, i.e. roughly the relationships to the firms's non-commercial environmnet. Drawing on results from an admittedly very small sample Blake concludes that headquarter's involvement is higher in the formulation of public affairs policies than in the implementation and evaluation of such policies. However, its involvement is low throughout, as is that of subsidiaries. Whether this means that the MNC as a whole is too little concerned with public affairs or that managements do not (yet) recognize it as a function cannot be answered by this study.

I trust that the reader will find the articles interesting and challenging. The thoughtful businessman will find ideas, suggestions for change and well substantiated recommendations. The researcher or student will find insights from the world of MNCs as well as some solid pieces of conclusive findings.

In the final chapter we shall try to synthesize some of the ideas put forward and see what broad conclusions can be drawn from this first attempt at collecting what the world has to offer in terms of research on how MNCs really function.

# 2 Rana K. D. N. Singh:

# Policy Issues and Trends in Parent-Affiliate Relationships in Developing Countries

The last decade has witnessed important changes in relations between developing countries and trans-national corporations (TNCs), which are likely to have significant impact on the relationships be-tween parent companies and their subsidiaries and affiliates in these countries. Varying patterns of foreign investment and technological participation by TNCs have emerged in several countries, largely in response to deliberate policies of host-country governments. Several of the policy issues with which governments in these countries have been most con-cerned revolve around the question of parent-affili-ate relationships and the degree of autonomy that TNC subsidiaries and affiliates can, and need to exercise.

There is no uniformity in the extent of control exercised over foreign branches and subsidiaries (over 50 % ownership by parent companies), or TNC affiliates, by parent companies. This has not only been a function of historical and socio-economic circumstances but also varies from sector to sector and is dependent on several factors including local managerial and technological capability, availabili-ty of skilled personnel and other production and service inputs and, increasingly, on national poli-cies in host countries towards foreign investment and technology. Measurement of the extent of autono-my at subsidiary/affiliate level is difficult, though several empirical studies have been made in

Director, Information Analysis Division, UN Centre on Transnational Corporations New York. The views in the paper are those of the author.

this regard. This is largely because comparable information is difficult to obtain and analyse and because conclusions usually have to be based on qualitative, and often subjective, assessments of management personnel. By and large, however, it is generally recognised that effective control on basic issues related to investments and returns is sought to be retained by parent companies, while varying degrees of autonomy are exercised by subsidiaries and affiliates in day-to-day operations. Since decisions relating to investments and returns can cover a wide range of activities relating to financing, procurement, production and marketing operations, the nature and extent of control by parent companies can be very significant, in a large number of cases. The approach towards global rationalisation of production and distribution by major transnational corporations in several production sectors has also resulted in a tendency to view the problem of parent-affiliate relationships as principally a global management function. This would, at best, be only partially true in countries and situations where a free market mechanism, in terms of enterprise operations, does not wholly prevail.

It has to be considered, in this context, whether parent-affiliate relationships in developing countries need to be considered on a different footing. The difference arises largely from the fact that, in several countries, governmental policies are increasingly being oriented towards varying degrees of regulation and monitoring of the activities of TNC subsidiaries and affiliates, with a view to effectively integrating these activities with host country objectives. As specific policies and measures on various aspects of foreign investment and foreign technology and services are implemented in different countries, the concept of global rationalisation of production may need to be reoriented and adjusted to national country situations. In some cases, the impact of such policies on parent-affiliate relationships may not have been significant so far, but trends in governmental policies undoubtedly require much greater adjustment on the part of transnational companies in respect of subsidiary/affiliate operations. This would, in principle, be equally applicable in the case of wholly-owned or majority-owned subsidiaries or in respect of joint ventures, though in the case of the latter, the fact of a different ownership structure may have more direct implications on parent-affiliate relationships.

The changing industrial conditions and bargaining capability in several developing countries are reflected in a wide range of policies towards TNCs. Because of major variations in political philosophy, socio-economic conditions and levels of development, policies towards TNCs vary considerably. Some developing countries, which regard the market mechanism as being adequate to channel investment resources into desired growth sectors, have accorded considerable freedom of action to TNCs while other countries have set up various mechanisms to regulate the operations of such corporations. The latter approach is often related to the growth of domestic industrial enterprises, both in the public and private sectors. In general, however, greater national participation and control are being exercised over utilization of natural resources. The growth of domestic entrepreneurial capability, combined with considerable technological development in certain countries, has led to greater emphasis on national participation and control of TNC affiliates and towards alternative corporate and contractual arrangements instead of wholly-owned TNC branches and subsidiaries. Several countries have also built up a legal and administrative framework and introduced various degrees of regulation and control over TNC investments and operations with a view to channelling TNC participation for fulfilment of particular needs and priorities. Such regulation is intended principally to ensure maximum contribution of TNCs to industrial growth and harmonization of their activities to the objectives of host countries which, from a long-term viewpoint, would also be in the interest of such corporations.

During the 1980s, there has been a significant change in the pattern of foreign ownership of affiliate companies, largely in response to policies of host developing countries. In the petroleum and mineral sector, state enterprises have been set up in several developing countries, which have either assumed full ownership rights consequent on nationalization or a gradually increased share of ownership. A greater degree of national participation is also taking place in the downstream processing of such resources, particularly in new projects in petrochemicals and mineral processing undertaken either through state or nationally-owned enterprises, or through TNC affiliates. In the manufacturing sector, the trend is increasingly towards the establishment of joint ventures, with varying degrees of foreign capital ownership, particularly where domestic capital is available and forthcoming. This has been possible because of greater availability and active participation of national partners in several countries. Though these developments have had significant impact on parent-affiliate relations, effective control continues to rest with the foreign partner in a large proportion of joint ventures and is often embodied in management and technical-service agreements. The trend towards joint ventures is also primarily evident in new investment propositions while earlier TNC investments continue to remain in the form of wholly-owned or foreign-majority affiliates, though there is growing pressure in several countries for increased domestic participation in ownership.

An important variation to a joint venture is for national enterprises to acquire foreign technology and knowhow and to utilize foreign technological services through contractual arrangements. The direct costs on account of technology fees and royalties by developing countries are projected to increase from about $1 billion in 1975 to $6 billion in 1985, representing 15 % of direct trade in technology. Technology licensing and contractual arrangements for project implementation and for subsequent management, marketing, and other technical services are being increasingly used in several developing countries as an alternative to foreign capital participation. The pattern of parent-affiliate relations is obviously different in such cases and is governed largely by contractual terms and conditions.

The trends in TNC activities in developing countries indicate a wide range of alternative forms of capital and technological participation, which have varying implications in parent-affiliate relationships. This question has, however, to be considered in the light of the overall implications and impact of TNC activities and possible areas of divergence between TNC interests and those of host developing countries. In extractive industries, involving large capital outlays, TNCs have constituted an important channel for mobilization of financial and technological resources, including management expertise. In the manufacturing sector, the inflow of capital and technology through TNCs has brought about considerable industrial diversification in several developing countries and significant diffusion of technological knowhow and capability. Despite these positive contributions, the pattern of operations of TNCs in developing countries has also had negative results and adverse impact on national entrepreneurial development and growth of technological capability in certain fields and has posed several problems and difficulties. The areas of possible divergence of interest need to be identified and measures taken to harmonise such interests in order that the potential contribution of TNCs to development and industrialisation is maximized. Since most of these issues relate to the pattern of operations of TNC subsidiaries and affiliates, the relationship between parents and affiliates on the one hand and between such affili-

15

ates and host country governments and institutions assume growing importance.

## AREAS OF POSSIBLE DIVERGENCE OF INTEREST

The potential areas of divergence between host country objectives and operations of TNCs may relate to activities external to the enterprise set up with TNC participation or to the nature and operations of such an enterprise. The former includes activities which constitute interference in internal political affairs and in the socio-political structure of host countries or which seek to subvert or violate national policies, laws and institutions, through corrupt and illegal practices. Areas of divergence in enterprise operations with which this paper is primarily concerned include (i) the nature of TNC investments, including the method of entry and areas of activity; (ii) the pattern of ownership and the degree of domestic participation in equity and in decision-making, both for new investments and existing TNC affiliates; (iii) the structure of production envisaged for developing-country affiliates, including the extent of downstream activities in resource-based industries and local content or value-added in manufacturing enterprises, together with policies related to domestic and foreign purchases and sales, including exports; (iv) financial implications of attracting TNC investments and of their operations, including the pattern of financing and inter-company transactions at various stages of implementation and operations; (v) the nature and conditions of supply of foreign technology and services to developing country affiliates, including development of technological skills, management and R and D, and (vi) management and service agreements with TNCs. The implications of these issues differ considerably in emphasis from country to country and also as between various sectors of production and services.

## ENTERPRISE-LEVEL AUTONOMY

Most of these aspects hinge around the issue of control and the relationship between parent companies and their subsidiaries and affiliates. Most developing countries are anxious to ensure that TNC affiliates exercise full autonomy in various aspects of decision-making. This is often considered as a prerequisite to effective integration of the operations of such affiliates in national economies of host countries. The various promotional and regulatory measures designed to channel TNC investments and participation in desired sectors of each economy are also intended to ensure that the decision-making process at enterprise level is related to the objectives and requirements of each economy. On the part of TNCs, while many corporations have been sensitive to policy developments and trends in these countries and have showed considerable flexibility and willingness to negotiate new forms of cooperation adjusted to the particular requirement of host countries, there has been continuing emphasis on treating the activities of their subsidiaries and affiliates as part of a global network of operations in particular sectors and branches of production. Consequently, the problem of how to reconcile national objectives and autonomy in decision-making with the global interest of parent TNCs remains unresolved. Policies are, in their nature, of general application and can only set the broad parameters. It is at the level of individual enterprises that such policies have to be implemented, both in letter and spirit; between these, there can be considerable divergence. While policies and institutional mechanisms can define the rules of the game, it is at the enterprise level of implementation and operation that effective autonomy may need to be exercised.

## PARTICIPATION IN OWNERSHIP

The issue of autonomy in decision-making by TNC affiliates has, in several countries, taken the form of greater national participation and control. While such autonomy may need to be exercised both by wholly-owned foreign subsidiaries or by TNC affiliates with minority foreign holdings, the policy trend in several developing countries, has been towards greater national participation in equity ownership, as it is generally considered that without such participation, effective autonomy at the enterprise level cannot be exercised.

Consequently, various forms of regulatory control have been adopted in several countries regarding foreign ownership. This can take the form of total restriction of private investment in certain sectors or permitting majority holdings in new enterprises for specified periods or permitting majority holdings only in certain sectors with prior government approval. Such regulatory control also extends to new investments by existing foreign branches and subsidiaries and gradual divestment of foreign holdings in such enterprises. From the viewpoint of effective national autonomy, however, increased national shareholding may not necessarily provide the answer. The acquisition of foreign shareholdings in the case of divestments or national participation in ownership in new enterprises can take various forms - purchase of equity by government, government enterprises or State financial agencies, purchase of equity in new projects, or divestment of holdings either to na-

tional industrial groups or in the open market in
these countries - and the implications for autonomy
may differ significantly in these cases. Where
foreign ownership is acquired by government or State
enterprises, it would normally be assumed that adequate autonomy would be exercised. However, the
critical issue in this regard is that of management
control. Mere ownership is not enough to ensure the
exercise of effective autonomy in the operations of
the local enterprise as rapidly as possible. The
experiences of several nationalized industries in
developing countries, particularly in the petroleum
and mineral sector, have amply demonstrated that
national control and autonomy can be exercised fairly rapidly and effectively. On the other hand, there
have also been several cases of foreign interests
through management and service contracts. In cases
where national participation is undertaken through
State financial agencies, the exercise of effective
national autonomy and control is even more difficult,
largely because such institutions tend to be primarily interested in returns on investment and their
participation in decision-making at the enterprise
management level may be limited.

DIVESTMENT OF HOLDINGS

When divestment of foreign holdings is effected
through sales of shares through private sector groups
or in the open market, the extent of national participation and control largely depends on the nature
of the transaction. In cases where choice of the
pattern of divestment is left to the foreign enterprise, this is normally effected through maximum
sale of shares to individuals. Often these individuals are company employees, whose interests are
more identified with the interest of the subsidiary.
Where a larger volume of shares has to be sold and
sales in the open market are possible, such shares
are scattered among a large number of shareholders,
so that effective control is retained by foreign
interests, which have the highest share-holding
even though this may be below controlling interests
of 51 per cent. It is only in relatively few cases
that such divestment is effected through sale of
large blocks of shares to national, private interests, though this may become inevitable if the
stock market is not developed and other purchasers
are not forthcoming. In all such cases, foreign
partners may seek to retain effective control, even
though ownership may be greatly reduced and even
converted to minority holdings. Where this is not
possible, foreign investors may be inclined to sell
their entire holdings to national enterprises and
investor groups.

MANAGEMENT PERSONNEL

One aspect of national policies relates to insistence
in most developing countries on appointment of nationals in senior management positions in foreign
subsidiaries. This often takes the form of restrictions on the employment of expatriates beyond certain
periods. This has increasingly been found by TNCs
to be in their interest also. The shortage of senior
management personnel in industrialized countries,
their reluctance to reside in developing countries
for long periods and their much higher emoluments,
have ensured that this aspect of policy is increasingly being complied with, in most countries. This,
by itself, however, has little effect on the degree
of autonomy extended to affiliate companies. In many
cases, nationals appointed to such positions are
as representative of the transnational corporation's
global interests as expatriate personnel. The complex and fairly detailed links that exist between
parent transnational corporations and their subsidiaries also ensure that only limited local initiative can be exercised on basic management issues.
While national management personnel provide an appropriate local image, their overall significance in
policy determination can be quite limited except
where parent companies are willing to permit decision-making functions to be decentralized. Nevertheless, national personnel in top management positions can influence policies and programmes of
foreign subsidiaries/affiliates significantly over
a period of time and have been able to do so in
several instances, particularly on aspects such as
local purchase policies, marketing, product adaptation and greater adjustment to national policies and
objectives.

Similar considerations relate to nationals of developing countries appointed to boards of directors
by foreign subsidiaries and affiliates. Most such
board members provide a useful local image but tend
to play a relatively limited role in policies and
management of foreign subsidiaries. Where significant divestment of foreign holdings takes place,
however, and local nationals have to be appointed
to boards of such enterprises, it can be ensured
that the personnel so appointed participate effectively, within the limits of national ownership rights
that they may represent.

JOINT VENTURES

The issues and considerations relating to exercise
of local autonomy in foreign-majority enterprises in
developing countries apply, in equal measure, to

joint ventures having mixed foreign and national
ownership. From the viewpoint of autonomy in decision-making, national equity ownership of less than
50 per cent may have relatively little meaning.
Where foreign equity is 51 per cent or more, the
enterprise is under foreign control and its decision-
making process is similar to that of a wholly-owned
subsidiary. In some developing countries, certain
limited share-holding rights can be exercised by
local shareholders (institutional or individual),
with 25 per cent or more shares, but these do not
interfere with the basic control function which
rests with the foreign investor having the controlling share-holding.

The concept of a joint venture in terms of autonomy
in decision-making should, therefore, be primarily
conceived in terms of equal or minority foreign
ownership. It is only then that participation and
control can be 'joint' between foreign and national
interests. With the increasing tendency in several
developing countries to regulate foreign investment,
there is considerable scope and need for inflow of
technology on the one hand, and, on the other hand,
limited capital participation, particularly to cover
costs of imported machinery and equipment. As developing countries become increasingly knowledgeable
about technological alternatives in various manufacturing sectors, there may be an increasing
tendency to limit foreign investments to the levels
necessary to ensure adequate technology flow and
coverage of resource requirements.

The joint venture concept represents a basic depar-
ture from foreign-owned or foreign-controlled enterprises. It implies that all major decisions relating
to the venture shall be taken locally, with the
foreign partner contributing only such inputs of
finance, technology and know-how as are mutually
agreed. This implies that foreign and domestic
partners should each have something to contribute,
the former normally contributing technology and
initial management expertise and the latter participating with special knowledge of domestic market conditions, laws, labour management and other local
factors. If domestic participation is purely financial with domestic partners having only 'sleeping'
interests, the purpose of a joint venture is not
really served. A real joint venture calls for a
complementary relationship between the foreign partner holding a minority interest and domestic shareholders willing and competent to participate in
management and operational decisions of the enterprise in question. This may necessitate that such
ventures should primarily be promoted either by

(i) State investment agencies who are willing and
in a position to exercise participation in the
management and operation of such enterprises or
(ii) national companies or industrial groups having
an equal or major share-holding.

A pertinent question is whether any appropriate percentage of foreign equity holdings can be prescribed
for joint ventures which would ensure adequate effective national participation and control of TNC affiliates. Effective domestic autonomy may be difficult to exercise with a foreign TNC having capital
ownership of 49 per cent unless this is part of
corporate policy of the parent company. It would
obviously be easy for a foreign company to ensure
that 2 per cent of ownership is taken by national
share-holders who would be purely nominal and would
not effectively participate in decision-making, but
provide a national image and compliance with national
laws. The practice of <u>presta nombres</u> (name lenders)
is fairly common in several developing countries
and needs to be replaced by local partners with
knowledge and capability for effective participation. The extent of effective TNC control would be
less in the case of foreign holdings of around 40
per cent, but the same principle would apply. In
such cases, however, it is possible to visualize
domestic investor groups and institutional agencies
such as state-owned finance corporations, industrial
development banks and the like sharing the remaining
60 per cent, in suitable proportions. Such agencies
can acquire a block of shares which could constitute
the determinant share-holding interest, as between
foreign partners and national investor groups. Thus,
a share-holding pattern of 26-40 per cent being held
by the foreign TNC, and a similar percentage being
held by a national investor group, with an institutional financial agency taking up the remaining
share-holding, may emerge as an appropriate pattern
in several cases. The role of the institutional
share-holder, in such cases, would be to ensure that
the enterprise is run as an autonomous corporate
entity, whose operations are not necessarily
tailored to the global interests of foreign partners.

It must be emphasized, however, that if a joint
venture is to be successful, it must involve a give
and take process, and the development of a stable
and harmonious relationship between the principal
partners. The fact that the foreign TNC has a financial stake in the enterprise must be reflected in
effective participation by the TNC to the extent
of his capital ownership. At the same time, there
must also be an effective compromise between the
interests of the TNC and those of major national

participants, and both should be consistent with national policies.

In terms of programmes and activities at the enterprise level, this may imply, _inter alia_, that (i) initial and subsequent investments are directly related to meeting critical production gaps in the economy; (ii) there is adequate reinvestment of profits in the same or allied fields of manufacture; (iii) investment programmes are related to the growth potential of the enterprise in terms of domestic needs and external demand; (iv) such investments initiate and assist the growth of ancillary units in allied production sectors; (v) the production, marketing and purchasing strategies are related to sectoral and national programmes; (vi) the inflow of technology from the foreign partners or other external sources is appropriate to domestic endowments; (vii) there is adequate growth of local skills, including those at managerial and supervisory levels, and (viii) there is an adequate programme of R and D at the enterprise level, so as to develop adaptive and innovative capability. Whether such objectives can be more effectively served through joint ventures with minority foreign holdings, or can be adequately achieved by greater local autonomy in management decision-making, would depend on the circumstances in each developing country. It would not be practicable to prescribe uniform principles to cover all cases, and most developing countries would need to develop appropriate policy mechanisms to ensure that an adequate degree of autonomy in decision-making is possible in such enterprises.

## TECHNOLOGY TRANSFER

The need for greater local autonomy also assumes growing significance in supply of technology and services by transnational corporations. Terms and conditions of supply of technology and technical services, including management, are generally embodied in technology agreements, management and service contracts and other contractual arrangements. The development of national technological capability is an important policy objective in most developing countries and TNC subsidiaries and affiliates need to ensure not only rapid absorption but adaptation and innovation to suit local conditions. These may necessitate an approach to technological absorption, adaptation and R and D at the enterprise level which can best be achieved through adequate autonomy, as there may be considerable divergence in approach regarding the nature and process of technology transfer between TNCs, as suppliers of technology and expertise, and recipient, licensee enterprises in developing countries, besides technology regulation agencies which have been set up in many countries. Technology transfer must be adjusted to objectives, conditions, and policies in developing countries. At the same time, technological choice has to be related to basic developmental goals and to domestic factor resources and conditions of application.

While the import of advanced technologies through TNCs may be essential for most countries, such technologies need to be modified or adjusted to suit local market and factor conditions in most branches, or alternative technologies to those available from TNCs may need to be considered. This would be particularly necessary in the case of the less-industrialized developing countries and regions, and may relate to size of plants and scales of production; the degree of labour versus capital intensity; use of local materials, and several other factors. For this purpose, potential licensees should evaluate technological alternatives from various sources. This presupposes, however, that developing-country licensee enterprises can exercise autonomy in technological choice, within the framework of national policies.

In several developing countries, the acquisition of technology through TNCs is increasingly being considered in relation to the various elements of technology and services. From the viewpoint of host countries, it may be desirable to 'unpackage' investment from the technology elements and also to further disaggregate the latter in terms of patented and unpatented know-how and technological services. This enables closer scrutiny of the costs and implications of each element in the package and can also ensure the growth of domestic technological capability though maximum use of domestic inputs, including project engineering and management and other technical operations. The extent to which 'unpackaging' may be practicable, would, however, largely depend on the extent to which recipient, licensee enterprises have the necessary autonomy in negotiating acceptable terms and conditions for acquisition of foreign technology and services.

An essential aspect of technology transfer through TNCs relates to the terms and conditions of supply of technology and services. The screening of such agreements by regulatory agencies in several countries has had a salutary effect both on technology payments by licensees in these countries and on principal contractual conditions, and has also generally provided an adequately flexible framework for negotiations. Technology regulation can be, and has been

used as, a valuable instrument in development of
domestic technological capability, apart from improving terms and conditions of contracts.

## R AND D

The growth of innovative technological capability
is also an important objective in developing countries. With R and D activities of TNCs generally
centralized in home countries or in other industrialized economies, R and D in TNC subsidiaries/affi-
liates in developing countries have largely been confined to limited product adaptation to local tastes
and conditions. At the same time, while patents re-
gistered by TNCs constituted almost 90 % of regi-
stered patents in several developing countries, their
utilization has been very low, often falling below
1 % of such registration. TNC affiliates have also
maintained little or no links with scientific and
research institutions in most of these countries.
It is essential that activities of TNC affiliates
should provide for greater R and D expenditure and
growth of innovative capability at the enterprise
level, if host country objectives are to be adequately realised. This may also only be possible through
greater decentralisation and autonomy.

## CONCLUSION

This paper has sought to highlight some of the major
policy issues and trends in developing countries
which may have significant impact on headquarter-
subsidiary relationships in transnational corporations. With growing regulation and monitoring of
foreign investment and technology in many of these
countries, the pattern of parent-subsidiary/affi-
liate relations may need to change substantially
and greater autonomy and decentralisation of decision-making may become necessary. With greater national participation in ownership in new enterprises
and changes in ownership patterns for existing TNC
investments, the operations of TNC affiliates will
need to be increasingly adjusted to national situations and requirements. External considerations
will of course continue to exercise considerable
influence, and close links with parent corporations
will continue to be essential, but a marked shift
would be required, and may be inevitable in most
cases, towards greater integration of the activities
of TNC subsidiaries/affiliates within national economies in these countries, instead of being linked
primarily to the global interests of parent corporations.

In most sectors and branches of production, such a shift in perspective would not affect the interests of TNCs adversely and may, in fact, provide new opportunities for investment and technological participation, particularly in developing countries having large internal markets or possessing scarce natural resources or special factor advantages. It would, however, require considerable reorientation in corporate policies and approach on the part of TNCs seeking to obtain or retain long-term investments and participation in these countries. It would also require significant adjustments in head-quarter-subsidiary relationships in TNCs operating in developing countries in the coming decade.

# 3 Gunnar Hedlund:

# Autonomy of Subsidiaries and Formalization of Headquarters-Subsidiary Relationships in Swedish MNCs

This paper is based upon a research project conducted at the Institute of International Business at the Stockholm School of Economics. The empirical material comes from an in-depth study of 24 subsidiaries of six large Swedish MNCs. The research design aimed at varying the ownership structure (wholly owned/minority joint venture) and location (developed country/less developed country) in each MNC. This succeeded almost completely. An average of ten interviews were conducted at each central headquarters and/or appropriate division, all subsidiaries were visited and 2-6 people interviewed, and the researchers had full access to documents, telexes, and correspondence between HQ and the subsidiaries selected for study.

This article will summarize the results from the project as regards the autonomy of the subsidiaries and the formality of headquarters-subsidiary relationships. Some comparisons with parallel studies of MNCs in other countries will also be made.

METHOD OF MEASURING DEGREE OF AUTONOMY

The degree of autonomy of a subsidiary was assessed in three different ways. First, during interviews in the subsidiaries, the respondents were asked to indicate the degree of influence, that the subsidiary and HQ, respectively, had on a number of specified types of decisions. Various averages over decisions were computed to yield indices representing the degree of subsidiary autonomy. (See table 1 for a listing of

Institute of International Business, Stockholm School of Economics

the decisions.) A five-point scale similar to the one used by Peccei and Warner (1976) was used. This is a very common method of measuring the degree of centralization of decision-making. Similar procedures - in either interview or questionnaire version - were followed also by Aylmer (1970), de Bodinat (1975), Garnier, Causse and Boudeville (1978), and Picard (1978) The method has several advantages. It allows comparisons between different types of decision and between different categories of subsidiaries for identical type of decision. It reduces the risk of drawing too general conclusions about the degree of autonomy, and it utilizes the cumulated experience of the respondent in asking him to provide estimates on the basis of this experience. However, the method also has some drawbacks. The respondent is biased by culture, organizational affiliation, position in the hierarchy, etc. Therefore, valid comparisons between firms are methodologically difficult to make. The fact that many categories of decision have to be covered means that the interviewer often does not have time to go through all of them with the necessary care and rigour. If a questionnaire method is used, the respondent easily gets tired of thinking about a long list of decisions, many of which he may not know much about. If, in order to address this last problem, several respondents are questioned, problems of adjusting for differences in respondent biases occur when indexes are computed and comparisons between decisions are made. In the present study, in most cases only one respondent was questioned. A conscious attempt was made to choose a similar person for each subsidiary. Most of them were Swedish managers at the level immediately below the general manager of the subsidiary, or the general manager himself, if he was a Swede.

Second, in order to expand the sample of companies, basically the same approach as the one described above was taken in the questionnaire study on 39 parent companies with 77 subsidiaries. In this study the respondents were HQ officials. The sample of decisions and the results are reported in table 2.

Third, the researchers made an estimate of subsidiary autonomy in strategic and operational matters respectively, on the basis of the total information collected during the research. Of particular importance here is that real decisionmaking processes were investigated in detail, and influence patterns observed in a number of ways; though interviews at several managerial levels both in the subsidiary and at HQ, through study of documents, letters and telexes, etc. Also these estimates were coded on a five-point scale. Many of the disadvantages inherent in the two previously mentioned procedures can be coped with by adding information processed in this third way. Apart from drawing on information from many sources, this method allows us to take into account the more indirect methods of influence through the use of targets, planning and reporting systems and face-to-face exchanges of opinion. There is a risk that these kinds of influences are not captured by the interview or questionnaire methods, even though in the in-depth study they were asked also to consider these indirect mechanisms of exercising power. (For a discussion of the difficulties involved in measuring the degree of influence in MNCs, see de Bodinat, 1975. in particular chapter 2, and Takamiya, 1979. The latter suggests that to examine actual decision-making processes might be the only way to resolve the difficulties that more formalized and economical methods suffer from.) Therefore, we have a good basis for a discussion of the autonomy of subsidiaries of Swedish MNCs. [17] When, in the analyses below, different measures give different conclusions, this will be mentioned.

AUTONOMY AT LARGE

Table 1 reports the results for the 15 different types of decisions used in the in-depth study. On a five-point scale, the average over 24 subsidiaries was 4.10, indicating a rather high degree of autonomy. The range was from 2.60 to 5.00, and the variance 0,281, showing that the autonomy varied considerably over subsidiaries. It could be argued that one could as well consider the results as indicating low autonomy. Indeed, why should we regard 4.10 out of 5 as "high" in terms of autonomy? If other types of decisions were chosen, the figure would be different, as is evidenced in table 2, which reports the results of the questionnaire study. Here, the average subsidiary autonomy - calculated as an average of answers to 48 questions similar but not identical to the ones used in the in-depth study - was 3.67.

Although we recognize the problems indicated above, nevertheless we would like to argue that the overall autonomy is rather hing. There are two sets of arguments to support this statement.

First, in table 1 it is also shown that HQ influence - measured in the same way as subsidiary influence - was higher than subsidiary influence for only 3 of the 15 decision categories. Also for such important decisions as the introduction of new products on the local market and the use of expatriate personnel (from HQ), the subsidiary is estimated to have more influence than HQ. In no case is there a big and

TABLE 1 Subsidiary and HQ influence for various types of decisions.
(Scale 1-5, 1=low subsidiary (HQ) influence, 5=high subsidiary (HQ) influence)

| | Subsidiary's influence[1] | HQ's influence[1] | (Strategic decisions) |
|---|---|---|---|
| Subsidiary's training program | 4.29 | 1.96 | |
| Lay offs of workers | 4.63 | 1.58 | |
| Use of expatriates | 3.71 | 3.33 | S |
| Appointment of chief executive officer | 3.21 | 3.63 | S |
| Maintenance of production facilities | 4.46 | 2.17 | |
| Setting aggregate production schedule | 4.08 | 2.96 | |
| Increase of production capacity | 3.38 | 3.88 | S |
| Choice of advertising | 4.96 | 1.08 | |
| Service of products sold | 4.63 | 1.08 | |
| Pricing of products sold | 4.08 | 2.29 | S |
| Introduction of new product on local market | 3.75 | 3.38 | S |
| Choice of public accountant | 3.04 | 3.57 | S |
| Extension of customer credit | 4.63 | 1.83 | |
| Use of cash flow in sub | 4.54 | 1.88 | |
| Borrowing from local banks | 4.50 | 2.14 | |
| Average | 4.10 | 2.49 | |
| For Strategic decisions | 3.51 | 3.32 | |
| For Operational decisions | 4.50 | 1.94 | |

1/ As rated by respondent in subsidiary. Averages over 24 subsidiaries.

TABLE 2  <u>Subsidiary autonomy for different types of decisions.</u>
(Scale 1-5; 1=low autonomy, 5=high autonomy.)[1]

| | | |
|---|---|---|
| 1. | Change of sub organization | 3.47 |
| 2. | Hiring top management in sub | 3.32 |
| 3. | Salary level for top management in sub | 3.18 |
| 4. | Hiring and firing of workers | 4.97 |
| 5. | Payment routines for employee wages | 4.78 |
| 6. | Responsibility for collective wage bargaining | 4.97 |
| 7. | Training program in sub | 4.60 |
| 8. | Transfer of employees between departments | 4.88 |
| 9. | Restructuring of work tasks | 4.86 |
| 10. | Taking disciplinary action - warnings, fines etc | 4.97 |
| 11. | Security against industrial espionage | 4.60 |
| 12. | Extent of over-time work | 5.00 |
| 13. | Vacations for employees not legally fixed | 4.40 |
| 14. | Choice of suppliers | 4.18 |
| 15. | Purchasing methods | 4.54 |
| 16. | Yearly production volume | 3.40 |
| 17. | Increase in production capacity | 2.62 |
| 18. | Quality control norms | 3.36 |
| 19. | Changes in manufacturing process | 3.65 |
| 20. | Maintenance of production facilities | 4.66 |
| 21. | Choice of costing system | 2.85 |
| 22. | Decision on work efficiency studies | 4.84 |
| 23. | Choice of work methods | 4.68 |
| 24. | Entering new markets within country | 3.75 |
| 25. | Entering new markets outside country | 2.24 |
| 26. | Introduction of new products | 2.79 |
| 27. | Choice of distribution channels | 3.79 |
| 28. | Adaptation of standard products | 4.05 |
| 29. | Setting sales targets | 3.17 |
| 30. | Preparing market plans | 3.84 |

(continued)

Table 2 (continued)

| | |
|---|---|
| 31. Level of advertising budget | 4.16 |
| 32. Choice of advertising agency | 4.88 |
| 33. Pricing of products sold locally | 4.19 |
| 34. Delivery times or order priorities | 4.84 |
| 35. Customer credit | 4.25 |
| 36. Product design | 3.49 |
| 37. Advertising approach | 4.35 |
| | |
| 38. Preparing financial plans | 3.03 |
| 39. ROI criteria | 1.85 |
| 40. Loans from local banks | 3.08 |
| 41. Raising equity capital | 1.48 |
| 42. Dividend policy | 1.54 |
| 43. Royalty payments and central overhead costs | 1.77 |
| 44. Use of cash-flow in sub | 2.49 |
| 45. Choice of public accountant | 1.91 |
| 46. Spending unbudgeted capital on investments | 2.31 |
| 47. Organization of budget work | 3.07 |
| 48. Internal transfer prices | 3.24 |

Average     3.67

1/ 1 = Decided by HQ alone, 2 = Decided by HQ after consultation with subsidiary, 3 = Decided by subsidiary but subject to approval by HQ, 4 = Decided by subsidiary after consultation with HQ, 5 = Decided independently by subsidiary.

clear difference in favour of HQ. This shows that head office very rarely, if ever, dictates decisions without involving the subsidiary in discussions and letting it influence the outcome. Certainly the picture of MNCs as centrally controlled monoliths ordering their subsidiaries around, has been shown not be true for this sample, as it has in other studies. (For a review, see Takamiya, 1979.)

Second, the autonomy of Swedish-owned subsidiaries can be compared with the results from the international study. Table 3 shows that Swedish subsidiaries are significantly more autonomous than comparable samples of U.S. and Japanese corporations. The best measure is probably the difference between the value for subsidiary influence and the value for HQ influence. In this respect, the Swedish companies appear to be more like the Japanese than like the U.S. ones.

TABLE 3    Influence of subsidiaries and HQs of Swedish, U.S., and Japanese MNCs.[1/]  (Scale 1-5; 1=low, 5=high influence.)

|  | Subsidiary's influence (A) | HQ's influence (B) | Diff (A-B) |
|---|---|---|---|
| Swedish MNCs (24 subsidiaries) | 4.10 | 2.49 | 1.61 |
| U.S. MNCs (21 subsidiaries) | 3.39 | 2.72 | 0.67 |
| Japanese MNCs (31 subsidiaries) | 3.93 | 2.18 | 1.75 |

1/    Average for the 15 decisions listed in table 1. U.S. and Japanese data were collected by Anant Negandhi, Ram Baliga and Martin Welge, through interviews in subsidiaries of U.S. and Japanese MNCs.

Thus, on the basis of these results, we can confidently say that the subsidiaries investigated enjoy a considerable degree of autonomy. A certain qualification to this statement needs to be made in light of the results in the questionnaire study. Table 6 compares the ratings for 13 identical decisions in the in-depth study and the questionnaire study. Although the fact that the samples are different has to be taken into account, it is interesting to note that the HQ officials responding to the questionnaires see more of centralization in the relationship than the subsidiary officials interviewed. Slightly different scales were used in the two studies, which may explain some of the variations. In the reseracher's ratings of autonomy in strategic and operational decisions, a five-point scale was also used. However, here the rating was based upon the relative influence of the subsidiary visavi HQ. Thus, a value of 3 indicated that HQ and subsidiary had equal influence, 4 that the subsidiary had more influence, and 5 that it had all or almost all influence. For strategic matters the average for 24 subsidiaries was 2.79, and for operational matters 3.96. Again, the conclusion is supported that there are no decisions clearly in the sole hands of headquarters.

Why is it that the subsidiaries are autonomous to such an extent? Some of the differences between Swedish companies on the one hand and U.S. and Japanese on the other might be attributable to differences in the sample of companies and subsidiaries. However, since the studies were made in cooperation, all efforts were made to get comparable samples. [4/] The only respect in which we were not very successful was in controlling for the size of the parent company and the size of subsidiaries. Both the U.S. and the Japanese companies were larger than the Swedish ones. The same goes for the subsidiaries. Brooke and Remmers (1970) found that the autonomy of a subsidiary decreased with the size of the parent company. However, Picard (1978) found the inverse relationship for marketing decisions. Thus, it is not probable that all of the large difference is attributable to this factor alone. Neither can the size of the subsidiaries explain the results, since previous research as well as our own (see p. 34 below) suggests that the autonomy increases with the size of the subsidiary. So we are still left without an explanation of the difference between countries. Without pretending to capture the full explanation, we would like to offer a few suggestions based upon the industrial history of Sweden.

## Organization histories of Swedish MNCs

Many of the large Swedish MNCs went international very early in their development. A wave of inventions and industrial ingenuity around the turn of the century led to the formation of companies such as SKF, Alfa-Laval, AGA, Sandvik, and L M Ericsson. Due to the limited home market, they were forced to expand abroad almost from the beginning. The companies were managed by entrepreneurially minded individuals, in a very informal way. This particularly applies to the management of the foreign affiliates. "He (the president 60 years ago) sent out his friends to a foreign country with a pat on their shoulder and a checkbook, and after that they were supposed to take care of the business", was how the relationship was described in one case. Contacts between headquarters and subsidiary were managed in a very personal way, and there was little or no standardization of relationships. One subsidiary could be left almost completely alone for years, another attracted the interest of HQ, perhaps for no other reason than the fact that the president of the company liked to go and visit the general manager of the subsidiary. So, the management style was informal, variable, built on historical personal relationships, and subsidiaries were generally given a lot of autonomy. To a large extent, this still characterizes the companies.

The picture above went together with a mother-daughter structure of the international organization, with the subsidiary managing directors reporting directly to the group president, or even to the chairman of the parent company board. This structure is more typical of Swedish and continental European companies than of British or U.S. ones. (See Stopford and Wells 1973; Channon, 1973; Franko, 1976.) Relatively recently - in most cases in the 1960's - most of the large Swedish companies have adopted structures based on product divisions. In the majority of cases, however, the foreign subsidiaries have not been integrated into the divisions.

The picture above holds true for the large, established companies. In our sample of six MNCs, three of them still have mother-daughter structures and very closely conform to the development sketched above. In two of the remaining three, the foreign subsidiaries are subordinated to product divisions. These companies are more diversified than the first three. Since diversification in itself usually leads to greater subsidiary autonomy (see for example Skinner, 1968; Stopford and Wells, 1968; Alsegg, 1971; Picard, 1978; and below pp 22 ff), this could contribute to explaining the consistently high degree of autonomy. However, as we have measured HQ influence, we have defined HQ as everything that is not a subsidiary. Thus, if a product division exercizes a lot of influence on a subsidiary, this has been classified as high HQ influence, whether or not group headquarters have any influence or not. The last company has a matrix-type organization divided both according to products and according to regions. It is the only one resembling what Stopford-Wells (1968) called "global structures" It also has the highest degree of centralization (lowest subsidiary autonomy) of the six.

Thus, it seems as if the large autonomy given to subsidiaries of Swedish MNCs to some extent can be explained by the historically evolved mother-daughter structure of organization and by the mode of the early internationalization of the larger companies. However, even in companies having internationalized later and having adopted divisionalized structures, subsidiary autonomy is comparatively high. A reexamination of the hypothesis about the influence of the size of the parent company seems to be called for. It should furthermore be remembered that this second group of companies has internationalized through acquisitions to a larger extent than the first one. This should have as a consequence reduced parent control. (See for example Behrman, 1969.)

Of course one could also refer to "pure" cultural explanations. Indeed, there are in Sweden strong traditions of emphazising individual responsibility, a lack of feudal patterns of land ownership and an absence of respect for organizational hierarchies. (See Hofstede, 1978.) We hypothesize that cultural factors do have an effect upon the mode of managing Swedish MNCs, even if the tendency of exporting national tastes would be tempered by the necessities of accomodating to the international environment. For any serious test of this hypothesis, it would be necessary, however, to carefully define what is meant by "cultural factors" in terms that makes it possible to observe them and relate them to management practices. We agree with Ajiferuke and Boddewyn (1970) that the term "culture" often has been used with too little care in comparative management research. There is a tendency to refer to everything that cannot be explained by other factors as emanating from cultural traditions. In summary, then, we do not want to draw any firm conclusions as to the effect of culture on the autonomy of subsidiaries of Swedish MNCs, but would rather point to the organizational histories of the firms, connected with the pattern of late and rapid industrialization, to a large extent interconnected with international developments, of the country.

## Autonomy for various types of decision

It has become almost commonplace to say that HQ tends to centralize with regard to strategic questions and decentralize with regard to operational matters. Table 1 shows that this conclusion holds true also for this sample. The nature of the scales necessitates a certain care as to use of statistical procedures. Anyway, t-tests of the differences indicated in table 1 yield levels of significance below 0.001 for a two-tailed test. The designation of which decisions are regarded as strategic is reported in table 1. The choice was of course made before the results were available.

Looking somewhat closer at the results for individual decisions in tables 1 and 2, it seems as if there are three types of decision on which HQ has a consi-

derable say. The first encompasses decisions that
draw on or directly affect central resources. Use of
expatriate personnel, expansion of production capacity, raising equity capital, dividend policy, and the
determination of royalties and administration fees
are examples of such decisions.

The second group of decisions includes items such as
the introduction of new products, and choice of export markets. These are decisions which constitute
long-term-obligations on part of the company.

The third type of centralized decisions are those
that are made in order to ensure standardization and
a common framework of organizational routines and
practices throughout the company. Choice of public
accountant, transfer pricing policies, quality control norms, choice of cost systems, product designs
and the organization of work on the yearly budget are
good examples. A subcategory in this group are decisions on targets set for subsidiary performance, such
as determination of sales objectives, preparation of
financial plans for the subsidiary, and setting of
return on investment goals.

Previous studies have sometimes attempted to compare
the degree of autonomy for various functionally defined groups of decisions. Garnier et.al. (1978),
using a sample of French subsidiaries of U.S. corporations, found that "organization and personnel" is
the least centralized and "finance" the most centralized function, with "production and research" and
"marketing" occupying positions in between. Our questionnaire study got almost identical results. The only difference was that Garnier et. al. put marketing
as somewhat more centralized than production and research, whereas we found the opposite relationship.
The difference in both cases were very small, however.

Although these and other similar results have some
use, we would like to argue that one has to be very
careful in assigning indexes of autonomy to functional classes of decisions in this way. A closer look
at table 2 shows that the variation over decisions in
degree of subsidiary autonomy was considerable also
within each functional class of decisions. Table 4
summarizes these observations. Depending on what decisions are used for the construction of an index,
one can obtain widely differing results for the autonomy of a certain function. To arrive at a "just" index, one would have to make the saple of decisions in
some way representative of the total area of responsibility of a given function. It could be argued that
in the questionnaire study, a dispropartionate share

TABLE 4  Subsidiary autonomy for various management functions. [1]/
(Scale 1-5; 1=low, 5=high autonomy.)

| | Average | Range |
|---|---|---|
| Personnel decisions (1-13 in table 2) | 4.45 | 3.18-5.00 |
| Production decisions (14-23 in table 2) | 3.96 | 2.62-4.84 |
| Marketing decisions (24-37 in table 2) | 3.82 | 2.24-4.88 |
| Finance decisions (38-48 in table 2) | 2.38 | 1.48-3.25 |

1/  Averages over decisions belonging in each class
for 66 MNCs.
Data obtained by questionnaires to HQ officials.

of the finance decisions chosen were of "strategic"
nature, whereas there are too many "operational" decisions in the organization and personnel lists.

Another disadvantage with this type of comparison is
that real decisions are rarely purely of one type or
the other, in particular if they are important decisions. A decision to introduce a new product on the
market has to be - and is - looked at from a marketing viewpoint, but also from production, financial
and personnel viewpoints.

13 of the 15 decisions used in the interview study
are also used in the qustionnaire study. Whereas the
interviews were conducted with managers of the subsidiaries, the questionnaires were answered by HQ officials. A comparison of the ranking of decisions in
terms of degree of subsidiary autonomy in the two
studies is made in table 5. Some interesting observations can be made. First, the average degree of autonomy over these decisions is seen to be 4.12 by the
subsidiary managers, and 3.62 by the HQ managers. To
some extent this might be explained by the slight
difference in definitions of the points on the scale.
We would hypothesize, however, that some of the difference originates in different conceptions as to how
large the autonomy really is. Our analysis of decision making processes - relying on interviews and document reading at both ends - lends support to this
interpretation.

Second, there are two decisions for which the views
at HQ and subsidiary differ sharply. They are both
financial decisions; "loans from local banks", and
"use of cash flow in the subsidiary". HQ managers

tended to see these decisions as centralized whereas for subsidiary managers they came far down on the list in terms of HQ influence. The in-depth study rather supports the view of the subsidiary managers. In spite of the fact that HQ wants to control these and similar operational financial decisions, they are often in reality taken by the subsidiary. The fact that decisions have to be taken very quickly and the local expertise needed to handle the matter were often mentioned by the subsidiary managers as reasons for this apparent inconsistency. HQ approval was very often just a formal sanctioning ex post of subsidiary decisions, and the subsidiaries often saw as their only obligation to inform HQ about their moves. One explanation of the probably exaggerated ratings by HQ officials may be that those people answering the questionnaire were not really familiar with how financial matters are handled in their corporations. Questionnaires tend to be answered by staff in organization, personnel, planning, external relations or similar departments rather than by finance executives. ANother explanation may be that the questionnaire study - due to the construction of the scale used - measured what Peccei and Warner (1976) called "policy centralization" rather than "de facto" centralization. That is, it measured intended (by HQ) rather than actual degree of centralization.

TABLE 5  Degree of autonomy by type of decision in the interview
(I) study and the questionnaire (Q) study

|  | I Rank | Score[1/] | Q Rank | Score[2/] |
|---|---|---|---|---|
| Choice of public accountant | 1 | 3.04 | 1 | 1.91 |
| Appointing CEO (I), Top management personnel (Q) | 2 | 3.21 | 6 | 3.32 |
| Increase of production capacity | 3 | 3.38 | 3 | 2.62 |
| Introduction of new product | 4 | 3.75 | 4 | 2.79 |
| Determining product volume for the year | 5 | 4.08 | 7 | 3.40 |
| Pricing of products sold on local market | 6 | 4.08 | 8 | 4.19 |
| Personnel training program for sub | 7 | 4.29 | 10 | 4.60 |
| Maintenance of facilities | 8 | 4.46 | 11 | 4.66 |
| Loans from local banks | 9 | 4.50 | 5 | 3.08 |
| Use of cash flow in sub | 10 | 4.54 | 2 | 2.49 |
| Customer credit | 11 | 4.63 | 9 | 4.25 |
| Hiring and firing of workers | 12 | 4.63 | 13 | 4.97 |
| Choice of advertising agency | 13 | 4.96 | 12 | 4.88 |
| Average score |  | 4.12 |  | 3.62 |

1/  Average score for 24 subsidiaries of 6 MNCs, scale 1-5, 1=low subsidiary influence, 5=high subsidiary influence.

2/  Average score for 66 MNCs, scale 1-5, 1 = Decided by HQ alone; 2 = Decided by HQ after consultation with subsidiary; 3 = Decided by subsidiary, but has to be approved by HQ; 4 = Decided by subsidiary after consultation with HQ; 5 = Decided by subsidiary alone.

# DETERMINANTS OF SUBSIDIARY AUTONOMY

We shall now discuss other determinants of subsidiary
autonomy than nationality of the parent company or
the type of decision that the autonomy refers to.
First, we will consider the effects of attributes of
the MNC as a whole; the type of business and technology it is involved in, its degree of diversification, its size, its international experience, the nature of its environment, etc. After that, characteristics of subsidiaries will be discussed in terms of
location, ownership structure, degree of integration
into the total system, absolute and relative size,
performance and market structure. It should be noted
that some factors do not unambigously belong in any
one of these two groups. Some company characteristics
are really made up of subsidiary characteristics,
such as the degree of interdependence between units
in the company.

## Characteristics of the MNC system as a whole

Exact comparisons between parent companies are difficult to make, since the quantitative measures of autonomy are calculated by subsidiary. Since furthermore only 3 to 5 subsidiaries are studied in-depth in
each company, and since it was not possible to have
sets of subsidiaries fully comparable between companies, the suggestions offered below should be read
with care. Therefore, the analysis here is more based
upon qualitative data gathered about the way that the
total company is managed. Probably, there is a certain HQ bias in our interpretation, since the information on this general level was generated mainly at
HQ. Of course, the data obtained in the interviews
and document analyses at the subsidiaries that were
visited are also used. However, strict comparisons on
the basis of these are not appropriate.

The technology of the company has been used as an
explanatory variable for the degree of subsidiary
autonomy by de Bodinat (1975) and Keegan (1972).
Picard (1978) did not find any relationship at all,
whereas de Bodinat found a positive relationship
between the complexity of technology and the degree
of influence on manufacturing decisions exerted by
the parent company on the subsidiary. Our results
tend to support this conclusion. In table 6, the
six companies are rated according to the degree of
technological complexity[2] of their main products on
the one hand and the degree of autonomy enjoyed by
the subsidairies on the other. As can be seen, the
relationship is fairly unambigous. It is, however,
not very strong. Within every company, there are
considerable differences between subsidiaries that we

investigated. (See table 6.) Of course, one has to be extremely careful in interpreting such simple measures of association as the one here discussed. The companies vary as to a number of other characteristics, and it is not easy to attribute anything to any specific factors. In spite of this, theoretical arguments (see de Bodinat, ibid) lead us to provisionally accept the interpretation given.

The degree of international experience of the parent company was shown to be positively correlated with high HQ involvement in marketing decisions by Aylmer (1970). Picard (1978) draws similar conclusions. Since 4 of the 6 companies here studied have been internationally active very long and with substantial (more than 50%) operations abroad, the variation in the supposedly explanatory variable is too low to allow any farreaching conclusions. It is interesting that the company allowing most of the autonomy to its subsidiaries also is the one that has internationalized most recently. Company No. 2 in table 6, however, is also relatively new and small (in relation to its own size) on the international market. In spite of this, it is the second most centralized company in the sample. This seems to be at least partly an extension of the management style that has prevailed within the company in general for a long time. The foreign subsidiaries have usually been built up from scratch, use the same advanced technology as the Swedish companies in the group, and have consequently been exposed to the corporate culture although they are relatively young. As will become evident below, we do not subscribe to the view that the mode of managing subsidiaries - or of managing the company at large - is so very heavily constrained by "contingencies" as the impression the format of this presentation may give.

The degree of interdependence between units in the MNC should be negatively correlated with subsidiary autonomy, since interdependence has to be managed, and that often requires that the centre takes an active role, constraining the subsidiaries. There are several types of interdependence between units. The most visible form of it is when there are big and important flows of goods and information between the units. However, the interdependence may also be less direct, such as when in an oligopoly market the behaviour. on the local market of subsidiaries I visavi competitior A influences the position of subsidiary II visavi A on another market. Common sources of supply or common customers are other examples of this type of interdependence. The results in table 6 give some rather weak support

TABLE 6    Aggregate company characteristics and
           centralization of decision-marketing to
           HQ[1]

| Centralization Company (rank): | 1 | 2 | 3 | 4 | 5 | 6 |
|---|---|---|---|---|---|---|
| Complexity of technology: | H | H | M | H | L | L |
| International experience: | H | M | H | H | H | L |
| Inter-unit dependency: | H | M | M | H | L | L |
| Geographical heterogeneity: | H | M | H | H | H | L |
| Market concentration: | H | H/M | H | H | H/M | M/L |
| Sixe of MNC:[2] | B | B | S | B | S | S |
| Degree of diversification: | L | M | M | L | H | H |
| Mode of entry on inter-national markets:[3] | BU/ AC | BU | BU/ AC | BU | AC | AC |

1    H=High, M=Medium, L=Low (relatively spoken).

2    B=Big, S=Small (relatively spoken).

3    BU=Build up, AC=Acuisitions (relatively spoken).

for the hypothesis that high interdependence leads
to low subsidiary autonomy. The hypotheses "fits"
for the extreme companies 1 and 6, but company 4
manages to combine a large measure of local autonomy with a high degree of interdependence between
units. The coordination mechanisms in this company
seem to build upon the sharing of norms and a strong
informal network of contacts, rather than on clear
allocation if integrative functions. This could be
interpreted as a case of organic coordination by
an organization in an uncertain, high-technology,
environment. (See Burns and Stalker. 1961.) However,
company 2 is anything but organic, and controls its
subsidiaries rather tightly. (See Hedlund, 1978).
The picture is thus not very clear, but the initial
hypothesis is supported to some extent.

The extent to which the company is diversified in
terms of products has been mentioned by several
authors as contributing to explaining the variation in degree of subsidiary autonomy. De Bodinat
uses the concept "heterogeneity of environment",
which probably amounts to much the same since diversification leads to heterogenity. The latter concept would include geographical heterogeneity
also, however, so they are not fully interchange-
able. In a diversified firm, central organs do not
have the knowledge necessary to tightly control and
guide the subsidiaries. However, and this is somewhat neglected in previous literature, the subsidiaries are often subordinated to product-based
divisions. These do have knowledge about the conditions in foreign countries and companies. For the
Swedish companies, three interesting points can be
made in this context.

First, as has been shown above, the mother-daughter
structure of organization still prevails, which
means that even if diversions do exist, they do not
have formal power over the foreign affiliates.
Companies 2, 3 and 4 in our sample have this structure. This may be part of the explanation for the
only moderately strong HQ involvement in the latter.
two.

Second, in the cases where the divisionalization
has been consistently pursued, and included the subordination of foreign subsidiaries to specific
divisions, the companies have found themselves
in rather severe lack of management resources to
cope with the international dimensions of business.
It is difficult enough to have one organization
capable of mastering the difficulties, let alone
two, three or four. Therefore, divisionalization
of the international organization - or interna-

tionalization from the divisions - may have the para-
doxical effect of <u>reducing</u> home country influence
and <u>increasing</u> subsidiary autonomy. To a large
extent, this dynamic depends on the fact that
Swedish MNCs are relatively small in an international perspective.

The <u>third</u> point also has to do with smallness. Because of indivisibilities and scale economies in
administration and sales, it is often not possible
to divide a foreign company up in several parts.
Admittedly, there is a tendency for the managing
director to become a "man in the middle", being
bypassed by direct contacts between product divisions at home and their counterparts in the local
company. However, the traditionally very strong
position that the managing director has enjoyed
in Swedish corporations has in most cases been
upheld in spite of the pressure from the divisions.

All these three points, together with the indication
that subsidiary autonomy may be undermined by a product division as well as by HQ, leads one to con-
template the complexity of the hypothesis between
diversification and autonomy. Table 6 shows that
the earlier results "fit" for the two diversified
firms, but the realtionship is less clear for the
rest.

The <u>geographical heterogeneity</u> of the MNC and its
environment would - one would suppose - be positively
correlated with the degree of subsidiary autonomy.
(See de Bodinat, ibid, although he does not use the
concept exactly as we do.) By geographical heterogenity we mean the spread and variation of environments in which the MNC is active. A company
with subsidiaries in all countries of the world
would have a highly heterogenous environment, one
with fairly many subsidiaries mainly located in
Europe and North America would be moderately hetero-
geous, and one with a few subsidiaries in (in this
case) the northern part of Europe would have low
geographical heterogeneity. As table 6 shows, we
do not find any indication of the hypothesized
relationship on our sample. Company 6, which should
be the most centralized according to the hypothesis,
is least centralized. Company 1, which should give a
lot of autonomy to its subsidiaries, is the most
centralized.

The <u>structure of competition</u> may be hypothesized
to have an effect on the degree of subsidiary autonomy. The more concentrated the market becomes
- in the sense that the whole world market is con-

trolled by fewer companies - the more reason is there for HQ to tightly control and inform the subsidiaries. The testing of this hypothesis is difficult, among other things because of the problems inherent in defining the appropriate product-market niche in which to measure the degree of concentration. Our effort to make a crude classification is reported in table 6. When two indications are given, this is because the company has several important product lines, the competitive structures of which are different. Again, the size of the sample and the lack of variation in the assumed independent variable calls for great caution. Nevertheless, so many incidents of how global oligopolies necessitate integration between subsidiareis or quick central action were observed during the field study, that we dare say that the hypothesis is supported. However, there are other ways of handling the needs for coordination than through strategic centralization. Companies 3, 4 and 5 are all active in global oligoplies, and still maintain fairly autonomous subsidiaries.

The effect of the size of the parent company cannot very fruitfully be investigated in this sample, since the size does not vary very much. In table 6 we have nevertheless divided the sample into two size-grups. The results at least do not contradict the contention that big companies control their subsidiaries more than small companies do.

The mode of entry on international markets is often hypothesized to have an effect on the autonomy of the affiliates. Companies that internationalize from within, building up their subsidiaries from scratch by forming new companies, are likely to exercise more control than those that internationalize through acquisitions. This is so partly because of the difficulties to control an entity with a long and influential previous history, partly because acquisitions are often undertaken precisely in order to buy competences that the buyer does not have, and therefore feels should not be interfered with. It may be interesting to know that one of the companies having internationalized chiefly through acquisitions recently turned to one of the present researchers to have the problem of integrating bought companies more closely into the group brought up at a corporate-wide seminar. An international task force was set up and wrote a report on the issue to corporate HQ. In this case there was in inclination not to want to disturb and irritate acquired companies, a feeling that one has to learn a lot before one interferes in the local situation.

Of course, there are acquisitions that are made in
rougher ways, sometimes as a means to reduce competition and with a view to close down plants later,
This is, however, not at all the common pattern
for Swedish MNCs, at least no sofar. Investments
abroad have been made in order to serve the local
market, or markets close to the country in question
rather than in order to prepare the ground for deliveries from other parts of the world. The basically
entreprenurial nature of the task to establish
abroad has thus led to a large measure of autonomy
being given to the subsidiaries, whether they have
been acquired or not. Therefore, it is perhaps
not surprising that our analysis does not provide
much support for the hypothesis at this general
level of discussion (see table 6). As is shown on
p. 38 below, analysis at the level of subsidiaries
yields results in the expected direction.

Just a cursory look at table 6 suggest that extreme
caution has to be observed in drawing even as mildly
phrased conclusions as we have done above. The previous literature in our view suffers from not paying
enough attention to the intricacies of the casual
relationships between the various factors indicated
in the table, and other ones too for that matter.
This research was not designed specifically to
address the questions implied here, but since the
material is so rich and our measures consequently
probably valid and reliable for the admittedly
limited sample, we have chosen to present an effort
of analysis anayway. Only further indepth studies
on larger samples will resolve the issues. Thus,
the temptation to go either for large samples and
rather superficial data or a few rich cases must
be resisted if research is to progress.

With these caveats in mind, we would like to summarize by suggesting that our research supports
hypotheses of a causal and positive relationship
between the autonomy of subsidiaries and: the
simplicity of the technology used by the MNC;
the lack of international experience of the parent
company; the degree of product diversifiction;
the degree of market fragmentation; the lack of
links of interdependency or common environmental
condition; the smallness of the MNC; the tendency
to internationalize through acquisitions rather than
by building up own companies.

We would furthermore suggest that these relationships are strongest for low to medium values on the
variables mentioned. Or - in other words - almost
all companies giving a very large degree of autonomy to their subsidiaries will exhibit the charac-

teristics mentioned, whereas the picture is more
mixed for companies with medium to very high centralization. Table 6 leads us to this interpretation. This view can also be supported on the theoretical level. It turns out that most of the arguments for centralization are either arguments claiming tht it is possible to centralize (because of
experience, being big and not too much diversified, having built it up from scratch), or arguments calling for integration between units (integration of product flows, market information,
pricing policy, competitive strategy at large),
which does not necessarily mean centalization and
drastic loss of autonomy. The mature MNC has a
choice of what kind of integration mechanisms it
wants to foster. A further indication that this is
indeed the case is the large differences in approach
by Swedish companies as compared to - for example -
US ones. We shall elaborate this point further in
the succeeding chapters.

## Characteristics of the subsidiaries

We are in a better position to assess the effects of
subsidairy characteristics than in the case of aggregate systems attributes. The size of the sample
allows some careful use of statistical treatment.
As before, we place prime importance on "soft"
data. When the results using qualitative data contradict the conslusions of quantative manipulation,
this will be stated. Luckily, there are rather few
such cases, probably because most of the quanti-
fication is nothing else than writing down the results of the in-depth studies in a compact, non-
verbal format. Therefore, the agreement between
the modes of analysis should not be taken as a
license to use remote, impersonal methods to obtain data for the purpose of discussing these or
similar questions.

First, let us look at the two variables that guided
the design of the study: the ownership structure
of the subsidiary and its location in terms of type
of country. Table 7 shows that, contrary to our
initial hypothesis, it matters little whether a
subsidiary is wholly owned or a joint venture, in
terms of the degree of autonomy of the subsidiary.
All the different measures show the same lack of any
clear tendency. The negative result contradicts
earlier studies, which have hypothesized and/or
found that wholly owned subsidiaries are more
tightly controlled than joint ventures.

Several types of reasoning would lead one to expect that subsidiaries located in so-called less developed countries would be differently treated than those in developed countries. The distance both in the geographical and the cultural sense should lead to more of local autonomy. On the other hand, the need to transfer know-how of technical and managerial kind should work in the opposite direction. Therefore, the lack of any clear differences is not that surprising at a first glance. It is difficult to separate the effect of geographical distance from the effect of the different state or type of development, since for Swedish companies they are highly correlated. The cultural distance was measured separately. The classification of Forsgren-Johansson (1975) was used. No clear relationship between cultural distance and measures of subsidiary autonomy was found.

We are thus left with the hypothesis of probably rather weak and contradicting tendencies. We would like to suggest that the character of the host country will become of less and less importance for the degree of autonomy given to the subsidiary, for reasons of increased knowledge and communication and because of global standardization of the management culture. At least this will be true for relatively open economies. Countries which are very different from the base country of the parent company and which close themselves off by prohibitive tariff walls and - probably more important - indigenization of personnel requirements will probably enjoy the presence of more autonomous subsidiaries. The price to pay for this will be later and less effective access to the knowledge and products of the company.

The questionnaire study gave the same conclusion as to the effect of ownership structure and location. Table 9 shows very small differencies between the various types of subsidiaries. Therefore. we may conclude that the results in the interview study were not only an artifact of a limited or skewed sample. (Although there are disappontingly few joint ventures and few LDC-located affiliates in the questionnaire study. The explanation for this is simply that the companies approached were not established through joint ventures and in LDCs to any greater extent.)

Affiliates in developing countries are often set up specifically to serve the local market, sometimes on outright demands from the local government that production has to be established if the company is to stay on the market. HQ involvement is in these

TABLE 7    Measures of subsidiary autonomy for wholly owned subsidiaries and minority joint ventures in developed countries/less developed countries

|  | Wholly owned subsidiaries (WH) (n=13) | | Minority joint ventures (JV) (n=11) | | | |
|---|---|---|---|---|---|---|
| Developed countries (DC) (n=13) | SUBDEC[1] | 3.96 | SUBDEC | 4.04 | = all DC | |
|  | SUBSTRAT[2] | 3.26 | SUBSTRAT | 3.36 | SUBDEC | 4.00 |
|  | SUBOP[3] | 4.43 | SUBOP | 4.50 | SUBSTRAT | 3.31 |
|  | AUTSTR[4] | 2.71 | AUTSTR | 3.00 | SUBOP | 4.46 |
|  | AUTOP[5] | 3.86 | AUTOP | 4.00 | AUTSTR | 2.85 |
|  | | | | | AUTOP | 3.92 |
| Less developed countries (LDC) (n=11) | SUBDEC | 4.11 | SUBDEC | 4.32 | = all LDC | |
|  | SUBSTRAT | 3.58 | SUBSTRAT | 3.93 | SUBDEC | 4.22 |
|  | SUBOP | 4.52 | SUBOP | 4.58 | SUBSTRAT | 3.74 |
|  | AUTSTR | 2.83 | AUTSTR | 2.60 | SUBOP | 4.55 |
|  | AUTOP | 4.00 | AUTOP | 4.00 | AUSTR | 2.73 |
|  | | | | | AUTOP | 4.00 |

| = all WH | | = all JV | |
|---|---|---|---|
| SUBDEC | 4.05 | SUBDEC | 4.17 |
| SUBSTRAT | 3.41 | SUBSTRAT | 3.62 |
| SUBOP | 4.47 | SUBOP | 4.54 |
| AUTSTR | 2.77 | AUTSTR | 2.82 |
| AUTOP | 3.92 | AUTOP | 4.00 |

1. Averages over subsidiaries indicated. SUBDEC is measured on a 1-5 scale, 5 indicating very high influence for the subsdiary. The score is calculated for each subsidiary by taking the ratings given by the respondent in the subsidiary on 15 specified decision areas and averaging to a composite index.

2. As 1., but for 6 of the 15 decisions areas considered as strategic.

3. As 1., but for 9 of the 15 decisions areas considered as operational.

4.5. Averages over subsidiaries indicated. AUTSTR (AUTOP) is measured on a 1-5 scale, 5 indicating very high autonomy of the subsidiary. The ratings were made by the researchers, on the basis of in-depth study. AUTSTR refers to autonomy in strategic matters, AUTOP to autonomy in operational matters.

cases heavy while actually establishing the local
company. After having got it going, however, the
attention turns to the bigger and closer markets,
where there is more interaction between the subsidiaries. Several cases of this nature are represented in our sample.

The      uncertainity of the subsidiary's environment
should be positively correlated with autonomy. Uncertainty requires rapid access to information, flexibility and capacity for fast response, which prohi-
bits too centralized forms of decision making. (We
need not here refer in detail to all the literature
on environment-organization interaction.) The degree
of uncertainity was measured by computing an un-
weighed index of answers given by a respondent in the
subsidiary to questions about the uncertainty of market, political, supply, labour, and financial conditions. A five-point scale was used. Table 9 shows a
weak positive relationship, significant at the 0.19
level. Controls were made$_3$ for variables such as
the subsidiary's size, market share, profitablity,
and impacts from the parent company. No strong
relationship between degree of uncertainty and
autonomy of the subsidiary was found, although the
direction of the association was the expected.

It may be of interest to note that the relevant uncertainties are perceived differently in developed
and developing countries. The overall degree of uncertainty is significantly higher in LDCs, and uncertainties connected with political conditions,
supply and capital markets are much more important
than in developed countries, However, market conditions is still seen as a primary source of uncertainty also in LDCs, as in the industrialized countries, where this factor was rated considerably
higher than the others. (See table 10.)

The clearest determinant of subsidiary autonomy
was the degree of cross-shipments of goods between
the subsidiary and other parts of the corporation.
(See table 9.) Purchases from the parent company
as a proportion of total sales was negatively correlated with autonomy. (Pearson's r=0.45, significant
at the 0.02 level.) The figure is not much affected
- in fact somewhat heightened - if first-order
partial correlations controlling for size, result
of subsidiary, and other variables possibly influencing the relationship are calculated. This can be
explained by the greater need for operational
coordination that cross-shipments of goods imply,
and the fact that the behaviour of the subsidiary
may have strategic implications for the company
as a whole. A closer look at the data and the

TABLE 8   Degree of subsidiary autonomy[1] for various
          types companies

|      | WH   | JV   |
|------|------|------|
| DC   | 3.64 | 3.73 |
| LDC  | 3.70 | 3.68 |

1. Based on questionnaire to 53 companies with together 117 affiliates abroad. Scale 1-5, 5 indicating high autonomy.

TABLE 9   Spearman coefficients of correlation between subsidiary
          autonomy[1] and various characteristics of the subsidiaries
          (n = 24)

|                                           | r      | Level of significance |
|-------------------------------------------|--------|-----------------------|
| Uncertainty of subsidiary's environment   | 0.18   | 0.19                  |
| Cross-shipments of goods                  | - 0.45 | 0.02                  |
| Technology transfer from HQ to sub        | - 0.21 | 0.16                  |
| Technology transfer from sub to HQ        | - 0.19 | 0.18                  |
| Size of subsidiary (turnover/year)        | 0.37   | 0.04                  |
| Relative size of subsidiary               | 0.38   | 0.04                  |
| Intensity of competition for sub          | - 0.24 | 0.13                  |
| Market share of subsidiary                | - 0.39 | 0.03                  |
| Performance of subsidiary                 | 0.20   | 0.17                  |

1.   Measured through interviews at the subsidiaries.
     Scale: See table 1.


TABLE 10   Level of uncertainty for various areas as estimated
           by respondents in subsidiaries, in DCs, and LDCSs.
           (Scale 1-5; 1= very easy to predict, 5=very difficult
           to predict.)

|                       | DCs  | LDCs |
|-----------------------|------|------|
| Market condition      | 2.92 | 3.18 |
| Political conditions  | 2.53 | 3.36 |
| Supply conditions     | 2.08 | 2.91 |
| Capital markets       | 2.23 | 2.91 |
| Labour markets        | 2.54 | 2.91 |
| Average               | 2.46 | 3.06 |

cases reveals that the influence of head office is indeed mainly directed at operational matters, and somewhat less at stratetig ones. Problems of logistics, transfer pricing, short-term financing and production take a lot of energy. The Pearson correlation coefficient is significant at the 0.002 level for operational autonomy and only at the 0.12 level for strategic autonomy.

If the subsidiary exports goods or services, it comes under closer scrutiny at HQ. However, often those subsidiaries that did export were either big, established, successful and powerful, or they were forced to export because of government pressure. The latter applies primarily to developing countries. In this case, mutual interests were sometimes formed between the government and the mangement of the subsidiary, countering the urge at HQ to control export flows. In the former case, the subsidiary had enjoyed considerable autonomy for a long time, and continued to do so even though its activities started to interfere with the rest of the corporation. It should be mentioned that most subsidiaries today supply the local market only, wherefore the effect of increased export interdependence cannot be fully analyzed for this sample.

Antoher type of interdependence is created by technology transfer between the parent company and the subsudiary. Again the results show a weak correlation with autonomy in the expected direction. (Table 9.) It is interesting to note that technology transfer from the parent to the subsidiary mainly (negatively) affects the operational autonomy rather than the strategic. As in the case of product flows between units, strategic matters seem to be dealt with more similarly in highly integrated and less integrated companies. For technology transfer from the subsidiary to the parent company, the relationship curiously enough is stronger for strategic matters. This could be explained by the fact that subsidiaries that are able to contribute knowledge to the group as a whole may develop a certain power base because of this. Indee, some of these subsidiaries were acquired because they could make such contributions. On the other hand R&D capacity is a critical strategic resoruce which HQ feels it has to control. Therefore we do not want to draw any farreaching conclusions from these data, particularly as there were very few subsidiaries that did transfer much technology to HQ.

The size of the subsidiary has previously been shown to be positively correlated with autonomy. From a theoretical standpoint, one can detect two conflicting forces at work. On the one hand, increased size means that the subsidiary can build up its own resources and become less dependent upon management. On the other hand, a very large subsidiary is of great importance to the whole company, and may therefore require a lot of attention. Indead, one would expect a curvilinear relationship here. A close inspection of the data reveals such a tendency. If the joint ventures - which are in some cases rather big and some of them rather special - in the study are taken our of the sample, it turns our that the remaining large subsidiaries are not more autonomous than the medium-sized ones. Therefore, we would hypothesize the following relationship depicted in figure 1 to hold:

The zero-order Pearson correlation coefficients for our measure of autonomy with size of subsidiary is 0.37 (See table 9.) The relationship is not significantly affected by the influence of third variables such as product flows, technology transfer or market share and profitability of the subsidiary.

FIGURE 1  Relationship between size of subsidiary and
          degree of autonomy

Autonomy

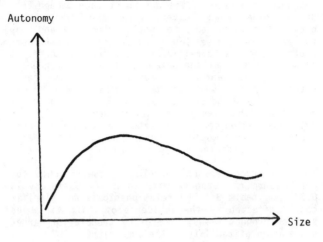

FIGURE 2  Degree of subsidiary autonomy by size of
          subsidiary for big and small MNCs

Autonomy

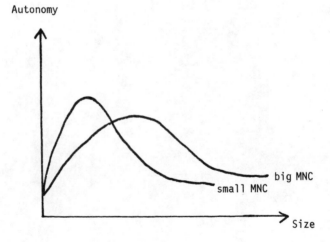

Some authors (see for example Aylmer, 1970) use the
size of the subsidiary relative to the parent company
rather than the absolute size as the relevant measure. Since the six parent companies in our sample do
not vary very much in size, the results are almost
identical if a measure of relative size is used.
We cannot separate the effects empirically. One would
assume on theoretical grounds that a subsidiary of a
given size would have larger autonomy in a small
corporation than in a large one, as long as it was
not so big that it constituted a very essential part
of the corporation. The curve in figure 1 should thus
be read as indicating the degree of autonomy <u>given</u>
a certain size of the parent company. For a smaller
company, the curve would be steeper and flatten out
earlier (Figure 2.)

In summary, previous findings about the positive
effect of size of subsidiary on its autonomy are
supported, but a declining degree of autonomy is
hypothesized for subsidiaries very large in relation
to the parent company.

We have dealt with the overall competitive position
of the total corporation above. Now, we will be concerned with the effects of <u>structure of competition
at the level of the subsidiary</u>. This aspect has not
been discussed at length in the literature.
Khandwalla (1973) (mentioned in de Bodinat, 1975)
found a positive relationship between degree of central control and the "illiberability" of the environment. An "illiberable" environment is an environment
in which there are severe pressures on the organization. Mostly, it is interpreted in the sense of competitive pressure. De Bodinat (1975) finds a very
weak support for the hypothesis in his study on influence in MNCs. Our results agree with his. There
is a weak relationship in the expected direction,
significant of the 0.13 level, between the autonomy
of subsidiaries and the <u>intensity of competition</u> on
the local market. (See table 9.) The latter variable
was measured by charting impressions of subsidiary
managers, so it is open to the criticism that impressions do not necessarily depict the "true" state of
the environment.

A more powerful determinant of autonomy in our sample
was the <u>market share of the subsidiary</u>. It seems as
if HQ influences subsidiaries with substantial market
shares more than those with small shares. This holds
true also when size of subsidiary and product flows
between subsidiary and parent are held constant. The
simple regression coefficient is significant at the
0.03 level. (See table 9.) It would be difficult in
this sample to separate the effect of local market

share from the effect of the global competitive
structure in the industry the company is active in.
From a close inspection of the specific cases, it
seems as if a subsidiary with a large market share
operating in an industry which is competitive (in
the structural sense, i.e., with many independent
sellers) on the global scale could still enjoy a
high degree of autonomy. Since its competitors on
the local market would be different from the competitors in other countries, the need for coordinated
corporate strategies would not exist. It turns out,
however, that the subsidiaries finding themselves in
this situation are mostly only the first MNC to get
involved in a country, "restructuring" the industry.
Other companies from other countries are often
knocking on the door. In these cases, HQ is anxious
in the first place to keep these potential - competitors out of the market and - if they manage to get
in - fight them with the whole arsenal of weapons
that only HQ can mobilize. This state of high market
share and lack of large international competitors is
probably only a temporary phenomenon. Only companies
with very specific and unique products, or with very
good contacts with the local government, will be
able to extend this golden period very long.

The performance of the subsidiary has been shown to
affect its autonomy by Aslegg (1971). We had difficulties in obtaining valid and reliable profit figures for all subsidiaries. Therefore, we use as a
measure of subsidiary performance the view of top
managers in the parent company. They were asked to
rate the subsidiaries on a 1 to 5-scale in terms of
their performance during the last five years. A weak
relationship in the expected direction is shown in
table 9. Control for size, imports from HQ, market
share, ownership structure and location does not
change the basic result.

Three qualifications to the simple hypothesis about
the effect of performance on autonomy seem desirable
after looking at the specific cases. First, performance seems to have to drop to a critical limit before anything is done. If results are only moderately bad, not much is done from HQ. Also, if performance is exceptionally good it may even attract the
attention of HQ and lead them to interfere with the
company. Second, performance is a relative measure.
If other subsidiaries, or - more importantly - the
parent company itself, is not doing well, the subsidiary may not notice any increased involvement. In
one of the companies, it was very clear that the
power struggles and anxieties initiated by a general
crisis of the company distructed HQ officials from

even informing themselves about some of the foreign
subsidiaries. Third, the companies studied here - as
Swedish companies in general - tend to react to problems in the subsidiaries rather by replacing the
managing director than by remote control of the company. The principle is autonomy and power exercized
by an independent and capable manager. Rather than
compromising the principle, the companies respond to
crises by trying even harder to find somebody who can
live with it. Indeed, some of the companies felt that
at a time when there were severe problems in a subsidiary, it would be particularly inappropriate to try to
guide things from the centre, since it would be even
more difficult to effectively do so than when conditions were more normal. (Of course one should inter-
prete our measures of autonomy in the light of this
discussions, since they do not capture this mode of
influencing the subsidiaries.)

Acquired subsidiaries tend to be given more autonomy
than those built up from scratch. This is in line
with previous research and with the discussion above
about the effect of modes of internationalization.
Within a given corporation, those subsidiaries that
had been acquired recently were more autonomous than
the rest. Since three of the corporations in the
sample had not acquired any of the companies studied,
except for a few joint ventures, no aggregate results
are presented here. A one-by-one comparison in the
cases where this was possible strongly supports the
hypothesis, however. The questionnaire study on a
large sample gives the same result. The average degree of autonomy on a 1-5 scale was 3.95 for companies acquired after 1971 and 3.60 for the rest.

The degree to which the subsidiaries were involved in
the production and selling of products based on the
core technology of the corporation seemed to influence their autonomy. Affiliates that only were active
in areas peripheral to this core were more autonomous
than the others. It was striking how one subsidiary
of a corporation could be tightly controlled whereas
another subsidiary in the same country acted rather
independently due to its marginal importance to the
top decision makers in the parent company. Particularly in companies with a mother-daughter structure
of organization, these peripheral units may be almost
unnoticed as long as they perform reasonably well.
Only the controller's department worries about them
in normal times. These subsidiaries tend to be managed in more formal ways, whereas - as will be
discussed at length later - the rule in Swedish
companies is a very informal management style.

Even <u>within</u> a specific subsidiary, different parts enjoy differing degrees of autonomy depending on their involvement in the core of the MNC's business.

In summary, we found strong support for a positive relationship between degree of subsidiary autonomy and: lack of integration with the MNC in terms of product flows; low market share of the subsidiary; establishment of the subsidiary through acquisition; lack of involvement in the core technology of the parent firm. Weak support for a positive relationship was found for: lack of technology transfer between the subsidiary and the parent company; size and relative size of the subsidiary; low intensity of competition on the local market; low concentration of suppliers on the local market; high performance of the subsidiary. No correlation was found for cultural distance. Finally, no definite conclusions can be drawn about the effect of ownership structure and location of the subsidiary.

As in the case of determinants of autonomy on the corporate level, one has to be very careful in the interpretation of analyses carried out stepwise, variable by variable. There is considerable interaction between many of the "independent" variables, and the structure of the interdependence varies with the stage of development of the internationalization process of the firm. Furthermore, some of the relationships can be expected to be curvilinear rather than linear. We have made efforts to check the results by computing first-order partial correlation coefficients and by breaking the material down in subcategories. The size of the sample puts severe limits on the statistical sophistication of the analysis that is possible and desirable. More important than this is that we can substantiate our conclusions by reference to in-depth studies of specific subsidiaries. This allows us to chart the causal relationships in more detail and with greater accuracy than is possible by statistical methods. It also allows us to observe an intricate interplay of forces that makes one want to leave the paradigm of cause-effect analysis for more holistic and processual interpretations. The correlations presented above are supported by in-depth analyses. For reasons of space and confidentiality, of course, we cannot present all this material. However, we will describe the characteristics of two of the most autonomous and two of the least autonomous of the subsidiaries at some length, in order that the reader may get the flavour of our type of data and mode of analysis.

## Subsidiary A - expansion on critical market

A is one of the most interesting subsidiaries in this
large Swedish MNC. The subsidiary is wholly owned and
located in a large developing country on the verge of
being heavily industrialized. The country is a market
economy with strong involvement by the government in
national economic planning. Its development strategy
has been and is to attract foreign capital through
investment and export incentives and very high cus-
toms barriers. A was established a long time ago, and
has produced simpler varieties of the company's main
product line for some time in addition to product imported from Sweden. In 1978, around 75 % of A's sales
was produced locally. Big investments have been made
lately and are being decided right now. In the future, A will produce also the most advanced versions
of the products. The parent company, and A, are involved in technology-intensive products sold to
large, institutional buyers. In this case, 80 %
of A's sales go to public or semi-public authorities.
During the last few years, negotiations about very
large deliveries have been conducted. Without exagge-
rating, one could say that the future of A is of
great importance to the company as a whole. A has
been rather successful during the last few years.
Before that, there were considerable problems both
in terms of profitability and in the form of confusion and conflict at the top management level.

The parent company has internationalized in a big way
rather recently. The policy has been to stick to
Sweden whenever possible, and only invest abroad when
this has been necessary to keep in the market. Cost
advantages abroad have not been of any importance.
Rather, what has triggered foreign investments has
been outright demands from the governments in the
markets served or potentially served, or tariff walls
prohibiting exports from Sweden at competitive
prices.

The company has a clearly recognizable management
style characterized by formality, the use of standardized methods and procedures, production-technology
orientation, and centralization to top management.
Its organization is the typical mother-daughter
structure, with the parent company being split up in
product divisions. There are also strong functional
departments for both production and marketing, however. Although the main products of the company require high technology and capital intensity in production and consumption, the company also produces
and sells lighter products. The competitive structure
for these is very different from the mature oligopoly
of the main product line. A is only involved in this

and competes solely against other MNCs rather than
with local producers.

The nature of A's business - oligopoly, government
involvement, and high technology - has lead headquarters to take great interest in the subsidiary.
The future of A is of strategic importance to the
parent company because of the fast-growing and large
market and because successful completion of some
large projects in the country would be a good argument on other, similar markets. Furthermore, build-
up of the production capacity requires transfer of
know-how from Sweden. Complex problems of coordination between headquarters, A, and the product divisions concerned have to be solved in this process.
The divisions are deprived of production and exports
and are at the same time asked to assist A. Since the
culture of the company is not very well developed in
terms of capacity to use informal channels, headquarters has had to take an active role in resolving
conflicts and making final decisions. Thus, in spite
of the relative novelty of international expansion
and the consequent lack of expertise in these
matters, the company has adopted a rather centralized
way of handling its relationships to A. New organizational units to address the problems have been created at the central level. Particular importance has
been put on specifying "who should produce what where
in the company". The top people in these new units
yield a lot of power over the subsidiaries.

HQ exerts influence on A in many ways. Because of
the important developments lately, there have been
many visits by top managers in the parent company to
A. Even the chairman of the board has taken an active
interest in the issues. Also at the operational
level, many trips - mainly from Sweden to A - have
been made. The plan is to cut down on trips as locals
are trained to run the production. In comparison with
other companies in the sample, there is much use of
formal mechanisms of coordination and control.
Written policies and manuals are important, and initiatives in the subsidiary are channeled to formal
institutions and follow reporting relationships.
During the build-up of production, around ten Swedes
are on site in A. However, the company does not primarily control through transfer of managers (see
Edström and Galbraith, 1977), but through systems.
The managing director of A is a third country national. The intention is to replace the Swedes in A
successively as local competence is built up.

The experience of A "fits" the hypotheses discussed
above rahter well. Technology intensity, large local
market share, important flows of products and techno-

logy, global oligopoly and strategic importance for
the MNC should all lead to centralization of decision
making. The relative lack of international experience
of the parent company and the success of A would be
expected to work in the opposite direction. It seems
as if the latter variable is not so important as the
opportunities for future success, which tend to
stimulate HQ interest in the initial stages of preparing for new moves. As for the international experience, the parent company has felt that it cannot
wait for experience to build up, and shyness in the
treatment of A has by no means been a characteristic
of the parent company's attitude. The management
style and philosophy must be attributed significant
importance. Also in other cases the foreign subsidiaries are not allowed any greater degree of autonomy,
in spite of not being of particular strategic importance, being involved mainly in less advanced
technology and competing in more perfect markets.
The strong influence of overall management style and
corporate culture on the management of the subsidiaries is further discussed in Hedlund (1977).

## B - the marginal joint venture

B is a joint venture formed about 15 years ago in
which the parent company of A (see above) has a minority share. The remaining share is controlled by an
important financial family in the country - which
happens to be the same as for A. One of the members
of the family is the managing director of B. The
Swedish company's motives for entering the agreement
were to start production and thereby avoid import
duties, to get access to the distribution network of
the partner, and to establish a more direct presence
on the market. B started producing one of the Swedish
partner's less sophisticated products. In addition to
this, the host country partner was involved in two
other lines of business, which by the way have been
more profitable throughout the period. B was in 1977
about three times as large as A. The Swedish firm has
received license fees from B, but lately national
legislation in the host country has prohibited
license payments to foreign parent firms. This has
caused tensions between B and - particularly - the
product division in Sweden responsible for B's products. The division exports parts to B, which has
somewhat alleviated the tensions. And - HQ personnel
at the parent firm point out - the profits of B partly go to the Swedish partner anyway in the form of
dividends.

B has acted very independently all the time. It
certainly belongs to the top four or five companies
in the sample in terms of autonomy. Contacts with the

parent company have been restricted to talks now and
then with its managing director or a few other top
officials. At the operational level, there are almost
no contacts. There is no Swedish personnel in B. B is
not subordinated to the same array of reports, manuals and routines as A. The relationship with the
parent company is rather informal and activated only
when immediate problems are at hand. Rather cordial
personal relationships seem to prevail. The Swedish
firm has not wanted to spend too much time and energy
on a business which is somewhat marginal to it in the
long term perspective. Moreover, good relationships
in the country have been regarded to be of strategic
importance for the main line of business.

This is a case where the stature as a joint venture
has undoubtedly had a big importance in providing B
with a lot of freedom. Wholly owned subsidiaries engaged in the same product line as B are controlled
much more tightly. The relatively low technology of
those of B's products that originate with the parent
firm, the lack of strong ties in terms of product
flows, the presence of a nationally respected partner, and the fact that management in Sweden had more
urgent matters to attent to - even in the same country - has "marginalized" B to such an extent that one
is content in Sweden as long as B provides a decent
return on capital invested. No doubt also the parent
firm's way of managing makes it difficult to introduce their systems half-way, as it were, in acquired
companies. Either you subscribe to the whole system,
or you are somewhat of an anomaly, which is best
dealt with at the central level. Since the threshold
of full acceptance has not been reached in this case,
a rather disembodied style of management by exception
and according to a philosophy of satisficing has been
adopted. This is looked upon with some resentment
among the next to the highest levels of management
in Sweden. There is a feeling that management in B
considers anything below the absolute top as too unimportant to pay attention to.

## C - the joint venture in search of a role

C was formed around 10 years ago by the Swedish parent firm and a local government controlled partner
in one of the fastest growing industrialized economies of the world. The Swedish firm had a 49 % share
of the venture. Lately, this share has dropped to
about half of this, since the parent company in
Sweden has not wanted to participate in increases
of the share capital in C. The venture imports around
a third of its sales from Sweden, and exports marginal quantities. Recently, plans have been discussed to
increase the exports by transfering production from

other plants, thereby specializing production by
company. C has had a couple of difficult years, as
has the parent company, which is the reason for the
reluctance to follow the local partner in raising
more equity. C is of approximately the same size as
A.

The Swedish parent firm is a mature, technologically
advanced MNC in a typical global oligopoly, where
competition is rather aggressive because of the entry
of a few new countries and companies on the world
market. The main product line of the company is organized in regionally defined divisions. In addition
to its main product, the company also has important
investments in related areas. These are subordinated
to other companies within the group, and not represented with subsidiaries in the country where C is
located. Global specialization of production has become an increasingly marked characteristic of this
company lately. This has necessitated quite complex
planning systems and heavy HQ involvement in restructuring and coordination.

C was tightly controlled by the Swedich firm until
the last few years. And in spite of the low share of
equity, Sweden still plays a very big role in the
running of the company. When the equity positions
were changed, a new managing director was appointed.
He was a local of the country, formally suggested by
the local partner, and thereafter accepted by the
Swedish parent firm. However, the previous Swedish
managing director was still on site, functioning as
the parent company's eye in C. The local partner did
not really know the technology and the market, so
they were rather passive, except when it came to
investment or divestment decisions. Being state-
controlled, the partner payed a lot of attention
to employment and - recently - to exports. From the
point of view of the partner, the best would be if
the Swedish firm took over the majority of the shares
and managed the company.

In this case, the parent firm exercises considerable
influence in spite of being in a minority position
and not even controlling the appointment of top management. Strict quality control standards are applied,
and C is dependent on central resources both for
transfer of technology and market knowledge. The
parent firm thus is in a position to be able to influence decisions. It also is in a position that
makes it want to exercise influence. Foreign-owned
competitors have been taking market share from C
recently, and are negotiating to set up new large
plants in the country, promising jobs and exports.
This is a strategic threat to the parent company

since not only the local market, but also export markets, is implicated. The industry is very capital-intensive, and dumping tendencies have been visible as new competitors have tried to gain volume.

Several factors - such as capital intensity, advanced technology, oligopolistic competition, and inter-unit product flow interdependence - have countered the tendency for power to be localized with the management of C and the majority partner. Also the fact that there is a clear reporting relationship to one of the divisions in Sweden has been of importance. In other similar instances, local management and the partner have been able to - as it were - play the divisions against each other, and top HQ management has not had the time or the specialized expertise necessary really to control developments. In this case, the profitability problems have led the parent firm rather to doubt whether it should go on supporting C than to tighten its grips on the venture. Now, when profits have gone up again, there is a renewed interest in contemplating the future of C. Whatever the outcome, the nature of the business of the corporation makes the fate of almost every unit of critical importance. Therefore, there certainly is a need for coordination. In this case, coordination has implied centralization. The corporation is probably the most centralized in the sample.

## G - a profitable step towards internationalization

G is a wholly Swedish-owned subsidiary in a European country. It was acquired a few years ago and is the biggest foreign company in the division to which it belongs. It is also very profitable. Formally, it is owned by the parent company, but the division has full responsibility for the operations. G produces and sells high-quality products, which are not, how-ever, very complex from a technological point of view. Production is not very capital-intensive. Competition is oligopolistic and conducted on unusually friendly terms. G has high market shares on the relevant market segments. There are no imports to G and only marginal exports to one other European country.

The parent company has grown very rapidly through foreign acquisitions during the last five years. Expansion has been concentrated to a few of the many divisions in this rather diversified company. There has been an explicit policy of internationalization through the buying of market positions held by profitable companies. The acquired firms are subordinated to the relevant division, and also initiatives for acqusitions are taken from the divisions rather than from group HQ, which is very small for the size of the firm.

The division to which G belongs was selected as promising in terms of international growth. After having studied many possibilities, G and a few other firms in other countries were bought. In the case of G, the fact that an old friend of the division managing director's was willing to take over management of G was of great importance for the closing of the deal.

G is left very free to manage its business. Contacts with the division are rather informal. The respective managing directors talk openly to each other when they meet. The reporting systems of the parent company have been introduced rather carefully, and no transfer of Swedish personnel to G has taken place. Before being taken over, G was a licensee of the division, and still is. In fact, one of the few problem areas in the relationship has been the organization of product development. This has not prompted the division to dictate decisions to G, however. A working group to discuss the problems has been set up to maximize the benefits of product development in both Sweden and G.

Illustrated in this case are the effects on autonomy of several factors; the fact that the industry sofar does not contain very many international companies, the diversified structure of the group, the lack of international expertise in Sweden, the particular conduct of competitiors (and, by the way, labour), the profitability of an acquired company, and the personal ties and trust between the key individuals involved. The clear subordination of G to one division has in this case not affected its position.

## Summary of caselets

These snap-shots illustrate and support our analyses at the level of aggregate data. Nevertheless, a few remarks qualifying the rather mechanistic treatment of data earlier should be made.

First, the specific tracing of "independent variables" is much more difficult for less extreme (in terms of degree of autonomy) cases. Complex interactions between factors, and a large degree of discretion as to the way the relationships are handled seem to be at work for the more normal cases. Also within the set presented above, similar "contingencies" are associated with very different outcomes in terms of autonomy.

The degree of complexity is increased by the fact that autonomy varies over time as a consequence both of changes in the supposedly determining factors and of rather random developments which when they have been initiated continue as if through pure

social inertia. An independent manager, a big order
in the subsidiary, a change at central headquarters,
priorities in other parts of the world, accidental or
intended involvement in politically sensitive projects in the host country; all these idiosyncracies
may shape the from and direction of development of
HQ-subsidiary relationships in general, and the autonomy of the subsidiary in particular. Brooke and
Remmers (1970) described how the relationship oscil-
lated between "open" and "close" as a consequence of
performance in the subsidiary. In order really to in-
vestigate these matters, one would best use lingitu-
dinal in-depth studies over long time periods. We
have not conducted such studies, and neither did
Brooke and Remmers. Nevertheless, on the basis of our
material, we would like to suggest that the variation
over time is much more complex, and much less determined, than implied by Brooke and Remmers. Certainly
performance has some importance, but at least for our
sample other variables were more important.

Finally, the influence of what - in lack of a better
word - one might call the management style of the
parent company is very strong and may cancel out
the effects of more specific determinants of autonomy. This is discussed in Hedlund (1978). Here,
suffice is to note that the effects of variables
such as degree of integration through product flow,
local market share, and local market concentration
seem to be stronger for operational autonomy than for
strategic autonomy. At the operational level, there
are clearly perceivable necessities for variations
in degree of central control depending upon the
characteristics of the subsidiary. For example,
intra-company deliveries require elaborate transfer
pricing schemes, inventory control systems, short-
term financing systems, coordination between deliveries and local marketing efforts, etc. All this requires that HQ takes an active role. At the strategic
level, however, the needs for coordination are satis-
fied in different ways in different companies, and
some of those ways do not involve primarily centralization to HQ.

THE FORMALITY OF THE RELATIONSHIP

After centralization, formalization is the most commonly discussed dimension of organizational structure and processes. Here, we will shortly report
some of the more general conclusions about the determinants of the degree of formality.

We define formality in terms of the degree to which
decisions are made and activitites carries out according to explicit routines and explicit lines of

authority and channels/fora of decision making. Ope-
rationally, for each subsidiary an index, based upon
the researcher's ratings is computed. A five-point
scale is used for each of the components in the
index, which is the unweighted average of the scores
on these four dimensions:

1. The degree of specification of channels and fora
   for decision-making in strategic matters.

2. As 1, but for operational matters.

3. The degree of specification of substance of decisions, rules for making decisions, and activities to be carried out, for strategic matters.

4. As 3, but for operational matters.

In addition to this, the respondents in the subsidiaries were asked to rate the extent to which
the subsidiaries relied on written policies from
headquarters to guide its decision-making (see
below), what manuals issued by HQ were used, and
what standard procedures were used. Moreover, the
whole arsenal of routines was investigated by in-
depth studies at headquarters. The conclusions
reported below are supported by all these sources
of information. As in the case of autonomy, it
should be remebered that the seemingly mechanistic
assigning of indexes to subsidiaries builds upon
very rich qualitative as well as quantitative
data.

## Formality at large

In general, the relationship between headquarters
and subsidiaries in our sample can be characterized
as informal. Since degree of formality is a relative
measure. the only way to justify this statement is
by reference to some standard comparison. Tables
11 and 12 show that the Swedish MNCs investigated
managed their subsidiaries much more informally
than did comparable U.S. corporations, whereas
the Japanese ones seem to be rather similar to
the Swedish in this respect. The larger size of the
U.S. companies might explain the difference between
Seden and the U.S., but this cannot be the whole
truth, since also the Japanese companies are bigger
than the Swedish. The larger size of the U.S.
subsidiaries may likewise have had an influence.
However, as will be seen below, for the Swedish
subsidiaries, formality decreased with size of subsidiary! We would like to offer the same type of
explanation in terms of the history of internationalization of Swedish MNCs for the high degree

TABLE 11

"To what extent do you rely on written policies from HQ to guide decision-making?" Answers from respondents in subsidiaries of Swedish, U.S., and Japanese MNCs. Scale 1-5, 1=a lot, 5=not at all. Number of answers.

|              | Swedish | U.S | Japanese |
|--------------|---------|-----|----------|
| 1=a lot      | -       | 3   | 1        |
| 2            | 4       | 14  | 3        |
| 3            | 6       | 2   | 9        |
| 4            | 4       | 2   | 8        |
| 5=not at all | 10      | -   | 10       |
| Total        | 24      | 21  | 31       |

TABLE 12

"For which of these areas do you have written manuals from HQ? Answers from respondents in subsidiaries of Swedish, U.S., and Japanese MNCs. Number of answers.

|                                             | Swedish | U.S. | Japanese |
|---------------------------------------------|---------|------|----------|
| Only technical design and manufacturing     | 2       | 1    | 5        |
| Only accounting                             | 4       | 2    | 5        |
| Only marketing                              | -       | -    | 2        |
| Only company philosphy                      | -       | -    | 3        |
| Only technical + marketing + accounting     | 10      | 2    | 5        |
| All or most of the above                    | 3       | 15   | 5        |
| None                                        | 5       | 1    | 4        |
| Total                                       | 24      | 21   | 29       |

of informality as for the high degree of autonomy. It would be difficult to argue in terms of cultural sterotypes here, since few would support the theses that the United States is characterized by a high degree of formality in general compared to Sweden an Japan. However, it is probably true that the professionalization and standardization of management as an occupation has gone furthest in the U.S. In Sweden and Japan, management is probably more of an activity exercized by traditional élites that build up a culture of its own, in which the members do not need formalized systems in order to interact and coordinate.

## Formality and company characteristics

The size and nature of the sample make it very difficult to study how aggregate company characteristics relate to degree of formality. Nevertheless, in table 13 we have ranked the firms in terms of degree of formality in managing headquarters-subsidiary realtionships. The following tentative remarks can be made.

First, there are very few clear relationships. The emphasis that was put on the complicated structure of causality and the high degree of management discretion in the discussion of autonomy applies also to formality.

Second, a rather clear relationship between centralization and formalization appears. Formal control instrument are thus in these firms not a substitute for influencing decisions in the subsidiaries, but a means to exercise such influence. Those firms that rely on informal mechanisms of coordination give much more autonomy to their affiliates. This is not unexpected. The chief alternative to formal methods is to send expatriates, or at least individuals well-known in and knowledgeable about the company as a whole, to the subsidiary. The presence of such individuals makes both autonomy and informality attractive. As is evident from table 14, very strong negative correlations between degree of subsidiary autonomy and various measures of formality were found for our sample.

Third, the two most formalized companies have their subsidiaries rather clearly attached to product divisions. The mother-daughter structure generally goes together with a high degree of informality.

TABLE 13 Formality of headquarter-subsidiary relationships and aggregate company characteristics[1]

| Company | I | II | III | IV | V | VI |
|---|---|---|---|---|---|---|
| Formality (rank): | 3 | 6 | 2 | 4 | 1 | 5 |
| Centralization (rank): | 2 | 4 | 1 | 3 | 5 | 6 |
| Inter-unit dependency: | M | H | H | M | L | L |
| Degree of diversification | L | L | L | M | H | H |
| Complexity of technology: | H | H | H | M | L | L |
| International experience: | M | H | H | H | H | L |
| Geographical heterogeneity: | M | H | H | H | H | L |
| Market concentration: | H/M | H | H | H | H/M | L |
| Mode of entry internationally[2]: | BU | BU | BU | BU/AC | AC | AC |
| Size of MNC[3]: | B | B | B | S | S | S |
| International organization[4]: | MD | MD | P | MD | P | P |

1    L=Low, M=Medium, H=High (relatively spoken).

2    BU=Build up, AC=Acquisitions (relatively spoken)

3    B=Big, S=Small (relatively spoken).

4    MD=Mother-Daughter structure, P=Product division
    structure.

TABLE 14  Pearson correlation coefficients for various measures
of formality of headquarter-subsidiary relationships
and subsidiary autonomy

| | Subsidiary autonomy[1] | |
| | r | level of significance |
|---|---|---|
| Formality[2] | - 0.60 | < 0.001 |
| Importance of budget[3] | - 0.66 | < 0.001 |
| Extent to which sub relies on written policies in decision-making[3] | - 0.66 | < 0.001 |
| Number of contacts with HQ through letters, telexes or personal meetings during a typical business month[3] | 0.42 | 0.02 |
| Number of visitors to sub from HQ last year[3] | 0.19 | 0.20 |
| Extents to which sub uses written manuals from HQ | - 0.35 | 0.06 |

1  Measured as described in table 1.

2  Measured as described in the text.

3  As rated by subsidiary respondents on 1-5 scale.

Formality and subsidiary characteristics

The ownership structure of the affiliate seems to
affect the degree of formality, as illustrated in
table 15. Joint ventures are managed in a more formal mode than in the case of wholly owned subsidiaries.

Affiliates located in developing countries tended
to be managed in less formal ways than those located
in developed for our sample. (See table 15.) An
explanation for this may be the tendency to staff
subsidiaries in LDCs with Swedes. There were on
average around 3 Swedes in developed country subsidiaries and 6 in LDC subsidiaries (here including
joint ventures). Also third country nationals were
more frequent in LDCs, almost 3 in average versus
less than half a person in developed countries.

The size of the subsidiary did not affect formality
according to our expectations. The relationship
was in the unexpected direction, low degree of
formality being associated with large size. (See
table 16.) It seems as if the tendency of high
autonomy to be associated with large size and low
formality would explain this surprising result.

High degree of product flow integration was positively correlated with formality. However, the result
is significant only at the 8% level. Even so, the
hypothesis that operational interdependence would
create a need for formal coordination mechanisms
was supported.

The "contingency school", litterature claims that
organizations working in uncertain environments
will adopt more informal modes of cordination and
control as compared to organizations enjoying
calmer conditions. (See for example Burns and
Stalker, 1961, and Lawrence and Lorsch, 1967.)
This hypothesis was supported for our sample, although again not very strongly. The relationship
was controlled for the influence of size of subsidiary, level of imports from HQ, and subsidiary
performance. The correlation coefficient was not
much affected.

The performance of the subsidiariy during the last
five years, as perceived by HQ management, was weak-
ly negatively correlated with degree of formality.
There was a tendency to use already existing formal
instruments more zealously when the subsidiary
became very unprofitable.

TABLE 15  Formality of headquarter-subsidiary relationships and
ownership structure and location of subsidiaries

|  | Formality[1] |
|---|---|
| Wholly owned subsidiaries (n=13): | 2.39 |
| Joint ventures (n=11): | 2.97 |
| Affiliates located in DCs (n=13): | 2.91 |
| Affiliates located in LDCs (n=11): | 2.14 |

1   Averages over subsidiaries. Index calculated as described
in the text.


TABLE 16  Formality of headquarters-subsdiariy relationsips and
subsidiary characteristics. Pearson correlation coefficients (n = 24).

|  | Formality r | level of significance |
|---|---|---|
| Size of subsidiary (turnover/year) | - 0.29 | 0.09 |
| Relative size of subsidiary | - 0.32 | 0.07 |
| Cross-shipments of goods | 0.31 | 0.08 |
| Uncertainty of sub environment | - 0.32 | 0.06 |
| Performance of sub | - 0.23 | 0.13 |
| Market share of sub | 0.03 | - |
| Frequency of conflicts on strategic matters | 0.58 | 0.001 |

The market share of the subsidiary was not correlated with degree of formality. We had expected
high local market share to be associated with more
intensive use of formal mechanisms. The Swedish tendency to treat important matters very informally
seems to have had an influence here, but we cannot
make any firm statements on this point.

Finally, an interesting correlation is the one between high formality on the one hand and frequence
of conflicts in strategic matters on the other. Formalized relationships were much more conflict-ridden
than informal ones. The direction of the causal
relationship is of course not evident. It could
very well be that relationships formalize when conflicts are encountered, as we indicated in the discussion of subsidiary performance. Nevertheless,
we could observe that formalization of headquarter-
subsidiary relationships in some cases had the effect
of letting potential problems cumulate and grow
for long times until they suddenly sprang up as
overt conflicts. More informal relationships generally helped in detecting and addressing problems
earlier, when tensions were not so high.

## SUMMARY

Our analysis yields a clear picture of autonomous
subsidiaries and informally managed HQ-subsidiary relationships for our sample of 24 affiliates of
Swedish MNCs. The picture is much less clear when
it comes to explaining these facts. A lot seems
to have to do with the historically given mode of
internationalization of Swedish industry. Some importance can probably be attached to the influence
of factors such as the inter-unit dependency in the
companies and the size of the MNCs and its subsidiaries. Factors such as these account better however, for the variation in degree of subsidiary
autonomy and, to some extent, formality. Particularly important is the degree of integration in terms
of product-flows to and from the subsidiary. This
"determinant" is more powerful for operational
than for strategic decisions. For the latter in
particular, management seems to choose between
different ways of relating to the subsidiary and
different distributions of power over units in the
company. The dominating archetype is one of high
autonomy and low formality, but also other combinations are represented in the sample. Management
style and management discretion thus appear to be
crucial concepts in the study of headquarter-subsidiary relationships, as already Brooke and Remmers
(1971) argued. We would therefore not agree with

those authors that deny the strong influence of
such seemingly intangible facts of organizational
life. (See for example de Bodinat, 1975.).

NOTES

1. The Pearson r correlation coefficient for the two measures SUBSTRAT (based upon respondents' answers on "strategic" decisions) and AUTSTRAT (based upon the researchers' rating, also for strategic questions) was 0.30. This is significant at the 7% level. For the operational decisions, r was 0.77, significant at the 0.1% level. This indicates that the measures appear to measure the same thing, although the discreapancy is rather large for strategic questions. Spearman and Kendall rank correlation coefficients give similar results. Kendall's tau = 0.68 for operational questions (significant at the 0.001 level), and 0.16 for strategic questions (significant at the 0.18 level). The Spearman rank correlation coefficients were 0.79 and 0.19 respectively.

2. For our sample, complexity of technology was very clearly associated with necessary scale of production units, so this distinction need not concern us here. It is possible, however, that these two factors work independently in the direction of decreased subsidiary autonomy.

3. By computing first-order partial correlation coefficients.

4. Ram Baliga, Anant Negandhi, Lars Otterbeck, Martin Welge and the author took part in the project. In the Swedish study here reported from, Gunnar Hedlund was project leader. Laurent Leksell, Ulf Lindgren and Lars Otterbeck also took part.

REFERENCES

AJIFERUKE, M. and BODDEWYN, J., "'Culture' and other explanatory variables in comparative management studies." Academy of Management Journal, June 1970, pp. 153-163.

ALSEGG, R.A., Control relationships between U.S. corporations and their European subsidiaries. AMA Research Study 107, 1971.

AYLMER, R.J., "Who makes marketing decisions in the multinational firm?" Journal of Marketing, October 1970, pp. 25-39.

de BODINAT, H., Influence in the multinational corporation: The case of manufacturing. Doctoral dissertation. Harvard University, School of Business, 1975.

BROOKE, M.Z. and REMMERS, H.L., The strategy of multinational enterprise. New York: Elsevier, 1970.

BURNS, T. and STALKER, G.M., The Management of innovation. London: Tavistock, 1961.

CHANNON, D.G., The strategy and structure of British enterprise. Boston: Graduate School of Business Administration, Harvard University, 1973.

EDSTRÖM, A. and GALBRAITH, J., "Transfer of managers as a coordinations and control strategy in multinational organizations". Administrative Science Quaterly, Vol. 22, No. 2, 1977, pp. 248-263.

FORSGREN, M. and JOHANSSON, J., Internationel lföretagsekonomi. Stockholm: Norstedts, 1975.

FRANKO, L.G., The European multinationals. London: Harper & Row, 1976.

GARNIER, G., CUASSE, G. and BOUDEVILLE, J., "Jusqu' où va l'autonomie de décisions des filiales?" Reveue Francaise de Gestion, Jan-Fev., 1975, pp. 42-52.

HEDLUND, G., "Organization as a matter of style." In Recent research on the internationalization of business. Ed. Mattsson, L-G and Widersheim-Paul, F., Uppsala, 1978, pp. 249-263.

78

HOFSTEDE, G., "Value systems in forty countries".
Paper presented at the Fourth International
Congress on the International Association
for Cross-Cultural Psychology, Munich,
July-August, 1978.

KEEGAN, W.J., "Multinational Marketing Control."
Journal of International Business, Fall
1972.

KHANDWALLA, P.N., "Uncertainty and the optimal design
of organizations". Working paper. Toronto:
McGill University, 1973.

LAWRENCE, P.R., and LORSCH, J.W., Organization and
environment: Managing differentiation and
integration. Boston: Graduate School of
Business Administration, Harvard University, 1967.

PECCEI, R. and WARNER, M., "Decision-making in a
multinational firm". Journal of General
Management, 1976, pp. 66-71.

PICARD, J., "Factors of variance in multinational
marketing control". In Recent research on
the internationalization of business, Ed.
Mattsson, L.-G. and Widersheim-Paul, F.
Uppsala, 1977, pp. 220-232.

SKINNER, W., American industry in developing economies. New York: John Wiley & Sons, 1968.

STOPFORD, J. and WELLS, L.T., Managing the multinational enterprise. New York: Basic Books,
1968.

TAKAMIYA, M., "Degree of organizational centralization in multinational corporations". International Institute of Management discussion
paper series. Berlin: Janauary, 1979.

# 4 Martin K. Welge:

# The Effective Design of Headquarter-Subsidiary Relationships in German MNCs

## PROBLEM AND METHOD

The percentage of foreign production in German MNCs
has significantly increased in the last few years,
having already exceeded the 50% mark in a number of
cases. As a reaction to the increasing importance of
foreign business, there have been extensive discussions in headquarters on problems of designing coordination between headquarters and foreign subsidiaries (see Arbeitskreis "Organisation international
tätiger Unternehmen" der Schmalenbach-Gesellschaft
1977, 1979). Until 1971, international coordination
in German MNCs was pretty much characterized by personalized control relationships with little formalization and standardization (see FRANKO 1976, p. 202).
Due to increasing degrees of competition, geographic
dispersion, and relevance of foreign markets, however,
a stronger emphasis of integrated global structures
can be observed recently (FRANKO 1976, p. 203). In
line with this structural reorientation, coordination
devices supporting structural coordination, such as
transfer of expatriates (cf. v. ECKARTSBERG 1979) and
planning, (cf. for example CHANNON and JALLAND 1979)
are discussed in theory and practice. Therefore, the
practical problem of designing the coordination intensity of headquarter-subsidiary relationships has
become considerably more complex, since the design
problem is no longer confined to structural coordination forms, but now also includes personal and technocratic coordination forms (for this differentiation
cf. WELGE 1975, p. 39). Consequently, the problem of
choosing the right coordination mix arises, and also
the problems of analyzing contextual influences, and
of analyzing the impacts of different design strategies on subsidiary effectiveness.

---

Fernuniversität Hagen, Hagen

It is the objective of this paper to explore these
relationships. Neither an organization interaction
analysis (for an overview cf. NEGANDHI 1975) nor the
dependence concept of the Aston-Group (PUGH et al.
1969) can be regarded as appropriate theoretical reference concepts for the conceptualizing of the headquarter-subsidiary variable in the above-mentioned
sense (for a more detailed elaboration of this point
cf. WELGE 1977, 1978). The conceptualization has
principally been oriented according to relational
dimensions of the organization interaction analysis,
but as far as dimensionalization of the different
categories is concerned, rather directly observable
and substantial categories of the interactions between headquarters and subsidiaries have been emphasized[1].

The data presented in this paper were collected in
extensive personal interviews conducted in six German
MNCs of the chemical industry and fifteen foreign
manufacturing subsidiaries, located in France, India
and USA. The six headquarters represent about 80% of
the total sales of the German chemical industry, and
can certainly be considered to be representative for
their industry. According to sales, the subsidiaries
studied were the most important foreign operations of
the respective MNC in the particular country. In
headquarters, members of the executive board, regional units, and product divisions were interviewed. In
the foreign subsidiaries, top executives, including
members of the finance and planning as well as product divisions were interviewed[2,3].

It is the purpose of this paper to explore differences with respect to coordination intensity between
headquarters and subsidiaries and interpret these
differences. Furthermore, influence patterns of the
internal context of subsidiaries on headquarter-subsidiary relationships are analyzed, and influence
patterns between context, headquarter-subsidiary-relationships and subsidiary effectiveness are explored.

DESCRIPTION OF HEADQUARTER-SUBSIDIARY-RELATIONSHIPS

Structural Coordination Intensity

The organizational structure of international relations[4] gives a first impression of the degree of
integration of foreign business into the whole range
of activities of a company. The means for structural
coordination intensity shown in Table 1 do not reflect any substantial differences with respect to the
structural integration of the subsidiaries interviewed in France, India, and USA. The means further seem
to show that all companies interviewed had a global
integrated structure, i.e. strategic planning deci-

sions and important policy decisions are taken in
Germany under a world-wide perspective. Which vari-
ants of the global structure dominated is exemplified
in Table 2.

| Dimensions of coordination intensity | all countries x | s | France x | s | India x | s | USA x | s |
|---|---|---|---|---|---|---|---|---|
| (1) Structural coordination intensity | 4.7 | 1.4 | 4.2 | 1.6 | 4.8 | 1.3 | 5.0 | 1. |
| (2) Transfer or expatriates | 3.1 | 1.9 | 2.6 | 1.5 | 1.8 | 0.4 | 4.8 | 2. |
| (3) Influence of parent company on the selection of expatriates | 3.1 | 1.9 | 2.4 | 1.7 | 3.4 | 1.7 | 3.6 | 2. |
| (4) Responsibility for intern. personnel decisions | 6.3 | 1.4 | 6.6 | 0.9 | 6.2 | 1.8 | 6.2 | 1. |
| (5) Motives to transfer | 3.3 | 1.8 | 3.2 | 1.6 | 3.6 | 2.3 | 3.0 | 1. |
| (6) Frequency of visits (to subsidiary) | 3.5 | 1.9 | 3.3 | 1.3 | 2.8 | 1.5 | 4.8 | 2. |
| (7) Hierarchical position of visitors (to sub.) | 5.8 | 1.9 | 6.2 | 1.8 | 4.6 | 2.5 | 6.6 | 0. |
| (8) Motives for visits (to sub.) | 4.9 | 1.8 | 4.4 | 2.4 | 5.0 | 1.6 | 5.4 | 1. |
| (9) Frequency of visits (to parent comp.) | 3.4 | 1.9 | 3.3 | 1.0 | 2.6 | 1.9 | 4.5 | 2. |
| (10) Motives for visits (to parent comp.) | 4.5 | 1.1 | 4.0 | 1.0 | 4.8 | 1.5 | 4.8 | 0. |
| (11) Ownership | 5.6 | 2.2 | 7.0 | 0.0 | 2.8 | 1.6 | 7.0 | 0. |
| (12) Responsibility for investment decisions | 4.7 | 2.0 | 5.0 | 2.1 | 4.2 | 1.9 | 4.8 | 2. |
| (13) Responsibility for credit decisions | 2.7 | 1.5 | 2.6 | 1.7 | 2.6 | 1.7 | 3.0 | 1. |
| (14) Degree of formalization of planning | 4.4 | 2.7 | 4.6 | 2.5 | 4.6 | 3.3 | 4.0 | 3. |
| (15) Degree of specificity of planning | 5.0 | 2.4 | 5.2 | 1.6 | 4.6 | 3.3 | 5.2 | 2. |
| (16) Mode of integration of planning | 4.4 | 2.7 | 4.6 | 2.5 | 4.6 | 3.3 | 4.0 | 3 |
| (17) Actors of planning | 3.3 | 2.2 | 4.2 | 2.9 | 3.0 | 2.0 | 2.6 | 1. |
| (18) Number of levels involved in the planning process | 4.6 | 3.0 | 4.6 | 3.3 | 4.6 | 3.3 | 4.6 | 3 |
| | N = 14 | | N = 5 | | N = 5 | | N = | |

x̄: arithmetic mean
s: standard deviation
1= minimal score
7= maximal score

TABLE 1. Means and standard deviations of headquarter-subsidiary dimensions by country (calculated with program CONDESCRIPTIVE of SPSS. Cf. NIE, N.H. et al. 1975, p. 185)

| Organization structure | absolute frequencies |
|---|---|
| Product divisions with world-wide responsibility | 7 |
| Grid structure (matrix-structure) | 6 |
| Product divisions with European responsibility and International Divisions with overseas responsibility | 2 |

TABLE 2. Organization structures of international activities (absolute frequencies) (N = 15)

World-wide responsibility of product divisions is most
frequent. This structural pattern offers favourable
conditions for the realization of world-wide, pro-
duct-group oriented decisions, especially with respect to sales and marketing policies. The international reporting systems work in such a way that
foreign subsidiaries report to their reference divisions in Germany what product decisions are concerned. Relationships with six subsidiaries were organized in terms of two- or three-dimensional grid structures. Which reporting line (functional, product,
region) dominated in a particular case, could not
always be found out with certainty. Due to qualitative impressions, however, it can reasonably be
assumed that in most cases product reporting lines,
and in some cases functional reporting lines, had the
greatest importance (for similar results see FRANKO
1976, p. 203).

Personal Coordination Intensity

A first relevant difference can be observed for the
dimension of "transfer of expatriates" (cf. Table 1).
In the American subsidiaries much more expatriates
with longer duration of assignment can be found, compared to the French and especially to the Indian subsidiaries. The high score for the American subsidiaries seems to be attributable to their size and
their higher degree of diversification, because
greater and more diversified firms necessarily have a
greater need for management personnel. In addition,
great und successful subsidiaries have a greater importance in the whole corporate strategy, more headquarter attention is paid to them, the investment
risk is greater. It now becomes understandable that
the corporate headquarter prefers to put the management of such subsidiaries in the hands of expatriates
in order to tie the network of personal coordination
as close as possible.

These rather rational arguments can be supplemented
by more or less irrational aspects. Beside Brazil and
Japan, the United States were perceived by the inter-
viewees as a country in which only highly qualified
managers are transferred, whereas India was regarded
as a host country for third-class managers. The low
score for India, however, needs further explanation.
Because of the Indian foreign investment code allowing joint ventures only, local partners might tend to
oppose the presence of foreign managers. In a Conference Board study a European manager, for example,
made this statement (NATIONAL INDUSTRIAL CONFERENCE
BOARD 1969, p. 72):

"Indian partners continually strive for greater
influence and try to take over the whole management by themselves. Experience has shown that

there are highly qualified Indian managers who
are perfectly able to establish and direct an
enterprise without foreign help, but there are
the even more frequent cases in which the lack
of Indian experts - in particular in the technical field, but not only there - becomes evident and necessitates the cooperation of appropriate foreign personnel. It is therefore indis-
pensable in the very interest of the company
that there be a reasonable number of foreign experts in the joint venture".

The Indianization policy, however, is not only the
consequence of personal preferences of local joint
venture partners, it is also part of the official
policy of the Indian Government (see GOVERNMENT OF
INDIA, 1975 - 1976, p. 12, JHA 1975, p. 8).

According to the impressions of our interviews in
France the reason for the not much higher score for
the French subsidiaries seems to be that headquarters
feel that successful subsidiary management crucially
depends upon the fact that a French manager is in
charge of the company who should be a graduate of one
of the Grandes Ecoles[5] and who, therefore, has
well-established connections with Government and
economic circles. In those cases in which such contacts were not so relevant, and in which subsidiaries
were more or less production units dislocated for
utilizing wage differentials, expatriates could be
found in important top management positions. These
people, however, had been in France for quite a long
time already -in one case more than ten years - so
that they were very knowledgeable with respect to the
French market and the French bureaucracy. It also
might have played a role that the rather small geographic distance between headquarters and subsidiaries can be bridged more easily by direct, sporadic,
and ad-hoc-contacts.

For the French subsidiaries, a further relevant
difference can be observed with respect to the variable of "influence of parent company on the selection
of expatriates". The low mean of 3.1 for the whole
sample is contraintuitive in itself. We expected a
higher score, i.e. a stronger influence of the parent
company because of the great importance of personal
coordination.

The low mean can partly be explained by the existence
of certain more or less formalized programs. The
score for this dimension tends to be too low, however, because of the selection decisions made more or
less on a case by case basis. Despite this mistake
induced by measurement error, the low value for the
French subsidiaries in comparison to other subsidiaries seems worth further exploration. Size does not

explain the difference because the Indian subsidiaries were smaller in terms of number of employees and sales. The Indian subsidiaries, however, scored much higher, almost as high as the much larger American subsidiaries. A good explanatory factor seems to be geographic distance from the parent company. Greater proximity enables a more frequent and direct control, and a faster correction of deviating behaviour which seems not possible to such an extent in the case of the US and Indian subsidiaries because of greater distance and higher cost of communication.

The parent company's influence on the selection of expatriates increases with increasing distance of the subsidiaries. A further argument for explaining the French data seems to be the tight integration of the French subsidiaries into the strategy of the reference divisions at home. By this, there are additional means to control deviating behaviour. A less strong influence of the parent company seems to be acceptable without any risk.

Country specific differences can also be observed with respect to the dimension of "frequency of visits". This holds for visits to subsidiaries as well as for visits to headquarters. The significantly higher scores for the American subsidiaries can primarily be explained by their size and their diversified production program. In some cases, the US-subsidiaries had a production program similar to their parent companies. Logically, there have to be more frequent contacts on the top management and the divisional level as well. Coordination by mixed boards which was already mentioned above, is another reason for intensive travelling. Size and diversification are reasons for great importance of a subsidiary within corporate strategy. These factors also mean a high investment risk because of the large amount of capital at stake. There is, therefore, not only the necessity for an intensive mutual exchange of information and thoughts, but also for the engagement of top level executives. The high score ($x = 6.6$) for the "hierarchical position of visitors" to American subsidiaries substantiates this point very well.

The respective scores for the Indian subsidiaries are much lower. They are smaller and less diversified than the American subsidiaries. Because of ownership restrictions (joint ventures), control of parent companies is much more limited. Consequently, there is less frequent travelling and, on average, the hierarchical position of the visitors is lower. These subsidiaries are not so important as to find the attention of high managerial levels in the parent companies. Because of the closed markets[6], the entrepreneurial risk is low, and the necessity for quick response to environmental change is not very great, which also might explain low frequency of travelling and low hierarchical position of visitors.

The French subsidiaries take an intermediate position. Travel intensity occupies an intermediate position, the score for hierarchical position of the visitors, however, is similar to the American subsidiaries. Size and diversification are again the explanatory factors. Frequency of visits seems to be dependent upon the context of the subsidiary, namely size and diversification. Hierarchical position always seems to be relatively high, if ownership pattern and peculiarities of the market do not oppose this strategy.

There is a close link between what we have said so far and the dimension of "motives for visits". The mean value of $x_G$ = 4.9 for the total sample leads us to the conclusion that motives like "strengthening of teamwork" and "coordination and adjustment" are the dominating reasons for most of the trips. The relatively low value (x = 4.4) for the French subsidiaries is rather instructive. For its explanation the great variance of 2.4 has to be observed. Subsidiaries managed by a German expatriate scored much higher for the dimensions of "motives for visits", i.e. "coordination and adjustment" dominated, whereas subsidiaries managed by French managers scored significantly lower. Obviously, the implementation of coordination and adjustment motives was resisted by French managers, perceiving their autonomy to be jeopardized. This impression can be substantiated by the background information from interviews with French managers.

In order to draw a preliminary conclusion with respect to the pattern of personal coordination, the following can be said: responsibility for international personnel decisions is highly centralized, visits play an important role for personal coordination since they allow personal insights and contacts. The visits have an additional weight due to the high hierarchical position of the visitors. Visits primarily serve coordination and adjustment as well as strengthening of teamwork. To one's surprise, the influence of the parent company on the selection of expatriates is fairly low despite the crucial relevance of personal coordination. Obviously, one does not so much rely on formalized programs, but rather on personal insights as far as the candidate is concerned. This procedure implies no risk, as long as expatriates have spent most of their career in the parent company. There is some doubt, however, whether this selection process will remain without risk in times of increasing demand for international managers. Some firms seem to respond to this problem. There were indications of systematic international career planning systems and internal programs to prepare managers for their foreign assignments.

## Technocratic Coordination Intensity

First, we would like to draw the attention to coordination by financial means. The scores for the respective dimensions are shown in Table 1. Except India, the companies prefer 100% ownership in the host countries studied. From a corporate policy point of view this pattern finds its justification by allowing a maximum of control with respect to market decisions as well as policy decisions in general. Only if 100% ownership is forbidden by local law, a deviation from this policy can be observed. This is the case for India and several other developing countries. The relevant paragraph in the "Guidelines for Industries, 1975 - 1976", p. 11 reads as follows:

> "Government's policy towards permitting foreign equity participation is selective. Such participation has to be justified having regard to factors such as the priority of industry, the nature of technology involved, whether it will enable or promote exports which may not otherwise take place and the alternative terms available for securing the same or similar technology transfer. The ceiling for foreign equity participation is 40% although exceptions can be considered on merits."

The ownership pattern just described does not necessarily mean that there are no joint ventures of German MNCs with local and/or foreign partners. We only wanted to point out that the companies interviewed preferred this pattern of ownership which, according to all respondents, offers better chances of control and coordination.

Responsibility for investment decisions is the second most important instrument of financial control. For describing this dimension the two closely connected aspects of the degree of centralization and programming are of interest. With respect to the degree of programming we could observe that in 60% of the cases investment decisions in subsidiaries were limited by defining maximum limits strongly dispersing in their absolute amounts, i.e. some kind of management by exception was practised; in 40% of the cases, there was no limitation, investment proposals were decided upon a case by case basis. The centralization scores are shown in Table 1. Subsidiaries never had full responsibility for investment decisions. At least, investment decisions were joint decisions of headquarters and subsidiaries.

The scores, however, show a trend toward a stronger
centralization of investment decision at headquarters. Control of investment decisions seems to be a
very important instrument of coordination in the
hands of parent companies (see also WELGE, 1977, p.
155).

Credit decisions seem to be less centralized and formalized. In more than half of the cases, there were
no limits of credit defined by the parent company.
Subsidiaries seem to be responsible for credit decisions, which is documented by the mean value of $x_G =$
2.7 for the total sample. This finding becomes more
understandable when it is added that in all cases the
host country was the most important capital market
for the subsidiary. The policy of raising money in
the host country requires some knowledge of the
conditions of the capital market in the respective
host country. This know-how is primarily available in
the subsidiaries. Consequently, this function is
delegated to the subsidiaries.

The companies interviewed obviously prefer a local
strategy in their credit decisions which is in line
with the local conditions of the money and capital
market. Credit decisions are polycentric. This strategy can also partly be explained by the desire to
avoid exchange risks.

A polycentric strategy could also be observed with
respect to the dimension of "transfer of profit"[7].
In no case could a universalistic pool strategy be
found. Strengthening of the equity capital basis of
the subsidiaries was the dominating motive for use of
profit. In 40% of the cases the entire profit was
reinvested, in 60% of the cases only that profit was
transferred to the parent company which was left
after making the investments necessary. There were no
arrangements such as transferring a fixed percentage
of the profit generated in the subsidiaries. A flexible strategy allowing for the profit situation of
the subsidiary and strengthening the equity capital,
was preferred to a strategy of getting a fixed and
continuous return of the capital invested. This
strategy of self-financing necessarily leads to a
greater independence of the subsidiaries because the
corporate headquarter is more likely to approve investments, if it does not have to transfer new funds
of its own (see BARLOW a. WENDER, 1955, p. 161).

Comparing the profit transfer behaviour of German
MNCs to American MNCs, a principal difference emerges. The German perspective of foreign direct investment is more or less motivated by the aspect of securing and building a long-term and continuous market
position, whereas American MNCs are more likely to
regard their foreign investment as a financial in-

vestment. Therefore, aspects of return on investment
and transfer of profit are much more emphasized. It
can only be mentioned here that this strategy might
be one reason for a higher conflict potential with
the host countries (cf. NEGANDHI a. BALIGA, 1976).

Taking the degree of formalization of planning as a
measure of intensity of integration, our data show
that half of the companies interviewed formalized
their international planning systems to a great
extent by intensive use of manuals and standardized
reports in the planning process with their foreign
subsidiaries. These companies seem to have realized a
high degree of unification and compatibility of
their planning system on a world-wide basis. To a
certain extent, this seems to be an indication of the
successful world-wide implementation of standardized
procedures. The other half of the companies interviewed show a very low degree of formalization of
planning. Whether this reflects a philosophy of
relative independence of the subsidiaries, whether
implementation of formalized international planning
systems is just at the beginning, or whether implementation of unified planning systems was successfully opposed by the subsidiaries, cannot definitely
be answered by our data.

The planning of "degree of specificity" and "mode of
integration" show a similar distribution. High formalization was combined with high specificity and
integration of national and international plans by
standardized reports and procedures. In the other
group, low degrees of specificity and personal means
of integration could be observed. These differences
also showed up with respect to the number of levels
involved in the planning process. In the first group,
often six or more different levels were involved in
the development of plans, in one case, however,
coordination of plans was achieved in a one-day-dis-
cussion between the subsidiary manager and the responsible member of the "Vorstand" of the parent
company.

Three different patterns emerge with respect to the
dimension of "actor of planning": in type 1 agencies
of the parent company (Vorstand, product and/or regional division) are the major actors in the planning
process. In this situation, the highest possible
actor-induced degree of integration is reached, the
planning process seems to function as a top-to-down
approach. In the type 2 situation, the subsidiary is
the major actor in the planning process. The planning
process carries elements of a bottom-up strategy, the
degree of integration is the lowest here. The third
type which could basically be observed in the planning process with the American subsidiaries, is an
intermediate solution. The board, as structural-ins-

titutionalized agency, staffed with managers from
parent company and subsidiary, is the major acting
force in the planning process. This variant induces a
medium degree of actor-induced integration.

It is striking to us that country-specific differences of technocratic integration dimensions are less
frequent than it was the case with respect to personal integration dimensions (see Table 1). Only the
"ownership" and "actor of planning" dimensions show
relevant differences. The low score for ownership in
the Indian subsidiaries was already explained by
legal influences.

The low "actor of planning" score in the American
subsidiaries seems somewhat surprising. It can be
explained by the dominating role of the mixed boards,
inducing a greater hierarchical distance to the parent
company and, accordingly, a lower integration intensity. The comparatively high score of the French
subsidiaries also needs an explanation. It is our
overall perception that the companies interviewed
consider the nations of the Common Market as one
single market. The organizational response to this
strategy was to integrate subsidiaries from EEC
countries into the responsibility of the product
divisions. This means a stronger integration into the
parent company's planning process, which necessarily
increases the actor-induced planning integration. The
Indian scores tending to be more similar to the
US-pattern can be explained with the joint venture
situation which forbids a stronger actor-induced
integration for reasons of ownership pattern.

Despite these two differences, the means of the
technocratic coordination dimensions show a universal
design of the technocratic coordination pattern, not
differentiated according to country-specific circumstances. Rules, procedures, programs and systems are
designed with a global corporate view. From the point
of view of corporate management, this strategy becomes evident because these means of standardization
create the basis for unified corporate management.
The effect of world-wide standardization would get
lost, if these rules would be designed in a country-
specific way.

CONTEXTUAL INFLUENCES ON HEADQUARTER-SUBSIDARY-
RELATIONSHIPS

We have learned that MNCs have different alternatives
for designing the relationships with their subsidiaries. Now the practical problem arises which mix of
different instruments of coordination they should
use, which instruments they should use in various
contextual situations, and what pattern of contextual

variables and coordination variables is associated with the desired success.

First of all, we would like to deal with the question of influences of internal contextual factors on various combinations of coordination instruments. In numerous studies of comparative bureaucracy relationships between contextual factors such as size, dependence, age, diversification, etc., and internal coordination have empirically been proved. Empirical studies analyzing the influence of internal contextual factors on external coordination, i.e. the pattern of coordination between parent companies and a system of dependent subsidiaries, however, are relatively rare.

The most comprehensive study based on qualitative impressions of a survey of subsidiaries of US MNCs has been submitted by ALSEGG (1971). According to his results, the coordination intensity of headquarter-subsidiary-relationships is decisively influenced by the size of the subsidiary. On the one hand, ALSEGG (1971, p. 99) argues that larger subsidiaries bear higher investment and market risks from the point of view of the parent company, which would favour a more intensive control by the parent company. On the other hand, larger subsidiaries are older in most cases, therefore having greater experience in their host country; they have already proved that they can operate successfully, they are better equipped with staff personnel, and they have a more qualified management potential.

Taking these factors together, and recognizing the fact that big subsidiaries usually operate in important markets and therefore have a greater weight in the corporate strategy, would, however, be in favour of a higher autonomy of large subsidiaries.

In his empirical study of subsidiaries of American MNCs, YOUSSEF could not find any significant relationships between subsidirary size and coordination intensity (YOUSSEF 1975, p. 139).

For his sample of 59 US manufacturing subsidiaries of European MNCs, ROCCOUR found a negative relationship between size and coordination intensity, i.e. the greater the size, the lower was the coordination intensity exercised by the parent company (ROCCOUR 1966, p. 15). ROCCOUR explains the great autonomy of the US subsidiaries by their particular role. They supply the biggest and most competitive market in the world, and therefore, they contribute to a significant extent to total MNC sales. This brings subsidiary management in a strong bargaining position vis à vis the parent company which cannot resist the autonomy of such strong subsidiaries without risk.

Age of subsidiary was found to be another influence factor by ALSEGG (1971, p. 100 ff.). Subsidiaries belonging to the parent company for a long time already have well-established connections to local stakeholders and extensive local experience. Since the subsidiary management tends to have good personal contacts to the parent company because of long affiliation to the parent company, there will be a good basis of mutual trust and cooperation. The risk of greater autonomy seems to be low. Therefore, older subsidiaries are more autonomous than subsidiaries with a shorter affiliation to their parent companies.

This relationship could be confirmed by YOUSSEF only for direct control, by which he means influence and supervision; according to his results, the extent of indirect control, including staff personnel, standardization of organization structures, processes, product development, and accounting procedures is increasing with increasing age of subsidiaries (YOUSSEF 1975, p. 140). ROCCOUR, however, could not find any relationship between age and intensity of coordination. Contrary to the opinion that US subsidiaries of European MNCs are relatively young, ROCCOUR points out that 41% of the subsidiaries interviewed started production before 1944, and 81% started production earlier than 1957 (ROCCOUR 1966, p. 15).

Ownership is mentioned as a further factor of influence. In cases of majority ownership, there are more chances of control and direction as in joint venture and minority ownership situations where interests and, possibly, resistances of local partners have to be taken into consideration (ALSEGG 1971, p. 103). This obvious relationship could be substantiated empirically by YOUSSEF (1975, p. 139).

Finally, ALSEGG points out the importance of the type of subsidiary. He hypothesizes that manufacturing subsidiaries are coordinated more intensively than sales subsidiaries, because "...production more readily lends itself to centralized direction, and engineers and technicians adhere more firmly to standards and regulations than do salesmen" (ALSEGG 1971, p. 7).

Because of the very heterogeneous results on internal contextual influences, a systematic data-based exploration of the contextual dependencies of external coordination seems to be in order. Since most of the existing material - except the ROCCOUR study - is related to American MNCs, it seems interesting to contrast our impressions with those findings.

The relationship between size of subsidiary and coordination intensity reflects a rather multiple and contraintuitive pattern (see Table 3).

| Coordination Forms / Contextual factors | Structural | Personal | | Technocratic | | |
|---|---|---|---|---|---|---|
| | | Pers. dec. | pers.coord. index | Invest. Dec. | Credit Dec. | Planning |
| Size (Number of employees) | 26 | -06 | 16 | -50$^x$ | -03 | 46$^x$ |
| Size (Sales) | 60$^x$ | -16 | 43 | -35 | -16 | 58$^x$ |
| Age | 00 | -30 | 36 | 29 | -10 | 37 |
| Type of foundation | -48$^x$ | -43 | 13 | 67$^{xx}$ | -42 | -06 |
| Ownership | 04 | 04 | 33 | 13 | 01 | 28 |

x  p $\leq$ 0,05
xx  p $\leq$ 0,01

TABLE 3. Correlations between internal contextual factors and forms of coordination (N = 15) (Spearman rank correlations, calculated with program NONPAR CORR of SPSS. See NIE, N.H. et al. 1975, p. 288).

Larger subsidiaries show a higher structural coordination intensity, i.e. more complex and multi-dimensional organization structures and more planning, when sales is taken as an indicator of size. This finding corresponds with results from studies of comparative bureaucracy concerning the influence of size on intra-organizational coordination (BLAU a. SCHOENHERR 1975; PUGH et al. 1969; CHILD 1972; KIESER 1973). Coordination in large subsidiaries is more highly bureaucracized than in smaller subsidiaries. Not only the extent of bureaucracy increases with size, but also the extent of personalized coordination devices (transfer of expatriates, visits in both directions) (r = .43).

There seems to be a three-dimensional response to subsidiary growth: intensive structural integration, more planning and personal coordination, i.e. stronger bureaucratization superimposed by stronger personalization. Coordination by control of certain decisions - personnel, investment, finance - decreases with increasing size. Case by case regulations are becoming less important than general rules with increasing size. The negative correlations between size and coordination intensity indicated in the studies above can be substantiated by our data only for coordination on an ad-hoc-basis, however, not for coordination by general rules. Higher market and investment risks associated with large subsidiaries seem to have a stronger weight than the autonomy arguments mentioned by ALSEGG (1971).

Correlations betweeen age of subsidiary, operationalized as duration of the affiliation with the parent company, and coordination intensity are realtively low. There seems to be some indication of more decentralization of personnel and credit decisions in older subsidiaries (see also PUGH et al. 1969). This might have something to do with greater mutual trust on the one hand, and greater familiarity with local money and capital markets as well as established connections to local banks, on the other hand. Decentralization of personnel decisions could be explained by the hypothesis that old subsidiaries develop managers familiar with local conditions, and therefore can participate in the selection decision to a higher degree.

On the contrary, planning, personal coordination and centralization of investment decisions increase with higher age. These findings seem to support STARBUCK's hypothesis of a positive correlation between age and bureaucratization. They also tend to support YOUSSEF who found positive correlations for indirect control and negative correlations for direct control (YOUSSEF 1975, p. 140). Similar to the response to size, there seems to be a complementarity of technocratic coordination (planning) and personal coordination (transfer of expatriates, visits), obviously typical of German MNCs (see WELGE 1977, p. 155).

The more extraneous influences are involved in the foundation of a subsidiary, either by participation of a local partner in the joint venture case or by takeover of an existing local enterprise, the less intensive is structural integration, the lower is the degree of bureaucratization, and the more centralized are personnel decisions. It is more difficult to implement such rules against the resistance of local partners or against existing and well-established organization and management structures in an existing local firm than in cases in which there are no such constraints (establishment of a new manufacturing subsidiary), or in which such difficulties can be overcome more easily because of greater influence (sales subsidiary). Centralization of investment decisions seems to be the most important instrument of coordination when foundation is influenced extraneously ($r = .67$).

The relationship between ownership and coordination dimensions is positive, indeed; but the low correlations indicate a weak relationship only. Our findings seem to support the expectation of positive correlation between ownership and coordination intensity raised by ALSEGG (1971) and YOUSSEF (1975).

Obviously, this hypothesis is true for personal coordination and planning, but not really true for the
other instruments of coordination. Since YOUSSEF
(1975, p. 141) found correlations similarily low, it
can be assumed that parent companies try to realize
the highest degree of coordination intensity possible, independent of the legally relevant ownership
patterns. This is not very difficult even in joint
venture situations, when either the joint venture
partner is very weak or when local capital is broadly
spread among small shareholders. In such a case, 50%
ownership allows a high degree of control and coordination. This differentiation between legal and factual ownership patterns which, unfortunately, is not
reflected in the measure seems to be an important
reason for the low correlations.

After having explored the relationships between
internal context and different forms of interorgani-
zational coordination, now the problem arises which
strategy of coordination is associated with above-
average <u>success</u>, and which constellations of context
variables and coordination variables are more successful than others, respectively.

INTERRELATIONS BETWEEN HEADQUARTER-SUBSIDIARY-
RELATIONS AND EFFECTIVENESS

The interrelations to be explored below are visuali-
zed in Figure 1.

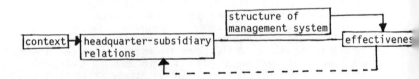

FIGURE 1: <u>Direct and indirect relations between
"Headquarter-Subsidiary-Relations" and
Effectiveness.</u>

In a first step we want to explore the <u>direct rela-
tionship</u> between headquarter-subsidiary relations and
effectiveness as postulated in Figure 1. Theoretical
and empirical results can hardly be found in the
literature. In his study based on qualitative impressions of American parent companies and their
Mexican subsidiaries, BARLOW points out that successful enterprises use totally different strategies of
coordinating their headquarter-subsidiary relations
(BARLOW 1953, p. 100). He substantiates this finding

by saying that control intensity depends upon <u>mana-</u>
<u>gement philosophy</u>. Nationally decentralized companies
prefer a more decentralized coordination pattern with
their foreign subsidiaries; companies managed more
centrally at home tend to adopt this strategy also
with respect to their foreign activities.

In view of these observations, headquarter-subsidiary
relations cannot be expected to be a good predictor
of subsidiary effectiveness. At the same time, BARLOW
points out the dysfunctional consequences of high
coordination intensity which interferes with the
initiative of local management, the quality of local
management, and the local flexibility. This would, at
least indirectly, have a negative impact on subsidiary effectiveness (BARLOW 1953, p. 101). According
to his impressions, a situation in which above-average success is to be expected can be described as
follows: a qualified manager is at the top of the
subsidiary, intensive information is demanded from
the subsidiary, but simultaneously it is in a position to maintain the greatest possible autonomy of
local management (BARLOW 1953, p. 109).

The findings of another study support the hypothesis
of positive correlations between formal, long-range
and integrated planning and effectiveness (KARGER a.
MALIK 1975, p. 60). They observed that companies
having a formalized international planning system
were more effective than companies without formalized planning systems (KARGER a. MALIK 1975, p. 63).
In this study effectiveness was operationalized by
financial criteria, such as sales per share, cash
flow per share, profit per share, etc.

Roughly similar conclusions can be drawn from a study
by STEINER and SCHÖLLHAMMER on "Pitfalls of Multinational Long-Range Planning". Their observations can
be summarized in the sense that mistakes in long-
range planning have a negative impact on planning
effectiveness and also on subsidiary effectiveness.
"... the greater is top management's awareness of the
importance of planning, and the more attention it
pays to a clear delineation of organizational objectives, the higher will be the effectiveness of the
company's planning effort. A company's planning
effectiveness can be reduced more significantly by
falling into these two traps than by any other planning pitfalls" (STEINER and SCHÖLLHAMMER 1975, p. 8).

A conceptually very fruitful extension of the perspective of looking at interrelations between headquarter-subsidiary relations and subsidiary effectiveness has been proposed by ALSEGG (1971, p. 111).
He puts this relation in a <u>dynamic</u> perspective, and
expects coordination intensity to vary according to
the <u>developmental stage</u> of the subsidiary. Small

subsidiaries are more autonomous at the beginning of their development; the necessity to limit local autonomy becomes greater with increasing number and size of subsidiaries.

Local managers then enjoy less independence, indeed, but their authority increases. The manager cannot decide himself on matters of finance and personnel, but he is responsible for a larger business volume.

In its static interpretation, this hypothesis implies a positive correlation between size and coordination intensity which was also basically reflected in our own data (see Table 5). Unfortunately, the dynamic implications of this hypothesis cannot be explored on the basis of our own data, because we have only crossectional and no longitudinal data.

ALSEGG introduces a further dynamic dimension by hypothesizing a positive correlation between below-average effectiveness and coordination intensity (ALSEGG 1971, p. 112). Subsidiaries not meeting the standards of effectiveness will be more strictly controlled in the next planning cycle; above-average subsidiaries, however, will be given more autonomy.

Similar to BARLOW, ALSEGG emphasizes the dysfunctional consequences of high coordination intensities by saying: "Incidentally, many experts argue that ever stricter controls stifle local initiative and are therefore counterproductive, and that a really capable man will not accept a managerial position where he is prevented from using the full range of his abilities" (ALSEGG 1971, p. 113).

These few existing data fully exemplify the complexity of the problem. From the data to be presented now, only incremental progress can be expected, particularly, because our data do not allow a controlled analysis of dynamic feedback relations.

The interrelations hypothesized in Fig. 10) have been explored by multiple regression analysis[10]. In order to get the right perspective of the patterns extracted by multiple regression analysis, some methodological remarks are necessary. The assumptions of multiple regression analysis - metric scaling of data and a great N, because there has to be an affluence of data when dealing with a great number of predictors - are not met in our data material. Since we do not want to test any hypotheses, but rather explore patterns of relationships, it seems acceptable to us to treat the data as if their scales were of metric quality (for this position, see also WEEDE 1977, p. 1 and the literature quoted in footnote 1). The problem of small sample size and a comparatively large number of predictors - a dilemma faced by any exploratory study$_2$ - is treated by using the adjusted $R^2$ instead of $R^2$ (see YAMANE 1967, p. 765). The following discussion has to be viewed against this background of limitations which would have to induce great modesty and caution in interpreting the results.

First of all, we have to raise the question whether internal contextual dimensions and design of head-quarter-subsidiary relations directly go together with subsidiary effectiveness. We will start with influences on the return on investment[11] of the subsidiaries[12].

Among the contextual factors, ownership seems to have the strongest influence on return on investment. Subsidiary size also contributes positively. The type of foundation, i.e. whether the subsidiary has been founded as a sales subsidiary, a joint venture with a local partner, by takeover of an existing local firm, or as a new manufacturing subsidiary, seems to have a negative impact on return on investment. All head-quarter-subsidiary dimensions seem to have unfavour-able effects on return on investment. Centralization of international personnel decisions, investment decisions, and high structural integration seem to have the strongest negative impact. Planning, perso-nal coordination, and credit decisions have a less negative impact. It is interesting to mention that these influences are clouded by the simple correla-tions. Here, some coefficients are positive.

Our description of the influence pattern of head-quarter-subsidiary relations seems to tend in the same direction as BARLOW's observations did (BARLOW 1953, p. 109). Decentralization of headquarter-sub-sidiary relations is more likely to generate an above-average return than high coordination inten-sity. In other words: a control strategy allowing more local autonomy is associated with better effec-tiveness than a more centralized strategy restricting local autonomy[13]. Autonomous subsidiaries are able to respond more quickly to environmental changes, they are more flexible, and provide able managers with more discretion than those subsidiaries managed centrally by their parent companies. Since selection of foreign managers is regarded as very important by parent companies, as was shown above, discretion for good managers seems to have an important explanatory power.

The design strategy unfolded by the data would be to choose 100% ownership, to keep within a certain size, and to keep the coordination intensity of headquar-ter-subsidiary relations as low as possible.

It is now interesting to analyze whether this design strategy is also adequate to the other effectiveness criterion of "satisfaction of management".[14) All in all, this question can be answered positively[15). Differences worth mentioning only result from the negative impact of size, and negative impacts of centralization of credit decisions as well as personal coordination.

Certainly, these observations bear some risk of interpretation due to the constraints mentioned above. On account of the satisfactory accordance with BARLOW's results, however, we can reasonably assume that our results tend in the right direction.

Further data, from longitudinal studies in particular, have to be added in order to deal with the complex feedback relations indicated in Fig. 1.

The same qualifications are also relevant when the management process[16) as a mediating variable is introduced into the interpretation. If additional variables describing the structure of the management system are put in the regression equation, only the variable of "concentration of decision making", i.e. the degree of delegation of decisions within the subsidiary, increases the explained variance to some extent. Decentralization of decisions within the subsidiaries favourably affects the return on investment. This observation corresponds with our arguments concerning the autonomy of headquarter-subsidiary relations. High centralization of decisions within the subsidiaries would counteract the advantages of flexibility and responsiveness which a relative independence from the parent company will imply.

Summarizing the results of efficient management in terms of "return on investment", we can propose the following pattern: decentralization of headquarter-subsidiary relationships together with internal decentralization within the subsidiaries seems to be most likely to be associated with above-average effectiveness of subsidiaries.

If this relationship is analyzed for the effectiveness dimension of "satisfaction of management", the same pattern emerges from the regression analysis as we have observed in the direct analysis. It is not surprising that the dimensions of the social component of the management system, i.e. authority and motivation, explain additional variance. Accordance of subsidiary management task design and motivation positively contributes to social effectiveness; the authority dimension, however, has a negative impact. In other words: low intensity of coordination of headquarter-subsidiary relations together with a job design adequate to the motivational structure of the managers, and low power distance, i.e. more participative leadership, seems to be an adequate constella-

tion for above-average social effectiveness of subsidiaries.

## CONCLUSION

The objective of this paper was the data-based exploration of relationships between German multinational
chemical firms and their foreign subsidiaries. In a
first step the question was explored whether coordination intensity is alike across the countries studied or whether there are differences. Primarily with
respect to the design of personal coordination,
differences could be observed, especially with respect to number of expatriates, duration of foreign
assignments, mode of influencing selection decisions,
frequency of visits and motivation of visits. With
the exception of ownership and actors of planning,
there was a stable and unified pattern of technocratic coordination.

The exploration of interrelations between internal
context and headquarter-subsidiary design revealed
size, type of foundation and ownership as important
factors of influence. In further studies, geographical distance and degree of diversification should be
explored in more detail.

As most important result from the exploration of
interrelationships between context, headquarter-subsidiary relations, and effectiveness, we can propose
that low coordination intensity of headquarter-subsidiary relations paired with internal decentralization
of decisions is most likely to be correlated with
above-average economic and social effectiveness. It
seems extremely necessary, however, to conduct
further studies on this subject in order to improve
our findings, and to deal more intelligently with the
dynamic feedback relations between the variables
analyzed in this study.

NOTES

1) For details of conceptualization, operationalization, and measurement of the headquarter-subsidiary variable see WELGE 1978, p. 328 and WELGE 1980.

2) For the complete interview guide cf. WELGE 1978, p. 579.

3) For further details on sample and research methodology cf. WELGE 1978, p. 76.

4) For the conceptualization and operationalization of this variable see WELGE 1978, p. 328. An overview of organization structures of MNCs is given in WELGE 1980, p. 1365.

5) Besides Polytechnique, the following institutions are considered as "Grandes Ecoles": Mines, E.N.S., St. Cyr, and H.E.C. See also WELGE 1978, p. 488.

6) For details see WELGE 1978, p. 482.

7) This variable is not shown in Table 1. Cf. WELGE 1977, 1978.

8) For details cf. WELGE 1978, p. 375.

9) For the entire conceptual framework cf. WELGE 1978, p. 110.

10) The analysis reported in this chapter implies certain assumptions of causality. Internal contextual variables are hypothesized to influence headquarter-subsidiary design, and coordination intensity of headquarter-subsidiary relationships is hypothesized to directly influence subsidiary effectiveness. In addition, it is assumed that the influence of headquarter-subsidiary relationships can also be mediated by the structure of the subsidiary management system. It has been mentioned before that cross-sectional data are not really suitable to test causal relationships of this kind. Under the exploratory objective of this study the following analysis seems to be justified, because the hypothesized pattern seems rather plausible, and because there is some evidence from the few longitudinal case studies available. The causality assumption, however, needs further empirical proof by data from longitudinal studies.

11) For details of conceptualization and measurement of this criterion of effectiveness cf. WELGE 1978, Chapter 3.

12) For further results cf. Table 5.2-17 in WELGE
1978. p. 426.

13) ALSEGG's analysis would suggest that inversion
of the argument makes sense as well. Subsidiaries will be given more autonomy because they
have been more successful. Unfortunately, this
hypothesis cannot be explored with our data
because of the lack of longitudinal data.

14) For conceptualization and measurement of this
criterion of effectiveness cf. WELGE 1978,
Chapter 3, especially p. 166.

15) For details of these results cf. Table 5.2-18 in
WELGE 1978, p. 429.

16) Cf. WELGE 1978, p. 213.

REFERENCES

ALSEGG, R.J.: Control Relationships Between American
Corporations and Their European Subsidia-
ries. AMA Research Study 107, American
Management Association, Inc. 1971.

Arbeitskreis "Organisation international tätiger Unternehmen" der Schmalenbach-Gesellschaft:
Entsendung von Führungskräften in ausländi-
sche Niederlassungen. Zeitschrift für betriebs-wirtschaftliche Forschung, 29. Jg.
1977, pp. 346-366.

Arbeitskreis "Organisation international tätiger Unternehmen" der Schmalenbach-Gesellschaft:
Organisation des Planungsprozesses in
international tätigen Unternehmen. Zeitschrift für betreibs-wirtschaftliche Forschung, 31. Jg. 1979, pp. 20-37.

BARLOW, E.R.: Management of Foreign Manufacturing
Subsidiaries. Boston 1953.

BARLOW, E.R.; WENDER, I.T.: Foreign Investment and
Taxation. Englewood Cliffs 1955.

BLAU, P.M.; SCHOENHERR, R.A.: The Structure of Organizations. New York, 1971.

CHANNON, D.F.; JALLAND, M.: Multinational Strategic
Planning. London-Basingstoke 1979.

CHILD, J.: Organizational Structure, Environment and
Performance: The Role of Strategic Choice.
Sociology, Vol. 6, 1972, pp. 1-22.

ECKARTSBERG, H. von: Auslandseinsatz von Stammhaus-
personal. Frankfurt 1979.

FRANKO, L.G.: The European Multinationals. A Renewed
Challenge to American and British Big Business. London-New York-Hagerstown-San Fran-
cisco 1976.

GOVERNMENT OF INDIA: Guidelines for Industries 1975-
76: Department of Industrial Development,
Ministry of Industry & Civil Supplies. New
Delhi 1975.

JHA, L.K.: Transnational Corporations and Developing
Countries. New Delhi 1975.

KARGER, D.W.; MALIK, Z.A.: Long Range Planning and
Organizational Performance. Long Range
Planning, Vol. 8, No. 6, 1975, pp. 60-64.

KIESER, A.: Einflussgrössen der Unternehmungsorgani-
sation. Der Stand der empirischen Forschung
und Ergebnisse einer eigenen Erhebung.
Kölner Habilitationsschrift 1973.

KOCH, H.: Die zentrale Globalplanung als Kernstück
der integrierten Unternehmensplanung. Zeitschrift für betriebs-wirtschaftliche Forschung, 24. Jg. 1972, pp. 222-252.

NATIONAL INDUSTRIAL CONFERENCE BOARD: Obstacles and
Incentives to Private Foreign Investment
1967-68. Vol. I: Obstacles. Studies in
Business Policy, No. 130. New York 1969.

NEGANDHI, A.R.; BALIGA, R.: Multinational Corpora-
tions and Host Government Relationships. A
Comparative Study of U.S., European, and
Japanese Multinationals. Reprint Series of
the International Institute of Management.
Berlin 1976

NIE, N.H.; HULL, C.H.; JENKINS, J.G.; STEINBRENNER,
K.; BENT, D.H.: SPSS-Statistical Package
for the Social Sciences. 2. edition. New
York 1975.

PUGH, D.S.; HICKSON, D.J.; HININGS, C.R.; TURNER, C.:
The Context of Organization Structures.
Administrative Science Quarterly, Vol. 14
1969, pp. 91-114.

ROCCOUR, J.L.: Management of European Subsidiaries in
the United States. Management International
Review, Vol. 6, No. 1, 1966, pp. 13-27.

STARBUCK, W.H.: Organizational Growth and Development. In: Handbook of Organizations, edited
by J.G. March. Chicago 1965, pp. 451-533.

STEINER, G.A.; SCHÖLLHAMMER, H.: Pitfalls in Multi-
National Long-Range Planning. Long Range
Planning, Vol. 8, No. 2, 1975, pp. 2-12.

WEEDE, E.: Hypothesen, Gleichungen und Daten. Kron-
berg/Ts. 1977.

WELGE, M.K.: Profit-Center-Organisation. Wiesbaden
1975.

WELGE, M.K.: Profit-Center. In: Handwörterbuch der
Betriebswirtschaft. 4. Aufl., hrsg. v. E.
Grochla u. W. Wittmann. Stuttgart 1975,
Col. 3179-3188.

WELGE, M.K.: Eine empirische Analyse der Gestaltung
der Beziehungen zwischen deutschen multi-

nationalen Unternehmungen und ihren Tochtergesellschaften in Frankreich, Indien und USA. Einige vorläufige Ergebnisse. In: Personal- und Sozialorientierung der Betriebswirtschaftslehre. Band 1, hrsg. v. G. Reber. Stuttgart 1977, pp. 134-159.

WELGE, M.K.: Einflussgrössen der organisatorischen Effizienz von Tochtergesellschaften deutscher multinationaler Chemieunternehmungen. Kölner Habilitationsschrift 1978.

WELGE, M.K.: Need for Grounded Theory of Headquarter-Subsidiary Relationships in Multinational Enterprises. In: Work Organization Research: American and European Perspectives, edited by A.R. Negandhi and B. Wilpert. Kent 1978, pp. 125-132.

WELGE, M.K.: Multinationale Unternehmungen, Organisation der. In: Handwörterbuch der Organisation. 2. Aufl., hrsg. v. E. Grochla. Stuttgart 1980, Col. 1365-1378.

WELGE, M.K.: Management in deutschen multinationalen Unternehmungen. Ergebnisse einer empirischen Untersuchung. Stuttgart 1980.

YAMANE, T.: Statistics. An Introductory Analysis. 2. edition. New York-Evanston-London 1967.

YOUSSEF, S.M.: Contextual Factors Influencing Control Strategy of Multinational Corporations. Academy of Management Journal, Vol. 18, No. 1, 1975, pp. 136-143.

# 5 Anant R. Negandhi and B. R. Baliga:

# Internal Functioning of American, German and Japanese Multinational Corporations

## INTRODUCTION

The research project upon which this paper is based began in 1976. The project is a collaborative effort by six academicians of three different national origins - German, Indian, and Swedish - and different academic training and orientation. The research is being supported by the International Instititute of Management (I.I.M), Science Centre, West Berlin, and the International Business Institute of the Stockholm School of Economics, Sweden. The project grew out of earlier research (Negandhi and Baliga, 1979) on a comparative study of multinational corporations in the developing countries. The research team consisted of Professors A. R. Negandhi, University of Illinois, Urbana-Campaign; Lars Otterbeck, Anders Edstrom, and Gunnar Hedlund, Stockholm School of Economics; B. R. Baliga, University of Wisconsin, Eau Claire; and Martin Welge, University of Cologne.

In this paper, we will examine selected aspects of internal practices of American, German, and Japanese multinational companies and explore the implications of these practices on external relations. Specifically, we will discuss the results of the study concerning,

(a) Level of decentralization or the degree of subsidiary autonomy.

(b) Headquarter-subsidiary relationships and the nature of major problems encountered in these relationships.

---

University of Illinois and University of Wisconsin

## LEVEL OF DECENTRALIZATION

Centralization versus subsidiary autonomy is a perennial and conflicting problem faced by most multinational companies. Increasing competition in the world market requires some measure of rationalization of production and marketing processes at a global level, thus requiring a higher degree of centralization of decision-making at the headquarter and/or regional headquarter levels. On the other hand increasing demands are being made by the host as well as by the home countries of the multinationals. A high degree of subsidiary autonomy is usually demanded by host countries.

To assess the relative influence of the headquarters and subsidiaries in decision-making, we examined the decision-making with respect to the following factors:

> Borrowing from local banks
> Use of cash flow by subsidiary
> Extension of credit to major customers
> Choosing public accountant
> Introduction of new product for local market
> Servicing of products sold
> Use of local advertising agency
> Expansion of production capacity
> Maintenance of production facilities
> Appointment of chief executive
> Use of expatriate personnel
> Layoff of operating personnel
> Training programs for local employees

These decisions were then identified as either strategic or routine. An Overall Delegation Index was then computed with strategic decisions weighted three times as much as routine decisions. The weighting factor was chosen to reflect the approximate ratio of time span of feedback of strategic decisions to routine decisions. Table 1 presents the findings for the Overall Delegation Index and the extent of delegation provided to the subsidiary's management along with a set of decisions.

As it can be seen from the table, the Overall Delegation Index is fairly low in absolute terms. Despite the headquarters' acknowledgment of less than perfect understanding of the subsidiary's operation and its environment, the subsidiary influence on major decision-making is minimal.

Relatively speaking, Japanese subsidiaries seem to enjoy the most autonomy, and the U.S. subsidiaries the least. German subsidiaries are in between these two extremes. Our results are consistent with earlier studies by Franko (1976) and Dyas and Thanheiser (1976).

Particularly, the executives working for U.S. subsidiaries in Western Europe, displayed the same frustrations in controlling their own organizations as those working in developing countries. Listen, for example, to some of their concerns voiced in our study in the developing countries.

An American executive in Thailand, complaining about the excessive control and reporting needed by the U.S. headquarters, stated:

> For these whiz kids who are playing around with the figures but really don't know what to do with the data. ... (The) more you supply, (the) more they want ... and my two (expatriate) assistants and I spend 60 percent of our time in generating reports and data, and I surely hope somebody is using them at least as toilet paper.

In a similar vein, another American expatriate, who had been posted to India after twenty-five years of service at the home office, said:

> Headquarters demand a lot of documentation from here ... (but) as far as top brass is concerned, they seem to know very little about what is happening in these countries.

Explaining his relationship with the home office, he pointed out:

> We take home leave ... take a week off to go to our headquarters ... socialize with the people we know, but communicate with nobody on substantial matters ... I sometimes wonder whether the president or even the vice-president of our international division will recognize me ... They simply do not care.

Yet another American executive in Thailand echoed his frustration, saying:

> I really question whether the top brass at the home office listen to what we say and report ... I think they are not mature enough to know the conditions prevailing here. ... We are just beating the drums, nobody cares to listen back home.

Japanese companies, on the other hand, seem to have mastered the so-called "Z" mode of operation in which

organizational members are acculturated and social-
ized toward a common set of organizational and
societal values (Ouchi and Jaeger, 1978). Given
such orientation, headquarters are not concerned
about losing their control in spite of higher
autonomy afforded to the subsidiary operations.
This is the most charitable explanation about
the Japanese subsidiary's greater autonomy. The
least chariable explanation may be that the Japanese
headquarters simply have not learned how to control
their subsidiaries and operate with a global concept.

TABLE 1

Comparison of delegation in the various areas for U.S., German, and Japanese MNCs

| | U.S. (N = 34) Mean | S.D. | German (N = 45) Mean | S.D. | Japan (N = 41) Mean | S.D. | U.S. (N = 34) Mean | S.D. | German (N = 45) Mean | S.D. | Japan (N = 41) Mean | S.D. |
|---|---|---|---|---|---|---|---|---|---|---|---|---|
| Overall Delegation Index | -1.68 | 4.33 | 0.14 | 3.72 | $2.89^x$ | 3.38 | -1.68 | 4.33 | 0.14 | 3.72 | $2.89^x$ | 3.38 |
| Local Personnel Decisions | 2.40 | 1.46 | 2.85 | 1.24 | $3.51^x$ | 0.93 | 2.40 | 1.46 | 2.85 | 1.24 | $3.51^*$ | 0.93 |
| Expatriate Personnel Decisions | -2.10 | 1.67 | -2.49 | 1.60 | $-0.65^*$ | 2.00 | -2.10 | 1.67 | -2.49 | 1.60 | $-0.65^x$ | 2.00 |
| Routine Production Decisions | -0.04 | 2.63 | $2.59^x$ | 1.43 | $2.24^x$ | 1.84 | -0.04 | 2.63 | 2.59 | 1.43 | 2.24 | 1.84 |
| Strategic Production Decisions | -1.78 | 2.21 | -1.54 | 2.21 | $0.07^*$ | 2.26 | -1.78 | 2.21 | -1.54 | 2.21 | $0.07^*$ | 2.26 |
| Routine Marketing Decisions | 1.27 | 1.62 | $2.42^x$ | 1.19 | $2.85^x$ | 1.11 | 1.27 | 1.62 | 2.42 | 1.19 | 2.85 | 1.11 |
| Strategic Marketing Decisions | -1.58 | 2.14 | -0.83 | 2.42 | $1.14^x$ | 2.35 | -1.58 | 2.14 | -0.83 | 2.42 | $1.14^x$ | 2.42 |
| Financial Decisions | 0.30 | 2.00 | $1.61^x$ | 1.50 | $1.90^x$ | 1.00 | 0.30 | 2.00 | 1.61 | 1.50 | $1.90^*$ | 1.00 |

$^x p \leq 0.001$
$^* 0.01 < p < 0.05$

Key

| -4 | 0 | +4 |
|---|---|---|
| max. H0 influence | equal inf. | max. sub. influence |

In examining the similarities and differences in decision-making influences in various functional areas,
we found no significant differences between U.S. and
German MNCs with respect to the decisions concerning
the local personnel. They were both relatively enjoying a greater autonomy in this regard, although
Japanese subsidiaries, here too, were the most decentralized.

With regard to expatriate personnel, we noted that
headquarters prefer to limit the delegation provided
to the subsidiary-executives and this is not surprising. Edstrom and Galbraith (1977) have pointed
out that expatriate personnel are significant links
in the control mechanisms employed by the headquarters. Interestingly, even here, Japanese subsidiary-executives appear to exercise greater influence than either their American or German counterparts. This could reflect a willingness on the part
of the headquarters' management to place greater
reliance on the judgment of their representatives
in the field. It could also reflect the fact that
being relative newcomers to MNC-systems (Tsurumi,
1976) they have yet to develop a field-tested international executive group at the headquarters to control their subsidiary operations.

It is easy to understand the high frustration of
U.S. subsidiary-executives when one looks at the
delegation accorded to them on routine production
decisions. They have the least authority of the
three MNC-systems studied. Here it clearly reflects
the need for rationalization and standardization of
operations practiced by U.S. MNCs. The relatively
larger size of U.S. operations may also contribute
to this quest for efficiency.

The headquarter's influence increases considerably on
strategic production decisions, though even here, the
Japanese subsidiary's executives appear to have more
influence. The delegation pertaining to operation and
strategic marketing decisions followed a pattern
similar to that for routine and strategic production
decisions. A senior U.S.-subsidiary executive seems
to have voiced the concern of many when narrated the
following episode:

> The opening of regional headquarters in Brussels
> has taken away much of our decision-making power
> and authority. Just recently we voiced strong
> objection to an advertising program that the
> regional headquarters was proposing to us in
> Britain. Our objections went unheeded and the
> advertising campaign turned out to be a dis-
> aster. We are also having problems recruiting
> managerial personnel because the job lacks any
> real challenge and decision-making authority.

The need to rationalize production on a global scale has generated additional pressure to the marketing operations.

This limited delegation of strategic marketing decision har posed problems for some Japanese firms operating in the United States. Sony, for example, could not react fast enough to competition surpassing some of Sony's higher quality products nor could they deal with erosion of retail price maintenance policies adequately.

From the above it appears that the headquarters' management is still relatively unwilling to recognize the differences of host-environmental conditions and their effects on the subsidiary's operation.

The delegation is also fairly limited on financial decisions. It is to be expected that in a multinational corporation system with numerous subsidiaries, finance would clearly be the language of management. However, practically all the subsidiaries studied had a functional form of organizational structure. The functional specialization leads to a lessening of the emphasis on financial management; for example, capital expenditure decisions get subsumed under decisions to expand production capacity, etc. The greater level of delegation in Japanese subsidiaries seems to be a function of size. Being much smaller than their American or German counterparts, the monetary sums involved in financial transactions are likely to be fairly small. An alternative explanation is suggested by the close relationship of Japanese organizations to Japanese banks (Caves and Uekusa, 1976). As a consequence of this close relationship between banks and headquarters, it is relatively easy to establish zones of authority (Burrage, 1972) within which the subsidiaries can function in a relatively autonomous manner.

We also examined the extent to with the various MNC-systems were formalized. Not surprisingly, there was a relatively high correlation between extent of delegation provided to the subsidiary's management and the extent of formalization. U.S. MNCs were the most formalized. As we saw earlier, many U.S.-subsidiary executives interviewed felt hampered by this formalization, especially in the developing countries.

## CRITICAL PROBLEMS BETWEEN HEADQUARTER AND SUBSIDIARY OPERATIONS

During the interviews with the senior executives of both headquarters and subsidiaries, we probed into some of the critical problems encountered in head-quarter-subsidiary relationships. Besides examining the nature and intensity of such focal issues between headquarters and subsidiaries, we also attempted to assess the relative influences of the headquarter and the subsidiary in resolving such issues.

Approximately one-half of the subsidiaries of the American, German, and Japanese multinational companies studied indicated that no serious problems existed in their relationships with the headquarters. Of the 48 critical issues narrated by the subsidiaries' executives, roughly one-third were concerning the lack of subsidiary's autonomy in dealing with the problems faced by them in the host countries; approximately one-fourth of these issues were concerning capital investment decisions. Table 2 shows the range of problems between headquarters and subsidiaries operations.

Comparatively, as we discussed earlier, Japanese subsidiaries enjoyed more autonomy in decision-making than those of the American and German multinationals and accordingly reported less frustration in this regard. Overall, there were no significant differences between the American and German companies. The global rationalization of production and marketing processes being practiced by the American and German MNCs seem to have resulted in similar challenges and problems. The following examples represent the nature of issues between headquarters and subsidiaries.

1.  The General Manager of an American subsidiary in Britain complained bitterly about the price for his exports being determined by the marketing manager at the European headquarter. Yet the subsidiary was responsible for meeting profit targets. This procedure led to a considerable degree of tension between the subsidiary and the European headquarter and the parent company has made no effort to resolve these differences.

2.  An American multinational wanted to terminate the operations of its subsidiary in Sweden as the plant was very old and productivity was low. When the plans were made public there was a considerable amount of concern. The Swedish government was very unhappy and started pressuring the local management to keep the plant viable. Ultimately, a compromise was reached to keep the subsidiary operations open for some time. The subsidiary's executives were not, however, sure about the next step headquarter may take.

TABLE 2

Nature of critical issues existing between the headquarters and subsidiaries

| Ownership of MNC | Capital Investment | Sales & Financial | Home Country Policies | Host Country Policies | Organizational Autonomy | No Issues | Total |
|---|---|---|---|---|---|---|---|
| | $N/q_0^1/q_0^2$ | $N/q_0^1/q_0^2$ | $N/q_0^1/q_0^2$ | $N/q_0^1/q_0^2$ | $N/q_0^1/q_0^2$ | $N/q_0^1/q_0^2$ | |
| U.S. | 3/10.3/27.3 | 2/6.9/22.2 | 1/3.4/14.3 | 1/3.4/16.7 | 5/17.2/33.2 | 17/58.6/27.9 | 29 |
| Germany | 5/12.2/45.5 | 3/7.3/33.3 | 2/4.9/28.6 | 2/4.9/33.3 | 8/19.5/53.3 | 21/51.2/34.4 | 41 |
| Japan | 3/7.7/27.3 | 4/10.3/44.4 | 4/10.3/57.1 | 3/7.7/50.0 | 2/5.1/13.3 | 23/59.0/37.7 | 39 |
| Column Total | 11 | 9 | 7 | 6 | 15 | 61 | 109 |

$q_0^1$ refers to Row percentages

$q_0^2$ refers to Column percentages

Chi square = 6.35   10 D.f.     Sig. 0.78

3. The U.S. parent company fired the marketing manager of its German subsidiary as he was not able to stay and manage within a budgeted amount. The Controller at the headquarter felt that the demonstrated skills of the marketing manager and his sales performance were not adequate to offset his overrun on the budget. His firing was seen as setting an example to other subsidiary executives to stay within budget at any cost. This incident had affected the morale of other senior executives.

4. The subsidiary of an American firm in France wanted to set up a profit sharing system with its employees. Headquarter was strongly opposed to such a move and asserted that they would rather divest than be a party to the new social policy. Despite insistent complaints by subsidiary management that the headquarter's personnel were insensitive to local issues, it refused to let the subsidiary negotiate the agreement. The net result was a series of strikes by the French subsidiary employees.

5. There was considerable argument between German headquarter and its Portugese subsidiary management about additional investment in a particular product line. The subsidiary had lost a considerable amount of money in the previous 15 years and the headquarter was very wary of additional investment. The subsidiary kept developing reports that showed that the investment was very desirable. Headquarter kept countering with studies which showed the investment to be undesirable. This process continued for nearly two years and was ultimately resolved in the subsidiary's favor only after they had managed to build up a very vocal lobby in the parent company.

6. The management of a Japanese subsidiary in Australia had to pay their employees a percentage of their salary during a strike as per Australian law. Headquarters personnel could not understand why this was necessary and tried to pressure subsidiary management to stop these payments.

With respect to the relative influences of headquarters and subsidiaries in the resolution of issues, our interview data analyses indicated that in approximately one-half of the cases, headquarters handed down the final decisions, and in less than one-third of the cases subsidiaries' viewpoint prevailed. Among the three sets of subsidiaries, Japanese and German subsidiaries seem to have more influence in resolving issues.

## SUMMARY AND IMPLICATIONS

Our results concerning the internal structure and processes of multinational corporations show that the quest of global rationalization has caught on and the German MNCs are in fact catching up with the U.S. MNCs in their pursuit of global reach, and the Japanese, although stumbling here and there, are not far behind. The centralization of decision-making is thus only a logical consequence of this quest. The needed autonomy of the subsidiaries to solve the specific socio-economic problems of the host countries is the victim.

Where do we go from here, is the question, for all of us to ponder, since we, academicians and business-men alike, were the ones who not long ago had pro-claimed the virtues of global rationalization.

TABLE 3    Profile of the Companies Studied

| | Country of Origin | | |
|---|---|---|---|
| | United States (N=34) | Germany (N=45) | Japan (N=41) |
| **Type of Industry** | | | |
| Heavy Engineering | 12 | 14 | 2 |
| Light Engineering | 5 | 6 | 14 |
| Chemical and Pharmaceutical | 7 | 21 | 4 |
| Electrical and Electronics | 0 | 2 | 6 |
| Automobile | 6 | 2 | 2 |
| Tires and Rubber Products | 3 | 0 | 0 |
| Foods | 1 | 0 | 1 |
| Mixed-Diversified Trading Companies with Manufacturing Investments | 0 | 0 | 12 |
| **Ratio of Equity** | | | |
| Wholly Owned | 32 | 44 | 31 |
| Majority Ownership | 2 | 0 | 1 |
| 50-50 Ownership | 0 | 1 | 5 |
| Minority Ownership | 0 | 0 | 4 |
| **Size: Number of Employees** | | | |
| 5000 and more | 5 | 6 | 2 |
| 1001 to 4999 | 11 | 11 | 2 |
| 501 to 1000 | 4 | 9 | 4 |
| 201 to 500 | 4 | 4 | 9 |
| 101 to 200 | 3 | 8 | 3 |
| 100 or less | 1 | 3 | 5 |
| Information Inadequate | | 26 | |

APPENDIX

THE RESEARCH DESIGN

As mentioned earlier, the project was conceived in a
comparative vein; we endeavored to study American,
German, British, and Japanese multinationals and
their subsidiaries. Our aim was to collect detailed
information on many aspects on multinational operations at both headquarter and subsidiary levels.
Subsidiaries of German, Japanese, and American multinationals operating in Europe (West Germany, United
Kingdom, Spain, Portugal, Belgium, and the Nether-
lands), U.S.A., Mexico, Brazil, India, and Iran and
their respective headquarters constituted the universe for the research reported in this paper. The
Universe was determined from investment directories
and listings provided by chambers of commerce and
manufacturing associations. Considerable efforts
were made to ensure that the listings were as current
as possible. The universe was restricted to firms
that were engaged in some form of manufacturing activity. Hence, firms in travel, banking, and other service sectors were omitted from consideration. The
chief executives of the firms were contacted. Letters
detailing the nature of the research project with
the request for a personal interview with the chief
operating officers and/or representatives of the top
management team were then mailed out.

At this juncture, it appears appropriate to make some
remarks on the sample that was utilized in the analysis. Ideally, in order to have some confidence (statistically) in the results, the random sample needed
to be large enough. Matching was impossible as historical patterns of Japanese, German and American investments in Europe have been quite different, with
Japanese multinationals being a more recent phenomenon. As there were considerable uncertainties about
the cooperation that could be obtained from multinational corporations' executives, a conscious random sampling procedure was not adopted. It can, however, be asserted that the final sample that did result was a random sample in a sense that every firm
in the universe had the same chance of participating
or not participating in the study. However, in order
to increase the generalizability and external validity of the study, considerable supplemental information was obtained both on the companies that had
participated in the study and otherwise. Despite
these efforts, the reader is cautioned to bear the
limitations of the sample in mind when reading
through the analyses and discussions.

120

# REFERENCES

BURRAGE, M. 1972. "The Group Ties of Occupations in Britain and the U.S." _Administrative Science Quarterly_, Vol. 17, No. 2, pp. 240-254.

CAVES, R.W. and UEKUSA, M. 1976. Industrial Organization in Japan. Washington, D.C.: The Brookings Institution.

EDSTROM, A. and GALBRAITH J.R. 1977. "Transfer of Managers as a Coordination and Control Strategy in Multinational Corporations." _Administrative Science Quarterly_, Vol. 22, No. 2, pp. 248-263.

FRANKO, Lawrence. 1974. "The Move toward a Multi-Divisional Structure in European Organizations." _Administrative Science Quarterly_ 19:493-506.

NEGANDHI, ANANT R. and BALIGA, B.R. 1979. Quest for Survival and Growth: A Comparative Study of American, European and Japanese Multinationals, Konigstein, West Germany: Athenaeum. New York: Praeger.

OUCHI, William and JAGER, A. 1978. "Type Z Organization: Stability in the Midst of Mobility." _Academy of Management Review_, Vol. 3, No. 2, pp. 305-314.

RUMELT, Richard. 1974. Strategy, Structure and Economic Performance. Boston: Division of Research, Harvard Business School.

STOPFORD, John and WELLS, Louis. 1972. Managing the Multinational Enterprise. London: Longmans.

THANHEISER, Heinz. 1972. Strategy and Structure of German Firms. Ph.D. dissertation, Harvard Business School.

TSURUMI, Y. 1973. "Japanese Multinational Firm." _Journal of World Trade Law._

# 6  Christopher A. Bartlett:

# Multinational Structural Change: Evolution Versus Reorganization

For most of this century Westinghouse's international
activities were managed through Westinghouse Electric
International, a separate organization based in New
York and maintaining only limited contact and interaction with the rest of the company.[1] In the 1960s,
Westinghouse tried to build its overseas strength
by acquiring strong national firms and linking them
to the U.S. parent through its international division. Difficulties arose not only in obtaining
companies (de Gaulle personally vetoed one key
acquisition) but also in integrating them into
Westinghouse. Thus, in 1971 the separate international organization was disbanded and the company's
125 division managers were given worldwide responsibility for the businesses they had been managing in
the domestic U.S. market.

By 1978, however, top management was concerned that
the company was gaining a reputation abroad for being
internally disorganized with a total lack of coordination between divisions. Several of its overseas
companies were in difficulty and had to be sold off.
Furthermore, foreign customers and governments were
complaining that the company was difficult to do
business with because of its insensitivity to local
situations and its inability to coordinate various
businesses in a given country.

In early 1979 the vice chairman's response was to
reorganize once again. He gave one of his key execu-

Harvard University Graduate School of Business Administration

tives 90 days to analyze Westinghouse's international operations and make recommendations for the organizational change required. The report recommended that the company supplement its worldwide product organization with a network of geographic managers reporting to a strong international chief. By July 1979 Westinghouse had begun installing a formal global matrix organization structure by overlaying the existing product organization with the new geographic organization. Newly appointed country managers reported to four regional presidents who, in turn, reported to an international president with a seat on the powerful corporate management committee. This reorganization, the company believed, would help it achieve the global integration it needed to remain efficient and competitive and the sensitivity to national environments it required to be effective locally.

The situation of Westinghouse provides a good illustration not only of the multiple strategic pressures that have confronted most companies as they have expanded abroad, but also of the typical structural responses in U.S. based multinational corporations (MNCs).

Like Westinghouse, many MNCs found themselves confronted by multiple, and often conflicting strategic demands as they grew internationally. Most became aware quite early of the need to develop an understanding of the diverse characteristics of the various national environments in which they operated. However, as foreign operations grew they began to recognize the opportunity and the need to rationalize these diverse worldwide operations to capitalize on their potential global efficiencies. As global competition intensified and, at the same time, pressures from host countries grew, managers of MNCs were confronted with the simultaneous need to be globally competitive and nationally responsive.[2] Responding consistently and appropriately to the variety of diverse, changing, and often conflicting demands has provided, for many companies, the major administrative challenge of the past decade. Their decision processes had to adapt to the challenge of becoming multidimensional - able to respond simultaneously to the global and the national strategic imperatives.

For many companies, the need for the decision making process to respond to these diverse and growing pressures led to a series of reorganizations similar to those undertaken by Westinghouse. So familiar did the pattern become that various "stages theories" of organizational development became widely recognized.[3] Some academics, consultants and managers

123

began to think of this series of reorganizations in normative rather than descriptive terms, and for some MNCs it seemed that organization structure followed fashion as much as it related to strategy.[4] Reorganizations from international divisions to global product or area organizations, or from global structures to matrix forms, became widespread. This, after all, was the classic organizational sequence described in the "stages theories".

Yet many companies that had expected such changes to provide them with the strategy-structure fit to meet the new pressures were disappointed. Developing a multidimensional decision making process that was able to balance the conflicting global and national needs was a subtle and time consuming process not necessarily achieved by redrawing the lines on a chart. Examples of failed or abandoned multinational organizations abound.[5]

While there were many companies, like Westinghouse, that appeared to concentrate largely on changes in the formal organization structure as a means to achieve the desired changes in their administrative processes, there were others that appeared to have developed successful multidimensional decision making processes without resorting to major changes in their formal organizations. Most notable was the substantial number of companies that had built large, complex and successful foreign operations while retaining their supposedly embryonic international division structures.[6] If these companies had been successful in achieving a strategy-structure "fit", they had done so without resorting to the sequence of traumatic reorganizations as described in the stages theories and as experienced by Westinghouse.

To understand why this substantial group of MNCs had not followed the stages model of organizational change, a detailed clinical study of nine of these companies was undertaken.[7] It was hypothesised that either the parameters of the generally accepted stages models were inappropriate, or there were alternative means of structural response that were not revealed in a simple classification of formal organizaton.

The companies studied were selected from two industries with diverse strategic characteristics: four from the food processing industry, and five from the health care industry (ethical and proprietary drugs, hospital supplies). In trying to understand why these companies had not evolved through the series of reorganizations described in the stages models, two quite different explanations emerged.

The companies in the food processing industry had retained their international division structure for a very simple reason: the key strategic demands of their operations were perceived as being undimensional. The nature of the business resulted in the key tasks being focused at the national level, with little long-term advantage to be gained by global operations. Product development, manufacturing, and marketing were all national rather than global tasks for a variety of cultural as well as economic reasons.$_{8}$ The conclusion reached was that increasing size and complexity did not cause these companies to abandon the "federal" organization structure needed to manage this business.

This paper concentrates on the findings relating to the five companies in the health care industry (ethical and proprietary drugs, hospital supplies). The administrative challenges confronting managers in these companies were more interesting, since they clearly did face the diversity of global and national demands and environmental conditions that had forced many other companies to follow the traditional stages of reorganization into global then matrix forms of organization. The companies studied, however, seemed to achieve their state of strategy-structure fit by a different process. Rather than focusing on "anotomical" changes, these companies seemed to spend more time modifying the "physiological" characteristics of their organizations. They appeared to view the required change form unidimensional to multidimensional organization as an adaptive, evolutionary process rather than as a series of powerful, yet perhaps traumatic, reorganizations. In contrast to companies such as Westinghouse and others which followed the "strategic crisis - structural reorganization" route, these companies developed, adjusted and integrated the required new skills, structures and processes gradually but continuously. It is this alternative process of adaptation from unidimensional to multidimensional organization that will be described in the remainder of this paper.

THE STRATEGIC DEMAND: MULTIDIMENSIONAL TASKS

Before describing the structural and administrative changes made by the various companies, it may be helpful to have an understanding of the overall task demands that provoked the changes. What were the strategic issues facing companies in the health care industry that prevented them from retaining the simple unidimensional "federal" organization structure that proved adequate for the food processing companies?

The task complexity facing the health care companies could be described briefly along three dimensions: The need to be simultaneously responsive at the national level yet efficient globally; the need to develop multiple functional expertise at multiple organization levels; and the need to be flexible in the way all of these demands were managed. Each will be described briefly.

- As they expanded abroad, these companies needed to understand and respond to the variety of local national demands that affected their success in each national market. They had to understand the structure and operation of national health delivery systems, the nature of government product registration processes, the formal and informal demands for local sourcing of critical products, and a variety of other such national pressures. However, they also had to recognize that if they were to be effective global competitors, their research efforts, manufacturing capacity, product policy and a variety of other tasks had to be coordinated and perhaps integrated on a worldwide basis. In short, they were faced with the challenge of being simultaneously responsive and flexible at the national level while maintaining the competitive efficiency that comes from global coordination.

- Unlike the food processing industry where the marketing function was the dominant success factor, in the health care industry the marketing, research, and manufacturing functions were all regarded as key success factors. Furthermore, in the food industry all the key tasks were concentrated at the national level (e.g, products developed to meet national tastes, local manufacturing due to freshness and transportation limitations, etc.). Key tasks in the drug industry however, needed to be managed at multiple organizational levels (e.g., for economic and quality control reasons active ingredients for most drugs were prepared centrally, while tablet and capsule plants could be operated efficiently on a regional or national basis; basic research obviously needed global coordination, yet product development was often handled on a regional basis, and local clinical trials were needed for national product registration).

- Unlike the food processing industry where the markets, the technology and the products were typically mature, the health care industry tended to present a much more dynamic operating environment. Particularly in the areas of new product development and government controls and regulations, changes were occurring at a very rapid rate in the 1960s and 1970s. Furthermore the stage of maturity and rate of change varied substantially by market.

## THE STRUCTURAL RESPONSE: MULTIDIMENSIONAL ORGANIZATION

Clearly companies could not hope to manage this set of complex, diverse, and changing demands through their simple, unidimensional "federal" organization structures. They were faced with the major challenge of developing complex, multidimensional "global" organizations. As stated previously, in the companies studied, such organization structures were developed not through the series of reorganizations described by the stages theories, but through a more gradual evolutionary process. This process appeared to involve three distinct yet closely interrelated changes, and although there was considerable overlap, these changes tended to occur sequentially. First, new management skills and perspectives were gradually, developed to reflect and respond to the growing range of task demands facing these companies; next, subtle modifications were made to the organization structures and systems to allow better interaction between the newly developed range of management perspectives; and finally, conscious efforts were made to change the organization "climate" in attempt to institutionalize the relationships required in an effective decision making process in a complex and uncertain multidimensional organization environment.

The purpose of these changes in the formal and informal structures and systems was to allow the organization's decision making process to evolve from a unidimensional to a multidimensional focus. Associated with each stage of the structural development was a change in what can be termed the predominant "management mode". Substantive decision management by senior management in the first phase tended to evolve towards a temporary coalition management mode, which in turn gave way to decision context management in the final phase. Each will be explained and illustrated in the following sections.

The nature of these structural developments and the changes in the decision making process that accompanied them will provide the focus for the remainder of this paper. Only one additional note needs to be added at this stage. Although each of the companies studied had made adaptions to skills, structure and "climate", it was also clear that they were not all at the same stage of development in creating their multidimentional organization structures and management processes. One had concentrated mainly on developing the range of management skills and perspectives required to respond to the diversity of task demands it faced and continued to utilize the substantive decision management mode. Others had supplemented such changes with varying degrees of change in their structures, systems, and basic administrative processes, and had broadened their repertoire of "management modes" in decision making. To illustrate the description of each of these modes however, examples are provided from the companies that most closely correspond to the phase of multidimensional development being described. It should be recognized, however, that none of the companies fitted neatly into such convenient categories: in effect, there were as many structural and administrative solutions as there were companies studied.

## DEVELOPING NEW MANAGEMENT PERSPECTIVES

### Organizational Changes

In their early stages of overseas expansion, all five of the health care companies studied had developed networks of strong independent country subsidiaries. The key strategic tasks were perceived as being first, to develop an understanding of the various national operating environments, and second, to use that knowledge to build strong initial market positions. Thus, country subsidiary managers with local expertise were granted considerable autonomy and independence to perform these tasks.

The organization structure that resulted could best be described as a "federal" structure in which the country managers' knowledge of their national operating environments gave them a dominant role in key decisions. Their power was formally recognized by the fact that geographic managers were line managers in organizations in which line authority was rarely challenged. Product and functional managers filled staff roles that were primarily defined as support functions for the country managers. Headquarters intervention into subsidiary operations was limited and infrequent, and the country managers' view dominated the strategic decision process.

As a consequence, even decisions with global implications were frequently made on the largely-unchallenged recommendation of country subsidiary managers. For example, in each of the companies studied, this early period of development was marked by the proliferation of manufacturing operations worldwide as country managers argued that a local plant was essential for the success of the national subsidiary. There was little resistance to such demands for two reasons. First, nobody in the organization had sufficient knowledge of the various national environments to challenge country managers' claims of customer demands or government pressures, and second, little if any analysis was being done to determine the global costs and efficiency of this multiple plant "strategy".

Although this "federal system" proved adequate for the early stages of establishing foreign subsidiaries, it became clear that a company's global strategy could not be defined by the simple sum of its various national strategies. Geographic-based demands had to be supplemented with product and functional views; national perspectives had to be counterbalanced by regional and global perspectives.

The major impediment to the goal of adding new perspectives to the decision process was that the product and functional managers who should have been able to provide such input were unable to do so. The dominance of the geographic perspective in the past had resulted in the development of product and functional managers whose major task was to service the needs of country subsidiary managers and act as headquarters links and information conduits. They had neither the expertise nor the organizational credibility to counter the country managers' proposals with arguments that took a more integrated global viewpoint. The first challenge in building a more multidimensional organizarion therefore was to develop managers who could represent these additional perspectives.

In all five health care companies, the process of developing the broader product and functional management skills and viewpoints followed a remarkably similar pattern. It began with the growth of a regional office and culminated with the establishment of management groups at the divisional level that had a substantial input to all major strategic decisions.

Ironically, it was the demands of the geographic line managers for more support at the regional level that gave product and functional managers an opportunity to develop their information access, their control role, and their coordination responsibilities. Through these changes their power and influence in the ongoing decision process increased substantially. In response to subsidiary criticism that the staff

groups at division headquarters were too distant and
often of too little experience to provide the required level of support, regional offices were established in all five companies studied. By working
closer to the various markets, product and functional
managers made important developmental advances as
they gained greater understanding of and credibility
in the subsidiary operations.

The next phase that was critical in the development
of the product and functional managers occurred
during the control period that tended to follow the
initial rapid growth abroad. As foreign sales and
overseas investment levels grew to a level of corporate importance, senior management began demanding
better information about and control over the largely
autonomous subsidiaries. The product and functional
management groups with their closer contact with
operations began to be seen as appropriate sources of
information and means of control. Increasingly, their
visits to subsidiaries were at the instruction of top
management to report on a problem rather than at the
request of the country manager to provide technical
information or support.

With increased market knowledge, access to regular,
current, reliable data, and power gained through
their new control responsibility, it was inevitable
that the product and functional managers eventually
would move to the third important phase in their development within the organization. In each of the
companies observed, these more sophisticated, more
powerful management groups began to recognize opportunities to coordinate and integrate activities being
managed separately by the various country operations.
While initial projects tended to concentrate on the
provision of regional services to subsidiaries (e.g.,
EDP systems and facilities, intercompany payments
netting), as soon as their credibility was established, these managers often began to take om major
coordination and integration responsibilities such as
regional manufacturing rationalization or regional
product management coordination.

The increased credibility that grew out of their
greater access to operations, the new influence that
derived from their control role, and the upgraded
power that flowed from their new coordination responsibilities, all provided the regional product and
functional managers with considerably greater impact
on the decision process. Their increasing importance
and power was symbolized by the growth of the regional office that took place during this period in each
of the companies observed. Country managers were par-

ticularly conscious of this change in influence of
product and functional managers, and in numerous instances tensions and even open conflict developed
between staff and line.

Nevertheless, senior management found the additional
information, services, and advice helpful in counter-
balancing the previously unidimensional analyses and
recommendations they had been receiving. To better
develop global perspectives and to obtain improved
access to the newly developed expertise, senior
management typically began to build the product and
functional management groups at the division headquarters level. Many of the stronger managers developed at the regional level were transferred to the
division level as part of this process.

This development resulted in the power and influence
of product and functional managers being developed
even more. First, their proximity to senior management enhanced their access to and influence in key
decision making processes. Equally important, however, was the role these managers began to play in
linking the international division to the rest of
the corporation. Their product or functional expertise gave them credibility in other parts of the
organization, while their greatly improved understanding of country level operations made them knowledgeable spokesmen on international issues. Typically these managers became international representatives to corporate bodies responsible for product
policy, research priorities, capacity decisions, and
other such global issues.

In all five health care companies studied the development of strong, credible product and functional
management groups appeared to be the first major
sted in supplementing the country level geographi-
cally dominated decision process. The pattern of
building a strong regional office then developing
strong division level management groups was remarkably consistent, and seemed to provide a means to
educate and legitimize the product and functional
managers close to country level questions before
bringing them to headquarters where they could input
more directly into major decisions.

## Management Process Change

Prior to the development of managers who could represent the global product and functional perspectives,
country managers' analyses and proposals to senior
managers went largely unchallenged. Even if a staff
manager did question the country manager's views,
his protests often went unheeded due to his low

status and credibility in the organization. Clearly
in these companies, decision influence was dominated by the geographic line managers.

As the new management skills and perspectives were
developed, however, the decision process on key
issues became more complex. Arguments for national
responsiveness faced strong counter proposals for
global integration, and the only means of resolving
the inherent conflict was to elevate it to the senior
management level. This mode of management can be
termed substantive decision management because senior
management's key role is as arbitrator on the merits
of issues in dispute.

This process arose largely due to the lack of any
other organizational means to resolve the inevitable
differences in opinions and recommendations. However,
it was also a process that seemed to suit senior
management, at least temporarily. By retaining the
integrator and arbitrator role, these managers were
able to develop a fuller understanding of the global
issues being raised by the newly developed product
and functional groups, and to appreciate the nature
and extent of the tradeoffs required between national
and global perspectives.

All of the sample companies found the substantive
decision management mode a convenient and simple way
to integrate new perspectives into the management
process in their early stages of multidimensional development. Not only did it provide a means for the
newly developed global skills and perspectives to
be integrated into the decision process, it also
represented a process of education for senior management, allowing them to form judgements on the relative importance of the various perspectives on different issues. Eventually, however, most of them found
it a cumbersome administrative system to maintain as
the prime decision making process.

There were three major classes of problems that these
companies seemed to encounter after using this management process over a period of time. The first related to the reliability of the inputs to key decisions. By having advocacy groups take frequently
opposing positions on issues, the analysis and recommendations being fed to senior management risked
being less than objective. Analyses were often based
on incomplete, conflicting or even biased data, and
decisions frequently had to be made from the limited
and sometimes extreme set of alternatives generated.

The second type of problem encountered in this decision mode related to top management overload. As the

only source of integration and resolution, senior
management soon became overburdened. The inevitable
slowdown in the decision making process that followed
had the effect of dampening the generation of proposals from within the organization, or of leading
middle managers to short-circuit the system by making
decisions without referral to others.

The third problem area was related to implementation.
Disputed issues resolved by senior management often
had to be implemented by managers who had fought
hard for an opposite outcome. Without the uncompro-
mising support of those responsible, implementation
effectiveness often suffered.

While these problems caused most companies eventually
to abandon the substantive decision management mode,
one of the sample group retained this as a key part
of its decision making process. Having developed
extremely strong functional management to counterbalance its geographic line managers, Merck and
Company had used a substantive decision management
style for many years and continued to use it as
its dominant decision process in 1979.

The main reason for the continued use of this management mode appeared to be that such a process was
neither unfamiliar nor uncomfortable in a company
with a historical origin rooted in the fine chemicals
business. Since this industry was characterized by
large scale centralized manufacturing and research
and a few big customers, centralized decision making
was the norm, and Merck followed the pattern.

The acquisition of Sharp and Dohm took Merck into the
international pharmaceutical business, and while its
traditional management style did not appear to re-
strict the growth of foreign subsidiaries with substantial autonomy, senior management at Merck recognized very early the need to control their activities and counterbalance their strong national perspectives with more integrated global views. The
division level functional staffs that were developed
in this company were substantially larger than equi-
valent groups in similar companies studied. The
international division marketing staff, for example,
numbered over one hundred and its manufacturing staff
over seventy - four to ten times the size of other
similar sized drug companies studied.

These functionally organized division staff groups
quickly established credibility with senior management and began to act as a filter and a control on
subsidiary proposals, elevating those with which
they did not agree for arbitration. A weekly inter-

national executive committee meeting, consisting of the division president and his geographic and functional vice presidents, was the center of major decisions. From the different perspectives presented on key issues, senior management felt it was able to obtain a broader appreciation of implications than any of the middle managers alone. They felt this put them in a better position to resolve differences in opinions. The strength of their division staff groups allowed extensive analyses to be made at senior management's request to help reach final decisions.

Yet despite its strong tradition of centralized decision making, even Merck seemed to be moving away from the substantive decision management mode as its primary administrative process. The senior vice president responsible for Europe said: "We centralize many more decisions than we should. Personally, I am trying to change this practice, primarily through my emphasis on grass roots profit planning". His expectations were that alternative structures and systems would be developed to allow more views to be integrated and tradeoffs to be made below the senior management level. This certainly had been the path followed by the other companies in the sample.

DEVELOPING NEW STRUCTURES AND SYSTEMS

Organizational Change

The process of developing appropriate and credible new management skills and perspectives clearly had implications for and impact on existing organization structures and systems. Regional offices were established, division level staff groups were strengthened in both quality and size, and management information and control systems became more sophisticated. These changes to the formal organization structure and systems provided the means by which the newly developed staff groups could enter the existing strategy decision making process. The regional and division offices gave them the legitimate power base, and the new systems provided them with the information flow and the communication channels they required to exercise their new skills and perspectives.

While these changes in formal structure increased the new product and functional managers' access to and credibility with senior management, the existing organizational structure and decision processes ensured that "geographic" managers retained the power implicit in their line positions. Thus, although the new formal structures allowed the product and func-

tional managers to influence the decision process,
it required them to do so through the existing formal
hierarchy. While most senior managements found this
process helpful in educating themselves to the new
perspectives being developed, in many situations the
administrative burden of consolidating and resolving
the conflicts generated by an evolving multidimensional organization created difficulties.

Most of the companies studied tried to alleviate
some of these problems by developing additional
structures and systems that would allow the required
integration of divergent points of view to take place
within the organization, rather than at the senior
management level. Through the use of temporary structures and systems, many of them were able to bring
together managers with different perspectives to
review complex issues before automatically elevating
any problems or conflicts for resolution.

As senior management became more familiar with the
implications of the multiple management perspectives,
they became more willing to delegate the responsibility of resolving the implicit conflict. Rather than
asking a product manager to critique a subsidiary
manager's proposal for example, a product-subsidiary
project team might be created to make a joint recommendation on the particular issue. Ongoing decisions that required continual balancing of input
were often passed through a standing committee that
incorporated managers representing the various relevant points of view.

In four of the companies observed, there was a proliferation of such temporary structures and ad hoc
groups soon after the newly established management
perspectives were in place in the organization. It
was through such task forces, joint teams, and
committees that the variety of management perspectives could be engaged selectively into various
decision processes. The key attribute of all of the
devices used was that they were flexible, allowing
management to continually shift the composition of
the inputs to various decisions and issues.

In the global recession of 1974/1975 Baxter Travenol
used a series of task forces to reorient subsidiary
managers from their traditional focus on the income
statement (and particularly on sales volume) to a
greater concern for the balance sheet. Corporate or
regional finance managers worked with subsidiary
managers to set targets, and often assisted in the
implementation. The new status of these staff managers was reinforced by the power they derived by
being appointed to this high visibility task force

by senior management. Their influence and achieve-
ments were very impressive, and senior management
was relieved of the task of continually resolving
arguments about the impact inventory reduction would
have on budgeted sales levels, for example.

Bristol Myers' senior management found itself getting
involved in product development disputes between
country managers with priorities and modifications
derived from their various market situtations, and
division product staff, whose priorities usually derived from existing corporate expertise and other
constraints. A pharmaceutical council was formed with
senior geographic line managers and business development staff managers as members. Debate in this
forum allowed a jointly agreed set of priorities to
be developed.

New plant capacity decisions were inevitably difficult ones in all companies, with various management
perspectives justifying vastly different manufacturing configurations. For example, country managers
typically promoted the need for local plants, finance
managers argued to maximize the use of tax sheltered
operations, and manufacturing staff groups pushed for
large specialized plants as regional or global
sources. Warner Lambert found one useful solution was
to create a joint task force of regional geographic
managers, together with manufacturing, finance, materials and marketing staff representatives to develop
recommendations on worldwide capacity needs.

## Management Process Change

Through the use of such teams, task forces and committees, senior management was able to ensure that
the diverse recommendations generated by the development of multiple management skills and perspectives were reconciled, or at least more focused, before being escalated. As such devices began to be
used more extensively, managers with different perspectives on the same problem developed an ability
to work together to find solutions. Senior management found itself having to intervene directly in
the substance of key decisions far less frequently.
Yet its control of the decision process remained
strong. By being able to decide the agenda, the
focus, the composition, the leadership and the power
of the particular overlaid structure, senior management could not only ensure that a particular issue
was dealt with from a multidimensional perspective,
but could also influence the direction of the resulting analysis, recommendations or decisions. This
mode of management can be termed <u>temporary coalition
management</u>.

The development of a variety of integrative structures and systems was a necessary phase for most of
the sample companies in assimilating the new skills
and perspectives that had been established. The use
of such means of integration had an important impact
on the interactions between managers with different
perspectives and responsibilities. If the interven-
tionist style of the "substantive decision management" phase served to raise senior management's
awareness and understanding of key issues from a
variety of viewpoints, the "temporary coalition
management" phase tended to broaden the perspectives
of the middle management group. Not only was this
phase important in exposing managers throughout the
organization to the complex tradeoffs required in
most decisions, but it also served to develop the
interrelationships and communications necessary in a
multidimensional decision making process.

Of the sample companies, Bristol Myers and Warner
Lambert seemed to have evolved to this stage. Not
only had they developed managers with the skills and
perspectives necessary to supplement and counterbalance the predominantly local national view, but
they had supplemented the traditional structure with
a variety of temporarily overlaid devices that
allowed these new perspectives to be integrated into
the decision process lower in the organization. In
effect, these companies had increased their decision
making repertoire by supplementing the substantive
resolution made with a coalition management approach.

In both companies the increased use of task force
teams and committees provided the vehicles by which
product and functional mangers could become involved in the decision process at an earlier stage.
Yet as the use of those temporary structures increased, country managers felt that corporate level
understanding of local needs was being increasingly
threatened. Their concerns derived not only from
the fact that product and functional groups were
being upgraded in size and status, but also because
they were positioned organizationally to leverage
their point of view. On the latter point, two factors
were important. First, they had the substantial advantage of physical proximity to senior management;
and second, they had strong well-established product
and functional counterparts elsewhere in the organization with whom they could form powerful alliances.
The country managers expressed the concern that because they were so distant from corporate headquarters and because they had no geograhpic counterparts there to defend their point of view, the proposals for global coordination and integration
presented by the product and functional managers
could easily swamp their arguments for local flexibility and responsiveness.

Senior management at both Bristol Myers and Warner Lambert were conscious that such concerns could be well founded. Therefore, while the product and functional managers were given greater access to the decision making process through their appointment to task forces and committees simultaneous efforts were made to reassert the role and power of the country manger and to ensure that his point of view was not overwhelmed by these changes.

Although the reality clearly was that there was a narrowing power and influence gap between product and functional staff managers and geographic line managers, in both companies a vigorous defense of the key role of the country manager was undertaken. At Bristol Myers management continually emphasized that the country manager was "king in his country" and that the growing product and functional staff influence was to help him supplement his entrepreneurial skills with technical and administrative capabilities. Warner Lambert's senior management also talked about the increasing role of staff managers as being "to help build rounded managers at the country level."

In the two companies that were using the temporary coalition mode to supplement their substantive decision management process, senior management seemed to concentrate on two key tasks: maintaining the legitimacy of the groups and individuals representing each of the decision perspectives, and ensuring the appropriate influence of each of these perspectives in key decisions. The achievement of the first objective led senior management in Bristol Myers and Warner Lambert to spend considerable time supporting and emphasizing the continuing key role of country managers, while simultaneously creating the temporary structures that allowed product and functional staff to input to important issues. In both companies, all groups of managers felt their influence and responsibility had increased - and impression that was probably well founded given their prior roles in a more "substantive decision management" process. It was this widespread sense of legitimacy and influence in the decision process that appeared to be a prerequisite for the successful operations of the temporary coalition mode of management. In the words of Bristol Myers International president, "As all managers began to be perceived as having legitimate points of view and viable influence on decisions the absolute distinction that has historically been drawn between line and staff managers is starting to have less meaning."

The second prerequisite of this mode of management was to ensure that the various management perspectives were appropriately represented in each of the many key decisions. It was here that companies experienced greatest difficulty.

Despite the clear advantage the "coalition management" process offered over the "substantive decision intervention" stage, demands on senior management were still substantial in forming, restructuring, and dissolving coalitons to manage the growing number of multidimensional problems. Furthermore, the mere creation of various coalitions did not ensure that the resulting decision process would be cooperative, and stress and devisiveness seemed an inevitable part of the operation of many teams and committees. In some cases the result was paralysis as opposing views became locked in impasse; in other instances decision making deteriorated to "horse trading" rahter than open interchange of views that was expected.

Thus, while task forces, teams, and committees often did provide useful means by which solutions to multidimensional issues could be found without continual intervention by senior management, they were limited when they degererated into forced alliances between reluctant colleagues. Some companies that had perceived the coalition management mode as being the solution to the bottleneck problems of their earlier substantive decision management process, began to recognize the need for further organizational adaptation. The open communication, cooperation and understanding that is required between managers in multidimensional decisions could not be legislated by changes in the formal organization alone.

## Developing a New Organizational "Climate": Decision Context Management

Just as they had recognized the difficulty of having senior management intervening in the content of key decisions, som companies began to recognize that to have them continually involved in structuring and controlling a large numer of complex, variable decision making processes was also very limiting. In the judgement of many managers a process that often depependend on forced alliances between reluctant colleagues, each protective of his turf probably would not be effective in the long run.

Having developed the appropriate management perspectives, then created viable structures and systems through which they could interact, the next major challenge for the developing multidimensional organization was to build an appropriate decision making environment. The goal was to create an organizational climate in which flexible, constructive and cooperative interaction between managers with different perspectives was institutionalized. Rather than having individual decisions being arbitrated or regulated from above, the objective was to achieve a more self regulating decision process in which managers themselves could negotiate the appropriate balance of views in multidimensional decisions.

In order to achieve this kind of environment, the managers had to supplement their ability and willingness to represent a particular viewpoint with an overall understanding of the corporations's broad objectives and a willingness to adapt, cooperate, and compromise to achieve those larger goals. Such changes could not be achieved overnight and required top management to focus on three major tasks:

1.  To broaden managers' perspectives and open multiple channels of communication through the creative use and control of manager movement and interaction within the organization;

2.  To change formal systems so as to facilitate and reinforce the desired cooperative and flexible decision making climate; and

3.  To create a value system that provided the organizational security required to encourage managers to take the risk involved in such flexible, broad perspective decision making.

Of the companies studied, Eli Lilly and Baxter Travenol appeared to be the most conscious of creating this type of flexible, cooperative decision environment. Examples of the changes made vill be drawn from these companies.

Management of both companies seemed to realize that flexible cooperative interactions would be difficult to develop solely through the limited channels and hierachical relationships provided by the formal organization. Management's considerable control over individuals movements and interactions in the organization gave it a powerful tool to impact two separate aspects of the decision environment. First, managers' understanding and appreciation of different organizational issues could be influenced; and second, interpersonal relationships and informal communications channels could be developed. For example, a subsidiary marketing manager transferred to a headquarters staff is likely to develop a far greater appreciation for both the local and the global issues involved in key marketing decisions. Furthermore, the personal relationships he develops in each assignment facilitate communications and cooperation on issues involving national and global marketing input.

Eli Lilly had a well established career development
system in which managers were transferred throughout
their careers from line positions to staff, from
country operations to headquarters, from product to
functional or geographic responsibility. Several
managers attributed the good contacts and cooperative
working relationships that were the norm at Lilly,
largely to this strongly institutionalized career
development track. While less well developed, Baxter
had also consciously begun to engage in a similar use
of temporary assignments and long term transfers.

Both companies also created forums in which multidimensional issues could be explored openly, without
the pressures or competitiveness that often existed
in task forces. Baxter, for instance, modified its
annual country general managers meeting to become a
senior management conference to which staff and line
managers were invited. For one week each year common
management problems were confronted by the entire
group, and joint recommendations and action plans
agreed to. The president explained that his objectives were twofold; to broaden the identifcation of
his top management from their parochial geographic
or functional views to a company-wide perspective,
and to create an environment in which they could
cooperate on key multidimensional problems.

By consciously focusing on transfers, assignments,
career paths, forums and meetings, senior management
was shifting its means of influence from the formal
to the informal organization structures and systems.

This conscious subtle use of transfers, assignments,
and meetings provided senior management with a means
of influencing the oganization's informal structure
and systems rather than the formal channels that had
previously been their main focus. Their ability to
influence the informal structure was strengthened
by the fact that in a multinational corporation
there were considerable barriers of distance,
language and culture that tended to limit contacts
and interactions between individuals. Managements'
control of the nature, frequency and composition of
interpersonal interactions therefore could have a
very strong influence on the development of an
informal structure.

In both Lilly and Baxter, senior management were
conscious of this important influence and used it
continuously. They also recognized that the behaviors and relationships that could be developed
through the informal systems needed to be reinforced
through the formal organization. Existing management
systems had to be changed to recognize the need for
cooperative flexible decision making behavior.

In Eli Lilly, for example, the formal evaluation process was changed so that a manager would be evaluated not only by his immediate line superior, but also by managers in other parts of the company with whom he had regular working relationships. Baxter also began broadening its evaluation process to allow product and functional managers to input into the evaluation of country managers and vice versa.

At Lilly, career path management had become highly formalized. There were personnel directors for each major function, product and geographic area who met frequently with senior management to review all actual and potential openings and all possible candidates. Managers were counseled on the importance of developing contacts and expertise in multiple responsibilities, and the broad career development histories of the senior management provided models for younger managers.

However, the process of influencing the informal system to develop cooperation and mutual understanding and realigning formal systems to reinforce such behavior could only be successful if undertaken in an operating environment that was extremely supportive. Asking a manager to abandon the simple certainty of defending his clear point of view from his defined position of organizational responsibility is asking him to take substantive personal and organizational risk. To foster the desired flexible compromising decision making process, an organization needs a strong, well established value system that provides the stability and security to allow an individual to take such risks.

Eli Lilly had an internal value system that not only had its roots in the founders' objectives, but also was continually reinforced by current management. In the words of the late Mr Eli Lilly, "Values are, quite simply the core of both men and institutions. By combining our thoughts and helping one another, we are able to merge the parts of the corporation into a rational, workable management system." The values he spoke of were also referred to frequently in the organization, and included openness, honesty in dealings with others, and the need for mutual trust. With strongly held corporate values such as these, the development of the desired cooperative, flexible interaction between managers was more easily achieved.

Although Baxter's corporate value system had tended to be more competitive and less supportive, over a number of years the international division president had been working to modify some of the accepted organizational norms. At every gathering of managers, his speeches and private remarks emphasized the need for cooperation and joint action between managers. He tried to make his own behavior and management style a model for the organization. He publicly applauded appropriate cooperative problem solving and decision making among management groups with diverse interests and perspectives. Gradually the adversary relationship that existed between country managers and headquarters staff gave way to a cooperative mutual respect.

## Management Process Change

There was a noticeable cumulative effect of helping to build a network of cooperative informal relationships, reinforcing such cooperation through the formal systems, and institutionalizing the resulting decision making behavior in a set of organizational values that strongly supported a flexible and cooperative management style. The companies that consciously worked on these changes began to develop an organizational climate in which managers recognized the broad corporate goals and worked cooperatively to help achieve them, even when this meant compromising some more parochial concerns. This management mode can be labeled decision context management.

Senior management's role in this mode was twofold: to support the organizational values, the informal structure and the formal systems that created the cooperative flexible decision process; and to communicate clearly and frequently the broad corporate objectives towards which such decisions should be directed. This represented a subtle and a delicate task, but less all-consuming than an involvement with individual decision outcomes or even with coalition building and management.

In the decision context management mode, the middle management level showed a much greater willingness to take multidimensional approach on key issues. In Baxter, for exampel, when the general manager of the Brazilian subsidiary wanted to build a local plant, he first discussed the matter at length with both the manufacturing manager and the product marketing manager at division headquarters, and with the corporate financial staff. When all views had been fully discussed, a mutually agreed set of alternatives and a recommended approach was submitted to top management.

It should be noted again that decision making in companies that pursued the decision context management mode were not all so easily self-regulated. On sensitive issues, senior management still had to intervene either by defining the coalition that was to make the analysis, recommendation, or decision, or by actually resolving specific issues where resolution by cooperation and compromise had not been possible. Like the other modes, this one simply broadened the repertoire of decision processes available to help resolve complex multidimensional issues.

CONCLUSION

The strategic challenges faced by the five health care companies are typical of the situations confronting many MNCs. Increasing pressure from host governments and global competitors increasingly force companies to develop and integrate its management capabilities at the local <u>and</u> the global levels; accelerating change in both arenas require that these multiple skills and perspectives interact flexibly.

While change in the formal organization has been thought of by many managers as the principal means of adapting the decision processes, the subtlety and complexity of a flexible multidimensional decision making process appears difficult to achieve solely (or even primarily) through formal organizational change. By retaining their simple international division structures, the five companies observed maintained a stability in their formal organization that allowed gradual changes in people, relationships, and processes to be introduced through more informal and less traumatic means. Rather than focusing their attention on the structure per se, managers of these companies seemed to be more concerned with the nature of decision process that the change was designed to achieve.

While their formal organization structures seemed to belie the fact, each of these companies had developed the flexible multidimensional decision process that its strategic environment demanded. Westinghouse's hope was that its newly installed matrix structure might take five years "to force product managers to interact with geographic specialists". Managers in the health care companies studied believed that their evolutionary approach achieved the same ends with less trauma.

NOTES

1. This account of Westinghouse's growth abroad is based largely on the article "Westinghouse Takes Aim at the World", Fortune, January 14, 1980, pp. 48-53.

2. Yves Doz has written extensively on the nature of these demands. See, for example, "Strategic Management in Multinational Companies", Sloan Management Review.

3. Perhaps the best known of the "stages theories" of multinational organization development was developed by John Stopford. See, for example, John M. Stopford and Louis T. Wells, Managing the Multinational Enterprise, New York: Basic Books, 1972. The first half of the book describes the patterns of organization structure evolution based on a study of 170 companies. The typical "stages" evolution is described as follows. A structure in which autonomous foreign subsidiaries are loosely linked to the parent company, is replaced by one in which subsidiaries are consolidated under an international division. Then a "global" product or area organization is typically installed, which, in turn, is replaced by a multidimensional (or "grid") organization structure.

4. Richard Rumelt noted a tendency for strategy to follow fashion in his study of Fortune 500 companies. See Richard P. Rumelt, Strategy, Structure, and Economic Performance, Boston: Division of Research, Harvard Business School, 1974, p. 149.

5. Perhaps the two most widely cited examples of multinational matrix organizations apparently have pulled back from their original structure. Davis and Lawrence describe the demise of Dow Chemical's global matrix, but point to the emergence of a more recent multinational matrix success: Citibank (Stanley M. Davis and Paul R. Lawrence, Matrix, Addison Wesley, Reading, MA, 1977, pp. 206-222). Recent reports indicate that Citibank has now abandoned its global matrix (see "Its a Stronger Bank that David Rockefeller is Passing to his Successor", Fortune, Vol. 101, No. 1 /Jan. 14, 1980/, p. 44).

6. A follow up study of the original Stopford sample of companies is planned. A preliminary estimate indicates that well over 30% of the

145

companies classified as having international
divisions in 1967 retained them twelve years
later despite their growth and the changing
environmental demands.

7. See Christopher A. Bartlett <u>Multinational Structural Evolution: The Changing Decision Environment in International Divisions</u>, unpublished
doctoral dissertation, Harvard Business School,
1979.

8. For a full exploration of the strategic demands
in the food industry, see Ulrich E. Wiechmann
<u>Marketing Management in Multinational Firms</u>,
New York: Praeger, 1976.

# 7 Tadao Kagono:

# Structural Design of Headquarters-Division Relationships and Economic Performance: An Analysis of Japanese Firms

As the environment surrounding large corporations becomes more complex and more uncertain, the corporate-wide structural design becomes increasingly difficult. In this paper the effectiveness of various structural alternatives in headquarters-division relationships will be empirically examined in terms of their economic performance. The purposes of this paper are to test several middle-range hypotheses about the effective headquarters-subsidiary relationships and to draw out theoretical and practical implications from the findings.

This paper is a part of a more comprehensive analysis of organizational structure and process of Japanese industrial firms (Kagono, 1980). The analysis is based upon data obtained by a mailed questionnaire sent to the largest 500 industrial firms and 33 other selected industrial firms in Japan and by interviews with selected managers which followed from 1976 to 1978. The questionnaires were sent to the office of the CEO of each firm, and 113 responses were received[1]. The industry and size composition of those firms are shown in Appendix A.

## I. THEORETICAL FRAMEWORK AND HYPOTHESES

Recent organizational research shows that the effectiveness of an organizational structure is successfully analyzed by focusing upon its information processing capacity (Perrow, 1967; Galbraith, 1973; Tushman and Nadler, 1978; Nonaka and Nadler, 1979). An organizational structure has a certain range of information processing capacity. The extent to which the utilization of this capacity contributes to the

---

School of Business Administration, Kobe University.

success of an organization depends upon the degree of fit between this capacity and the information processing load imposed upon the organization. The information processing load, however, differs in different environments. The most effective structure for the organization, therefore, is contingent upon its environment (Lawrence and Lorsch, 1967).

The above view on organizational effectiveness, which may be called "information processing paradigm", is the basic theoretical framework of the following analysis.

TASK ENVIRONMENT AS THE DETERMINANT OF INFORMATION PROCESSING LOAD AND STRATEGIC CONTINGENCIES

Those parts of the environment of an organization which are relevant or potentially relevant to organizational goal setting and goal attainment are called its "task environment" (Thompson, 1967). The task environment is the primary determinant of information processing load on the organization. The organization has to gather, transmit and combine information and make decisions in order to cope with the environmental contingencies that threaten its goal attainment. As the task environment is not given to an organization but is enacted by it, it is difficult to characterize the task environment by objective data. In this study the following factors are taken into consideration in order to characterize the task environment each organization faces; (1) market and technological environment, (2) principal technology, (3) size of organization, (4) diversification strategy, (5) R&D strategy, (6) major competitive issue in the principal market, and (7) goals. The methodology of measurement is explained in Appendix B.

The analysis of these variables (also shown in Appendix B) suggests that they could be combined into two composite dimensions.

The organization that has a higher score on the scale of the first dimension faces a more unstable environment, relies on new product competition rather than on price competition, adopts a less routine technology, relies on a more concentric diversification strategy and R&D, and is larger in size. This dimension indicates the instability of environment, the frequency of unpredictable changes, the variety of strategic options open to an organization and its competitors, the ambiguity of situation, and the difficulty of routinization of task, in short, the uncertainty of task environment.

The organization that has a higher score on the scale of the second dimension faces a more diverse and heterogeneous environment, adopts a less concentric diversification strategy, has businesses in more industries, and is larger in size and aggressive in diversification. This dimension indicates the diversity and heterogenity of contingencies imposed upon an organization, the unrelatedness of these contingencies, the vastness of environment, and the difficulty of internal control, in short, the complexity of task environment.

The two dimensions represent the two aspects of the information processing load imposed upon an organization and also are consistent with the principal dimensions suggested by previous studies (Thompson, 1967; Duncan, 1972, 1973; Nonaka, 1972). The two dimensions form the basis of the following theoretical and empirical analyses.

In the following analysis, the task environment will sometimes be divided into four cells, by dichotomizing the two dimensions. Figure 1 shows the typical industries in each cell of the task environment. The classification is based upon the industry averages in the two dimensions.

Those unpredictable events in an environment which threaten the success of an organization and, therefore, the control of which is critical to its success, are called strategic contingencies. The above analysis shows also that the first dimension corresponds to the types of the strategic contingencies that organizations face. In the lower score section of this scale, price competition based upon logistic efficiency is critical to the success of the firms, and, therefore, those events that threaten the logistic efficiency become the strategic contingencies. In the higher score section of this scale, new product competition is critical to the success of the firms and, therefore, those events that threaten the new product development become the strategic contingencies.

## ORGANIZATIONAL STRUCTURE AND INFORMATION PROCESSING CAPACITY

Three aspects of organizational structure, i.e. organizational form, structural arrangement of headquarters-division relationships, and interdepartmental power balance, will be examined in this paper. In the rest of this section the fit between the information processing capacities of various structural alternatives and the information processing loads of various task environments will be analyzed and, then, the hypotheses about what structure is fitted to what task environment will be specified.

## Organizational form

The first aspect is the choice of organizational form represented by the choice between "functional vs. multi-divisional form" or between "product vs. geographical form". Each organizational form has a certain range of information processing capacities.

The multi-divisional form is characterized by (1) the divisionalization of operating activities into more than one self-contained unit (or division) which has the authority and its own resources to make operating decisions concerning a geographic area or a group of products, and by (2) the establishment of a corporate headquarters which is freed from operating duties and concentrates its efforts on strategic decisions including the allocation of resources among divisions. These structural arrangements enlarge the information processing capacity in the following aspects.

(1) Complexity reduction: The multi-divisionalization makes it possible to reduce the complexity of task and the information processing load, because the creation of self-contained sub-tasks reduces the interdependencies among them (Galbraith, 1973).

(2) Strategic responsiveness: The multi-divisionalization advances the strategic responsiveness of the corporate headquarters, because it is freed from operating duties (March and Simon, 1959; Chandler, 1962).

(3) Operating responsiveness: The multi-divisionalization advances the organizational operating responsiveness towards external contingencies, because the divisionalization enables each division to deal with a smaller number of contingencies and to change its action program flexibly and independently of the other divisions (March and Simon, 1959; Walker and Lorsch, 1968).

(4) Differentiation: The divisionalization makes it easier for each division to create the structure and managerial behavior which fit to its particular sub-environment (Lorsch and Allen, 1973).

These capacities are better exploited in an uncertain or complex environment. On the other hand, the multi-divisionalization entails opportunity costs that otherwise would not be necessary.

(1) The divisionalization creates the redundancy of resources and, therefore, makes it difficult to capitalize on the economy of scale such as joint usage of common resources and knowledge, further specialization, etc.

(2) The divisionalization makes it difficult to realize the benefit of coordinated actions among various parts of an organization.

These opportunity costs exceed the benefits in a less uncertain and less complex environment where the economy of scale and the benefits of coordinated actions are easily realized. Although these opportunity costs are avoidable even in the multi-divisional form by establishing sophisticated integrative devices touched on later, they entail additional costs. In a less uncertain and less complex environment, therefore, the functional form organized with interdependent functional departments 'is more effective. But, as the uncertainty and/or complexity of task environment increase, the benefits of divisionalization increase and are to exceed its costs. In a more uncertain and/or complex task environment the multi-divisional form becomes the superior alternative.

From the foregoing discussion, it is hypothesized that the functional form is more suitable to the firm facing a less uncertain and less complex environment, while the multi-divisional form is more suitable to the firm facing a more uncertain and/or more complex environment (Hypothesis A-1).

The bases of divisionalization which are widely used among multi-divisional firms are geography and product. The difference between the two lies in the focus used to divide the contingencies with which each division deals. The geographical divisionalization focuses upon the difference of contingencies among markets or customers, while the divisionalization on the basis of product focuses upon the difference of contingencies among production technologies as well as among markets or customers. The difference suggests that the product division form is better suited to cope with a more complex (diverse in terms of technology as well as market) and/or more uncertain (unstable in terms of technology as well as market) environment. From the foregoing discussion it is hypothesized that in a highly complex and/or uncertain environment the product division form is more suitable than the geographical division form (Hypothesis A-2).

In this study the organizational form of each firm is classified into either of three forms, i.e. functional form (F), product-divisional form (PD) and geographical divisional form (GD), on the basis of the preliminary analysis of the responses to the questionnaire (Appendix C).

## Structural arrangement of headquarters-division relationships

The second problem is addressed to the following four aspects of structural arrangements of headquarters-division relationships in multi-divisional organizations:

(1) To what extent should an organization be divisionalized into self-contained units (degree of divisionalization)?

(2) How autonomous should the divisions be (degree of autonomy)?

(3) How complex should the integrative devices be that enable divisions to share human resources and advance cooperation among divisions (degree of complexity of integrative devices)?

(4) To what extent should the activities of divisions be coordinated (degree of inter-divisional coordination)?

The effectiveness of various structural alternatives in these four dimensions also could be analyzed in terms of the costs and benefits of their information processing capacity in various task environments.

The analysis of the information processing capacity of the multi-divisional form has suggested that the organizational capabilities to reduce environmental complexity and to differentiate managerial behaviors would be increased by the advancement of divisionalization and divisional autonomy. These capabilities are better utilized in a more complex environment. Hence, it is hypothesized that the organizations pursuing effectiveness advance divisionalization and divisional autonomy as the complexity of task environment increases (Hypothesis B-1).

The increase of uncertainty in task environment imposes two contradicting demands on the structural arrangements. The first is the demand for further divisionalization. In order to deal with a higher level of uncertainty effectively, an organization has to advance divisionalization and divisional autonomy so that each division can concentrate its efforts on a smaller number of contingencies and can make more prompt and flexible decisions. On the other hand, the increase of uncertainty demands the depression of divisionalization and the advancement of functional specialization within each unit so that each division can utilize more specialized knowledge and information to cope with a higher level of uncertainty.

The means widely adopted to reconcile these two contradictory demands is to create integrative units or interdivisional coordination networks. Such devices as group headquarters, functional integrating committees or departments, the direct interdivisional communication networks, etc. make it possible to take advantage of both divisionalization and functional specialization (Galbraith, 1973, 1977). These devices entail additional costs and impose difficult management problems because they create more complex communication and reporting networks within an organization. However, they are the sole alternative that enables organizations to reconcile the two contradictory demands.

Hence, it is hypothesized that as the uncertainty in task environment increases, the organizations pursuing effectiveness advance divisionalization and divisional autonomy and create more complex integrative devices and a closer interdivisional coordination network (Hypothesis B-2).

## Power balance among functional departments

The last aspect of organizational structure analyzed in this paper is the power balance among functional departments. The majority of previous studies on power phenomena within organizations have been focused upon their negative or dysfunctional side. In the following analysis, however, it is assumed that power phenomena are unavoidable to every organization and their existence in itself is not pathological. As suggested by Cyert and March (1963), Bower (1970) etc., the organizational goal setting and problem solving process is not a harmonic and mechanical process rigidly controlled by the top but a conflicting political process in which intergroup or interpersonal power balance plays a major role.

Whether a power balance in an organization is functional or dysfunctional is determined by the extent to which the goals and decisions created by the power balance are congruent with those demanded from the task environment. Perrow (1965), Thompson (1967), and Hickson et al (1971), suggest that the relative power of departments in the goal setting and problem solving process in well-managed organizations tends to be proportional to their relative contributions to the control of the strategic contingencies that the organizations face.

154

The analysis of task environment has indicated that the type of strategic contingencies is related with the degree of uncertainty of task environment. It implies that the effective interdepartmental power balance may be specified in relation to the degree of uncertainty.

In a stable environment, the price competition based upon logistic efficiency is critical to the survival of organizations and the events that threaten the internal efficiency constitute the contingencies. In this environment, the production department, which has the knowledge and information to cope with these contingencies, should have the strongest influence on the goal setting and problem solving process. As the uncertainty of task environment increases, the competition based upon the combination of various marketing strategies becomes more critical to the successful survival of organizations, and the events that threaten the effectiveness of the marketing mix become the strategic contingencies. In this situation, the marketing department, which has the knowledge and information to cope with these contingencies, should have the strongest influence.

In the extremely uncertain environment as is faced by the firms in science-based industries, the strategic contingencies that threaten the success of organizations exist in the technological or scientific environment. In this situation, the R&D department should have the strongest influence on the goal-setting and problem solving process.

Based upon the foregoing discussion, it could be hypothesized that in the organizations seeking effectiveness, the department that has the strongest power (or power center) should be changed from production department to marketing department and then, from marketing department to R&D department as the uncertainty of task environment increases (Hypothesis C).

The data about power balance was obtained by the mailed questionnaire. Each respondent was asked to specify the functional department that had the largest say in interdepartmental conflict situations among the three functional departments.

PERFORMANCE

The relationships hypothesized in this section are not the mere average or general relationships between task environment and organizational structure but the functional or effective relationships or better fit between the two. In order to test such hypotheses, it is necessary to have some measure of organizational performance and to examine whether the better fit actually brings better performance.

In this study, the economic performance of each firm was measured from two sources. One is the respondent's <u>subjective</u> judgement about his firm's performance compared with its competitors in terms of (1) profitability, (2) growth, and (3) financial stability. The other consists of two <u>objective</u> figures, i.e., return on equity and equity ratio. The overall performance measure was constructed by summing up the standardized scores of these 5 figures. The respondents also divided into high performers and low performers on the basis of the overall performance.

## II.  RESULTS OF EMPIRICAL ANALYSIS

The hypotheses specified in the previous section will be tested empirically by the following three methods in this section.

The first empirical test is the analysis of the relationships between task environment and organizational structure. This analysis does not take into account the performance which is critical to the test of "functional" hypotheses. The analysis, however, can be taken for the test of such hypotheses if we can successfully assume that most firms create the structures which fit to their task environments or that the survival of the firm is the most important evidence of its effectiveness. These assumptions, however, are sometimes problematic. Therefore, the first analysis should be thought to be a weak or proxy test.

The second test is the comparison between high performers versus low performers. Our hypotheses imply that high-performing firms would create the organizational structures better fitted to their task environments than low performers. If our hypotheses are valid, the relationships found among the high performers are closer to our hypotheses than those found among the low performers. This test is stronger than the first but has some limitations yet. The most important limitation is the possibility that high performers may not necessarily create the best fit with the task environment in every aspect of organizational structure.

The third test is based upon the analysis of the determinants of performance in several separate subsamples, each of which faces an identical task environment. Within this subsample, the structural characteristics that fit the task environment have a positive influence upon performance and the unfitted have a negative influence. By comparing the results with hypotheses, the empirical validity of the hypotheses will be tested. This is the strongest test but demands a sizable number of firms facing a common task environment.

THE ANALYSIS OF RELATIONSHIPS BETWEEN TASK ENVIRONMENT AND ORGANIZATIONAL STRUCTURE: WEAK TEST.

## Organizational forms

The distribution of the three organizational forms, i.e., functional form, product-divisional form, and geographical-divisional form in each cell of task environment is shown in Figure 2. It indicates that the ratio of the functional form is highest in the environment with below average uncertainty and complexity (cell I). The ratio of the product-divisional form is highest in the environment with above average uncertainty and complexity (cell IV) and lowest in the environment with below average uncertainty and complexity (cell I). The ratio of the geographical form is high in the environments where either uncertainty or complexity is above average. These findings are consistent with our hypotheses A-1 and A-2.

## Structural arrangement of headquarters-division relationships

The relationships between four dimensions of structural arrangement of headquarters-division relationships and the aggregate indicators of uncertainty and complexity are shown in Table 1. Among the standardized regression coefficients, only two, which show that the divisionalization has positive relationships with uncertainty and complexity, are statistically significant at .05 level. These relationships are consistent with our hypotheses B-1 and B-2. Among the other coefficients, two coefficients in the regression analysis of the degree of interdivisional coordination have slightly higher positive values. The positive relationship between uncertainty and the degree of coordination is consistent with our hypothesis B-2. The other figures do not support nor negate either hypothesis B-1 or B-2.

TABLE 1. Relationships between the Indicators of Information Processing Load and the Four Dimensions of Headquarters-Division Relationships

| Dimension (dependent variable) | Standardized Coefficients Uncertainty | Regression Complexity | $(R^2)$ |
|---|---|---|---|
| Degree of divisionalization | | | |
| (number of divisions) | .36** | .23* | (.17) |
| (average size of divisions) | .20 | -.00 | (.02) |
| Degree of divisional autonomy | .06 | .10 | (.02) |
| Complexity of integrative devices | .07 | .10 | (.02) |
| Degree of interdivisional coordination | .23 | -.19 | (.06) |

Size of sample for the first dimension;  69
Size of sample for the last three dimensions;  31
* $p < .05$    ** $p < .01$

### The power balance among functional departments

The relationship between power balance and uncertainty of task environment is shown in Table 2. It shows the average score of uncertainty for each group having the same power center. These averages indicate that those firms in which the production department has the largest influence on average face the lowest uncertainty, those in which the R&D department has the largest influence face the highest uncertainty, and those in which the marketing department has the largest influence locate in between. This order is consistent with our hypothesis C.

TABLE 2. The Relationship between the Location of Power Center and the Environmental Uncertainty

| Location of power center | average score (number of firms) of uncertainty |
|---|---|
| Production department | - 1.19 ( 9) |
| Marketing department | 0.06 (58) |
| R&D department | 2.95 ( 4) |
| F-ratio | 1.07 |

$p < .05$

The findings presented thus far should be interpreted
with caution, because the relationships statistically
identified are the general or average relationships
between organizational characteristics and task
environment and are not necessarily identical to the
effective relationships to which our hypotheses are
addressed.

COMPARISON BETWEEN HIGH PERFORMERS AND LOW PERFORMERS

## Organizational form

Figure 3 indicates the distributions of the three
organizational forms in each cell of task environment
separately for high performers and low performers.
The result contradicts our hypothesis. In the low-
performing group the ratio of the functional form
steadily decreases as the complexity and/or uncertainty increase. This relationship is consistent with
our hypotheses A-1 and A-2. In the high-performing
group, however, the ratio decreases until cell III,
but increases in cell IV. This turnover is contradictory to hypothesis A-1 or A-2. In all, contrary to
our prediction, the low performers show a closer
pattern to our hypotheses than the high performers.

## Structural arrangement of headquarters-subsidiary relationships

The relationships between the four dimensions of
structural arrangements of headquarters-division
relationships and the uncertainty and complexity of
task environment are shown separately for high performers and low performers in Table 3. It shows
interesting differences between high and low performers.

TABLE 3. Relationships between the Indicators of Information Processing Load and the Four Dimensions of Headquarters-Division Relationships in the High and Low Performers.

| Dimension (dependent variable) | High Performers | | | Low Performers | | |
|---|---|---|---|---|---|---|
| | Standardized Regression Coefficients Uncertainty Complexity ($R^2$) | | | Standardized Regression Coefficients Uncertainty Complexity ($R^2$) | | |
| | Uncertainty | Complexity | ($R^2$) | Uncertainty | Complexity | ($R^2$) |
| Degree of divisionalization (number of divisions) | .01 | .39* | (.11) | .54** | .20 | (.30) |
| (average of divisions) | .44* | -.04 | (.17) | .04 | .01 | (.20) |
| Degree of divisional autonomy | .25 | -.03 | (.08) | -.06 | .17 | (.04) |
| Complexity of integrative devices | -.30 | -.29 | (.09) | .25 | .02 | (.01) |
| Degree of interdivisional coordination | -.21 | -.30 | (.10) | .47 | .31 | (.28) |

Sample Size
first dimension N=29     Sample Size first dimension N=39
the other     N=11     the other     N=20

The regression analysis of the number of divisions indicates that the high performers advance the divisionalization in response to the increase of complexity while the low performers advance it in response to the increase of uncertainty. The regression analysis of the average size of divisions indicates that the high performers increase the size in response to the increase of uncertainty, while the low performers determine the size independently of the degree of uncertainty or complexity. These two regression analyses suggest that the relationship between divisionalization and uncertainty among the high performers is opposite to that among the low performers. Among the high-performing firms, the increase of uncertainty suppresses the divisionalization, while among the low performers the increase of uncertainty advances the divisionalization. The high performers' response to the increase of complexity is consistent with hypothesis B-1, but their response to the increase of uncertainty is inconsistent with hypothesis B-2.

The regression analysis of divisional autonomy suggests that the high performers advance divisional autonomy in response to the increase of uncertainty.

This relationship is consistent with hypothesis B-2. Among the low performers the degree of divisional autonomy is determined independently of the uncertainty of task environment.

The regression analyses of the complexity of integrative devices and of the degree of interdivisional coordination also show interesting differences between the high and low performers. In response to the increase of complexity and uncertainty in task environment, the high performers reduce the complexity of integrative devices and the degree of interdivisional coordination while the low performers advance them.

TABLE 4. A Summary of the Findings on the Structural Arrangements of Headquarters-Division Relationships

| | relationship with uncertainty of task environment | relationship with complexity of task environment |
|---|---|---|
| Degree of divisionalization | | |
| (number of divisions) | $\pm$ ( + ) + | + ( + ) + |
| (average size of divisions) | $\pm$ ( - ) $\pm$ | $\pm$ ( - ) $\pm$ |
| Degree of divisional autonomy | - ( + ) $\pm$ | $\pm$ ( + ) $\pm$ |
| Complexity of integrative devices | - ( + ) + | - ( ? ) $\pm$ |
| Degree of interdivisional coordination | - ( + ) + | - ( ? ) + |

Sign of relationship found among high performers (hypothesized sign) sign of relationship found among low performers
+ positive, - negative, $\pm$ neither positive nor negative,
? not hypothesized.

These results are summarized in Table 4 with a summary of our hypotheses. The most noticeable difference between the high and low performers exists in their response to the increase of uncertainty. In response to the increase of uncertainty, the high performers on average increase the divisional autonomy and the average size of divisions without increasing the number of them, and at the same time, reduce the complexity of integrating devices and the degree of divisional coordination. On the other hand, the low performers on average increase the number of divisions, increase the complexity of integrative devices and the degree of coordination, and reduce the divisional autonomy. The structural response of the low performers is closer to our hypothesis B-2 than that of the high performers. The unpredicted structural response of the high performers, however, may have some rationale with theoretical and practical meanings, which will be analyzed in the following section.

As to the response to the increase of complexity of task environment such a noticeable difference was not found between the high and low performers. The high performers' response, i.e., the increase of number of divisions and the reduction of the complexity of integrative devices and the degree of coordination among divisions, does not contradict our hypothesis B-1.

## Power balance among functional divisions

Hypothesis C about the fit between environment and interdepartmental power balance, which was supported by the weak test, is also supported by the stronger test. Table 5 is the comparison of the distribution of power centers between the high and low performers. In the high-performing group there is no firm that has the power center inconsistent with hypothesis C. The low-performing counterpart, however, includes firms that have the unfitted power center.

TABLE 5. The Relationships Between Power Center and Task Environment in High and Low Performing Groups

| Location of power center | high performing group | | low performing group | |
|---|---|---|---|---|
| | low uncertainty | high uncertainty | low uncertainty | high uncertainty |
| Production department | 4 | 3 | 1 | 0 |
| Marketing department | 16 | 13 | 14 | 11 |
| R&D department | 0 | 1 | 0 | 3 |

Another notable difference between the high and low performers is the fact that the ratio of firms where the production department has the strongest say is significantly higher in the low-performing group. Among the 8 firms in which the production department has the largest power, only one gains the above-average performance.

DETERMINANTS OF PERFORMANCE

If the degree of fit between task environment and organizational structure determines the effectiveness of organizations in a task environment the structural property fitted to the environment has a positive effect on performance while the unfitted have a negative effect. Based upon this premise, the determinants of performance of various subsamples were analyzed. Table 6 contrasts the determinants of performance in two subsamples, i.e., the subsample composed of the firms facing above-average uncertainty and the subsample composed of the firms facing below-average uncertainty. It reconfirms the findings of the second test. In this analysis three dimensions of structural arrangements of headquarters-division relationships which are defined only for multi-divisional firms are deleted, and other organizational characteristics and contextual variables are included as the independent variable. The notable findings are shown in the table.

First, in the uncertain environment subsample, the adoption of functional form has a significant positive effect on performance. This result is consistent with the result of the second test, but contradictory to our hypothesis A-1.

Second, to advance divisionalization has a positive effect on performance in the certain half of task environment but has a negative effect in the uncertain half of task environment. This result is also consistent with the result of the second test, which, contrary to our hypothesis A-2, indicates that the high performers depress the divisionalization in response to the increase of uncertainty.

Last, as suggested by the fact that the existence of the power center in the production department has a negative effect on performance in the environment with above-average uncertainty, the fit between power balance and task environment is one of the major determinants of organizational effectiveness.

III. ANALYSIS OF THE EIMPIRICAL RESULTS

The main findings of the empirical tests presented in the previous section could be summarized as follows:

(1) On average, the firms organized into functional form face the least uncertain and complex task environment, those organized into product division form face the most uncertain and complex task environment, and those organized into

163

TABLE 6. Stepwise Regression Analysis of the Determinants of Economic Performance

| low uncertainty task environment | | high uncertainty task environment | |
|---|---|---|---|
| independent variables | standardized regression coef. | independent variables | standardized regression coef. |
| flexibility of reorganization | .88** | number of product managers | -.64** |
| conflict resolution by smoothing | -.59** | power center in production dept. | -.82** |
| adoption of product division form | -.43** | adoption of functional form | .57** |
| flexibility of job description | -.18* | number of divisions | -.59** |
| average size of divisions | -.28** | conflict resolution by forcing | -.19** |
| adoption of product manager system | -.18* | adoption of long-range planning | .29** |
| emphasis on forward integration | .25** | emphasis on new product competition | .97** |
| emphasis on price competition | -.27** | R&D intensity | -.48** |
| risk avertiveness | .38** | routineness of technology | -.17* |
| R&D intensity | .35** | emphasis on diversification into by-product market | -.14* |
| N = 27    $\bar{R}^2$ = | .909 | N = 25    $\bar{R}^2$ = | .954 |

** $p < .01$    * $p < .05$

* dummy variables for each category.

The independent variables listed for the stepwise regression analysis were as follows: organizational forms (functional, geographical division, and product division forms)* location of power center (production, marketing and R&D departments)*, mode of conflict resolution (confrontation, smoothing and forcing)*, divisionalization (number of divisions and size of divisions), development activities (centralization, decentralization and mixed)*, adoption of long-range planning*, organicness (flexibility of organization change*, emphasis on flexibility*, flexibility of job description, and composite score), size, technology (routineness), direction of diversification (forward integration, backward integration, channel integration, concentric, technology-related, market related, unrelated, by product, and non-diversification), rate of diversification, variety of industries, R&D intensity, competitive strategy (product quality and specification, sales promotion, new product, marketing channel)*, risk aversion, emphasis on growth goal, and growth rate of principal industry.

geographic division form face a task environment in between.

(2) Corresponding to the increase of complexity in task environment, the effective firms on average advance divisionalization by increasing the number of selfcontained units.

(3) Corresponding to the increase of uncertainty in task environment, the effective firms on average depress the divisionalization, advance the divisional autonomy, and simplify the integrative devices and interdivisional coordination network or even regress to the functional form.

(4) As the uncertainty of task environment increases, the location of the power center in the effective firms moves from the production department to the marketing department, and, then, to the R&D department.

The first and second findings are not new to us, therefore, need no further explanation. The following analysis is addressed to the last two findings.

## THE STRUCTURAL ARRANGEMENT OF HEADQUARTERS-DIVISION RELATIONSHIPS IN AN UNCERTAINTY TASK ENVIRONMENT

Between high and low performers there is a significant difference in the structural response to the increase of uncertainty in task environment. The difference between them could be schematically depicted as Figure 4.

The figure indicates that the basic level of divisionalization is determined by the degree of complexity of their task environment. In this aspect no significant difference exists between the high and low performers. As the uncertainty of task environment increases, two kinds of responses appear. The high performers' response (left) is characterized by the depression of divisionalization, the advancement of divisional autonomy and the simplification of integrative devices and interdivisional coordination network. In some cases the depression of divisionalization is so extensive that organizations regress to the functional form. The low performers' response (right) is characterized by the advancement of divisionalization and the sophistication of integrative devices. The high performers' response may be characterized as the simplification of headquarters-division relationships and the low performers' as their sophistication. Why, contrary to our hypothesis B-2, was the latter model less effective than the former?

In order to answer this question, we have to reconsi-
der the inference process which leads to hypothesis
B-2. Our hypothesis was derived on the basis of the
assumption that, as the task environment becomes more
uncertain, the organization comes to face two contradictory demands. On the one hand, in order to cope
with the higher uncertainty, an organization has to
be divided into a larger number of autonomous divisions so that each division faces a limited segment
of environment and promptly responds to environmental
contingencies. On the other hand, an organization has
to advance functional specialization within each unit
so that each unit is able to possess more specialized
knowledge to process uncertain information. The
widely used means to reconcile these two contradicting demands is to create functional integrating
units and/or interdivisional coordination networks.
Hence, we expected that in response to the increase
of uncertainty in task environment a rational organization would advance divisionalization and, at the
same time, advance functional specialization by
creating more complex integrative devices and interdivisional coordination networks.

In reality, however, this response was not effective.
The high performers emphasized the demand for functional specialization by sacrificing the demand for
divisionalization, instead of adopting devices which
reconcile both demands simultaneously. The rationale
of this high performers' response will be consistently explained within our theoretical framework, if the
following two assumptions are to be admitted². The
first is that the advancement of functional specialization within a division is more effective as a means
to cope with a higher level of uncertainty than the
advancement of divisionalization. The second is that
the formal devices installed to reconcile the contradicting demands entail a large amount of cost. Are
these assumptions valid?

The first assumption may be supported by the tendency
of recentralization observed among Japanese firms
after the first oil crisis. In response to the increase in uncertainty brought by the first oil crisis
a lot of large firms have recentralized their structures by merging divisions or by returning to the
functional form. This fact suggests that the advancement of functional specialization is more effective
as a means to cope with uncertainty than the further
divisionalization.

The second assumption may be supported by the studies
on the two-bosses structure represented by matrix
form. The sophisticated integration device used by
the low performers is a version of two-boss struc-

ture, because in this structural arrangement a functional manager in a division has two reporting relationships; one for his division's general manager,
and one for the functional integrating units' manager[3].

Galbraith (1973, 1977), Davis and Lawrence (1977),
Knight (1976), etc., indicate that the two-boss
structure may bring about difficult management problems and can create such pathological situations as
power struggle among managers, anarchy, avoidance of
taking responsibility, etc. The sophisticated formal
structure is quite likely to entail unexpected costs
and to increase the time and efforts to make decisions.

TABLE 7. The Stepwise Regression Analysis of the Determinants
of Innovation Time

(Time span needed to Commercialize Innovation Idea)

| independent variables | standardized regression coefficients |
|---|---|
| emphasis on growth goal | -.37** |
| ratio of R&D personnel to total employees | .50** |
| decentralization of R&D activities | -.45** |
| emphasis on concentric diversification | .19* |
| adoption of product manager system | .28** |
| divisionalization (number of divisions) | .31** |
| expected growth rate of principal industry | -.41** |
| emphasis on unrelated diversification | -.17* |
| emphasis on integration of distribution channel | -.22* |
| emphasis on marketing channel competition | .13 |
| power center in R&D department | .15 |
| ratio of product improvement expenditure to total R&D expenditures | .16 |
| | $\bar{R}2$ = .779 |

** $p < .01$     * $p < .05$

Table 7, which is the analysis of the determinants of
the time span needed to commercialize a new product
idea[4], supports the above speculation. It indicates

that the adoption of a product manager system, which is another version of the two-boss model, and the advancement of the divisionalization prolong the time span of innovations. This result suggests the existence of difficult management problems in the formalized two-boss system.

The foregoing discussion and supporting evidences indicate that the high performers' response has its own rationale that is explainable within our theoretical framework. Two important implications of the foregoing discussion are as follows: First, that the advancement of functional specialization within each division may advance the organization's capability to cope with uncertainty more effectively than the progression of divisionalization. Second, that the sophisticated integrative devices may bring difficult management problems and demand a lot of time and effort when innovative decisions are made in the uncertain environment.

INTERDEPARTMENTAL POWER BALANCE

In this study it was assumed that organizational decision making is the outcome of internal political process and that the quality of the organizational decision making depends upon the extent to which the group or person who has the knowledge and information needed to control the organization's strategic contingencies has a proper influence on the political process. The findings indicate that the interdepartmental power balance is one of the most significant determinants of organizational performance.

The influence of the power balance upon organizational performance was significant and clear. The reason why such significant results were obtained may be explained by the organic character of the Japanese management system. It has often been claimed that Japanese firms' organizations are characterized by consultative or participative decision-making, lateral and information communication network, flexible and abstract rules and job description, control by socialization, etc. (Yoshino, 1968; 1971; Pascale, 1978; Ouchi and Jaeger, 1978). The interdepartmental or interpersonal power relationships play a more important role in such organic organizations than in the mechanistic organizations where members' role and authority are clearly defined by rules. The importance of power balance, however, is not limited to organic organizations or Japanese firms, as suggested by the studies of U.K. and U.S. firms (Woodward, 1965; Perrow, 1970).

The reason will be more effectively explained if one

admits the fact that the power balance reflects various organizational characteristics. The interdepartmental power balance is not a design parameter in its usual sense. Organizational designers can influence the power balance only partially and indirectly, because the interdepartmental power balance is the composite outcome of a variety of factors such as formal stractural arrangements, established promotion and recruitment policy, staffing, management control system, training and socialization process, organizational culture or climate, etc. The interdepartmental power balance is the proxy variable of these various characteristics. Hence, it is quite likely that the significance of the interdepartmental power balance is amplified by its proxy character.

## IV. CONCLUSION AND IMPLICATIONS

The research presented in this paper represents an effort to establish middle-range hypotheses about the effective structural design of headquarters-division relationships and related subjects. It was shown that the empirical findings from Japanese firms supported some of the hypotheses which had been derived on the basis of the information processing paradigm. It was also shown that the unpredicted findings could be explained within the theoretical framework of the information processing paradigm if only some assumptions were accepted. On this ground the general conclusion can be drawn that the amount of information processing load and the types of strategic contingencies are the major determinants of effective organizational design and, therefore, the organizational structure should be analyzed and designed by focusing upon its information processing capacity to cope with these determinants.

The analysis so far has been concerned with the structures in Japanese multi-divisional firms. It may be possible, however, to generalize our findings beyond Japanese multi-divisional firms because the validity of the basic assumptions on which the hypotheses were constructed and the analysis was made is not confined to Japanese firms or to multi-divisional firms. The rest of this section is devoted to the discussion on the generalizable theoretical and practical implications of the research.

The most general implication, which can be drawn directly from these conclusions, is that the effectiveness of any corporatewide structural design could be successfully analyzed in terms of its information processing capability to deal with the information processing load and the strategic contingencies imposed by its task environment. This general the-

oretical perspective could act as a bridge to transmit the design experience from one area to another
and to integrate the case by case experiences into a
more complete system of knowledge.

For instance, Fayerweather (1978, p. 471), asserts
that the organizational design of multi-national
corporations is "a never-ending subject of discussion
among MNC managers" in spite of the abundance of
research. Many researchers have drawn diverse, contradictory conclusions thanks to the difference of
the contexts among the researches. How diverse they
may be, the reconciliation of these conclusions or at
least some of them may become possibly by analyzing
various contexts in terms of the amounts of complexity and uncertainty and the type of strategic contingencies, and by analyzing the organizational structures in terms of their information processing capabilities to cope with them.

Another implication, which may be drawn from hypothesis C and related findings, is that the organizational information processing activities are the
outcome of an internal political process where the
interpersonal or interdepartmental power balance
plays an important role and that the effectiveness of
an organization should be evaluated also by the
degree to which it creates the power balance by which
the idea and opinion of the person or group with the
knowledge and information to cope with strategic
contingencies are given attention and emphasis in the
goal formation and problem solving process.

It should be noted, however, that the internal power
balance is very difficult to manage. Two points
should be made concerning this problem. First, the
formal structural arrangement is one of a number of
factors that create and maintain the effective power
balance. In order to create or maintain an effective
power balance, various devices, such as formal structural arrangement, management control systems, recruitment, promotion and staffing policy, training
and socialization program, etc. should be combined.
The second point is that the effectiveness of a
management system should be evaluated not only in
terms of its influence upon individual information
processing activities but also in terms of its influences upon the internal power balance and upon the
political process.

The third implication that could be drawn from the
research is addressed to the two-boss structure that
is the essential component of the matrix form which
has become increasingly popular among the firms in
electronics, engineering, aerospace industries, and

the diversified multi-national corporations (Davis and Lawrence, 1977; Knight, 1978). Our research results on the structural arrangement of headquarters-division relationships, however, suggest that the corporate-wide two-boss structure or the matrix may have practical limitations even in Japanese firms which are thought to have the culture fitted to the two-boss structure (Davis and Lawrence, 1977).

There have been two opposite views on the matrix among the researchers. The first, which is represented by Stopford and Wells (1972), asserts that the matrix is the ultimate form of corporate development, although admitting the difficult management problems it entails. The other, which is represented by Davis and Lawrence (1978), asserts that the matrix is inherently unstable and should be thought of as a transitory form from one stable simple structure to another. The findings presented in this paper support the second view. Our findings suggest that the matrix may be unstable, need a lot of time and efforts and may delay the timing of innovative decisions. If so, what alternative is left for those firms that need the matrix?

Davis and Lawrence (1978) have concluded that the matrix is the preferred structural choice when the following three conditions exist simultaneously: (1) the outside pressure for dual focus, (2) the pressure for high information processing capacity, (3) the pressure for shared resources. As these conditions are imposed by a highly uncertain and complex environment, the organizational response to the increase of uncertainty observed among the high performers in the complex environment may present an answer to the alternative structural arrangement to deal with these conditions.

Their structural arrangement is characterized by a smaller number of divisions, a larger average size of divisions, a wider range of divisional autonomy, a simple hierarchical integration. They deal with the pressure for shared resources by merging divisions into a larger division and increasing the size of divisions and deal with the pressure for high information processing capacity by advancing specialization within each division and divisional autonomy. They cope with the pressure for dual focus - divisionalization and functional specialization - by specifying the most important focus and create simple formal structure around the primary focus rather than by accepting the dual focus. The rationale of this design strategy will be understood, if one admits that the dual focus does not necessarily mean both are of equal importance and that secondary focus may be taken into consideration in an informal way.

Davis and Lawrence (1967) assert that "many aspects of Japanese culture are ideally suited to the matrix format" (p. 55) but paradoxically conclude that "the Japanese don't have to create a formal matrix structure ....., because matrix structure and behavior is an intrinsic part of their way of being." Our findings further indicate that the formalization of the matrix is not only needless to the Japanese firms but also harmful when they face uncertainty. Our findings suggest that in an uncertain environment the simple formal structure with a single focus is the superior alternative even for Japanese firms with the culture fitted to the matrix.

FIGURE 1.   Typology of Task Environments and Representative Industries

|  | COMPLEXITY | |
|---|---|---|
|  | LOW | HIGH |
| **UNCERTAINTY** HIGH | CELL II<br><br>PHARMACEUTICAL & FINE CHEMICALS, THE OTHER (PRINTING, MUSICAL INSTRUMENTS, ETC.) | CELL IV<br><br>GENERAL MACHINERY, ELECTRIC MACHINERY & ELECTRONICS, TEXTILE INCLUDING SYNTHETIC FIBER |
| LOW | CELL I<br><br>FOOD & DRINK, PAPER & PULP, CHEMICALS, PETROLEUM, RUBBER, GLASS & CEMENT, STEEL, SHIP BUILDING | CELL III<br><br>MINING, NONFERROUS METAL, METALS & METAL PRODUCT, AUTOMOBILE & PARTS, PRECISION MACHINERY |

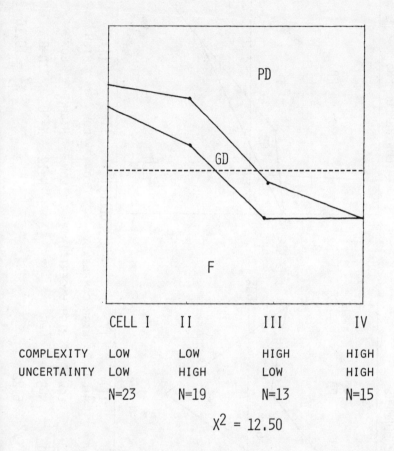

|  | CELL I | II | III | IV |
|---|---|---|---|---|
| COMPLEXITY | LOW | LOW | HIGH | HIGH |
| UNCERTAINTY | LOW | HIGH | LOW | HIGH |
|  | N=23 | N=19 | N=13 | N=15 |

$$X^2 = 12.50$$

FIGURE 2. The Distribution of Organizational Forms in the Four Cells of Task Environment

174

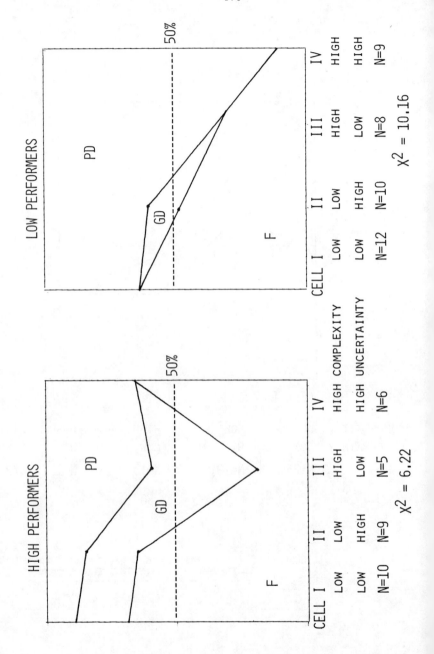

FIGURE 3.  Comparison of the Distributions of Organizational
Forms between High and Low Performing Groups

175

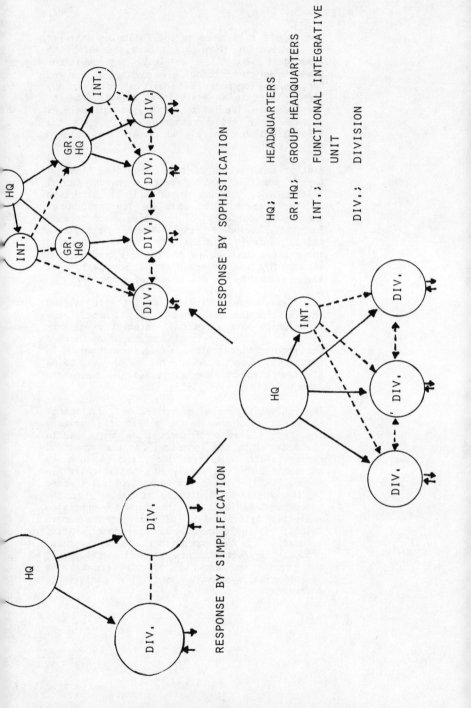

FIGURE 4. Two Patterns of Structural Response to the Increase of Uncertainty

NOTES

1.  The sample size used in the following analyses
    may be smaller than this figure, because each
    respondent was asked to leave any questions
    blank to which he cannot give precise answer and
    because any response with missing value in any
    item related to an analysis is deleted from it.
    The sample size also differ among analyses
    because only those responses which have any
    missing value in related items are deleted
    analysis-wise.

2.  Another explanation of the unpredicted findings
    may be possible if one admits a reverse causal
    relationship between organizational structure
    and performance, i.e. that the low performance
    create the scarceness of resources which demands
    for the sharing of the resources and for a
    closer control of divisions. The sophisticated
    integrative devices and the close interdivision-
    al coordination observed among low performers
    may be caused by the scarceness of resources.

3.  Only few Japanese firms adopted the formalized
    matrix structure when this study was made. Those
    firms which have functional integrative depart-
    ments in multi-divisional and those which have
    the product integrators (product managers) in
    functional form, however, may be thought to be
    at some stage of the evolution to the matrix
    structure (Galbraith, 1973).

4.  The innovativeness of organizations in terms of
    (1) rate of innovations within the primary
    industry, (2) rate of innovations that lead to
    the entry into new industry, (3) time spent to
    commercialize innovation idea, and (4) quality
    of innovation was analysed statistically in
    Kagono (1980). The following variables are added
    to the variables indicated at Table 6 as the
    independent variables of the stepwise regression
    analysis, heterogeneity of environment, uncer-
    tainty of environment, R&D personnel ratio,
    allocation of R&D expenditure (basic reserach,
    product improvement, new product development,
    and process improvement), expected growth rate
    of principal industry, and five performance
    indicators.

# A P P E N D I X   A

CHARACTERISTICS OF THE SAMPLE

## INDUSTRY

| | |
|---|---|
| Mining | 3 |
| Food & Drink | 8 |
| Textile (including Synthetic Fiber) | 5 |
| Paper & Pulp | 4 |
| Chemicals | 10 |
| Pharmaceutical & Fine Chemicals | 9 |
| Petroleum | 3 |
| Rubber | 2 |
| Glass & Cement | 4 |
| Steel | 7 |
| Nonferrous Metals | 6 |
| Metals & Metal Products | 3 |
| General Machinery | 12 |
| Electrical Machinery & Electronics | 20 |
| Automobile & Parts | 4 |
| Shipbuilding | 5 |
| Precision Instruments | 4 |
| Other (Printing, Musical Instruments, Housing Materials, etc.) | 4 |
| T o t a l | 113 |

## SIZE

### Sales Ranking (among Japanese industrial firms)

| | |
|---|---|
| 1st ---- 100th | 24 |
| 101st ---- 200th | 21 |
| 201st ---- 300th | 27 |
| 301st ---- 400th | 21 |
| 401st ---- 500th | 15 |
| 501st ---- | 5 |
| T o t a l | 113 |

APPENDIX B

MEASUREMENT OF VARIABLES WHICH CHARACTERIZE TASK
ENVIRONMENT

(1)  market and technological environment
     (1-1)     heterogeneity (the average of the
               following 4 items,
               reliability coefficient, =.742)
                    market heterogeneity*
                    technological heterogeneity*
                    input heterogeneity*
                    heterogeneity of competitive
                    strategies*
     (1-2)     instability (the average of the follo-
               wing items,
               reliability coefficient, =.671)
                    frequency of new product intro-
                    duction*
                    time span of facility renewal (re-
                    versed)*
                    length of product life cycle (re-
                    versed)*
                    instability of demand*
                    reliability of sales forecast
                    (reversed)*
                    magnitude of effect of price re-
                    vision*

(2)  technology (routineness)
               custom production (1-point), small
               batch (2-points), large batch (3-
               points), mass production (4-points),
               continuous process (5-points)

(3)  size (number of employees)**
               logarithm of the number of employee

(4)  diversification strategy
     (4-1)     direction of diversification (emphasis
               on each direction is measured by 3-
               point scale; 0-not adopted, 1-adopted,
               2-adopted as the main direction)
               -    backward integration
               -    forward integration
               -    integration of distribution
                    channel
               -    concentric diversification
               -    technology-related diversifica-
                    tion
               -    market-related diversification
               -    byproduct diversification
               -    unrelated diversification
               -    has not diversified in the last 10
                    years

<u>A P P E N D I X   B</u> (cont'd)

  (4-2) rate of diversification
       percentage of sales accounted by
       the new product lines introduced
       in the last 10 years
  (4-3) variety of industries
       number of two digit industries in
       which businesses are done

(5) R&D strategy
       R&D intensity (percentage of R&D
       expenditures to total sales)

(6) major competitive issue (major competitive issue
   in the principal market is classified into
  one of the following categories)
       product quality and specification
       pricing
       sales promotion including adver-
       tisement
       new product development
       marketing channel

(7) goals
  (7-1) relative importance of three goals
       ranking of three goals, i.e.,
       growth, profitability
  (7-2) risk avertiveness
       choice of the less risky alterna-
       tive from two presumed investment
       alternatives

   * measured by 7-point scale
   ** obtained from published sources

A P P E N D I X  B (cont'd)

Principal Component Analysis of Selected Context Variables

|  | 1 | 2 | 3 | 4 | 5 | 6 |
|---|---|---|---|---|---|---|
| - heterogeneity of environment | .099 | .410 | .134 | -.185 | .237 | .327 |
| - instability of environment | .329 | .123 | .085 | .303 | -.055 | -.022 |
| - technology (routineness) | -.254 | -.122 | -.171 | -.063 | .125 | .212 |
| - size | .327 | .231 | -.121 | .192 | -.088 | .247 |
| (direction of diversification) |  |  |  |  |  |  |
| backward integration | .119 | .026 | -.156 | -.111 | .098 | -.062 |
| forward integration | -.170 | .043 | .117 | -.020 | .173 | -.456 |
| integration of dist. channel | .053 | -.110 | .178 | .318 | .502 | .023 |
| concentric diversification | .246 | -.334 | -.125 | .010 | -.334 | .311 |
| technology-related diversif. | .134 | .364 | .087 | -.335 | .192 | -.153 |
| market-related diversif. | -.098 | .321 | -.073 | .415 | -.388 | .003 |
| unrelated diversifaction | -.073 | .077 | -.244 | -.282 | .198 | .382 |
| - rate of diversification | .355 | -.024 | .024 | -.099 | -.017 | -.293 |
| - variety of industries | -.117 | .456 | .034 | .163 | -.162 | -.160 |
| - R&D intensity | .413 | -.135 | -.120 | -.151 | -.008 | -.033 |
| (major competitive issue) |  |  |  |  |  |  |
| quality and specification | -.075 | .024 | .623 | -.196 | -.259 | .218 |
| pricing | -.254 | .047 | -.517 | .096 | -.008 | -.094 |
| new product | .415 | -.054 | -.152 | .034 | .167 | -.217 |
| - risk avertiveness | -.137 | -.385 | .264 | .167 | .003 | .091 |
| - growth emphasis* | .008 | .017 | .093 | .489 | .408 | 273 |
| EIGEN value | 3.072 | 2.025 | 1.828 | 1.410 | 1.309 | 1.199 |
| % | 16.2 | 10.7 | 9.6 | 7.4 | 6.9 | 6.3 |

*  dummy variable that takes 1 if growth goal is ranked higher than profitability goal

Based upon the principal this component analysis, two composite indicators are defined. The first, the degree of environmental uncertainty, is the non-weighted average of standardized scores of indicators whose loading to the first dimension is greater than .2. The second, the degree of environmental complexity, is the non-weighted average of standardized scores of indicators whose loading to the second dimension is greater than .2.

181

# A P P E N D I X   C

OPERATIONALIZATION OF ORGANIZATIONAL STRUCTURE

Each respondent was originally classified into either
of the four pure forms, i.e., functional form (f),
geographic-division (gd) form, product division
form (pd), and functional division form (fd), or
either of the six hybrid forms, i.e., six pairs of
the above four forms (f+gd, f+pd, f+fd, gd+pd, gd+fd,
and pd+fd). The functional division form means that
some functional departments are organized into divisions. This category was added because some Japanese
firms adopt the concept of multi-divisional organization only nominally or after changing the concept
significantly (Urabe, 1965).

Comparing the similarity of task environments, these
forms are reduced to the three groups. Product division form (PD) consists of those firms which adopt
either pd (19 firms) or pd+fd (9) or pd+f (14), geographical form (GD) consists of those firms which
adopt either gd (3) or gd+pd (7), and functional
form (FD) consists of those firms which adopt f(51)
or fd (4) or f+fd (4). One firm which adopts gd+f was
not classified to either, because it had a task environment significantly different from others. No
firm assume gd+fd.

The four dimensions of the structural arrangements of
the headquarters-division relationships in each firm
were measured by the following 9 indicators.

    (a)  Degree of divisionalization
        (1)   number of divisions
        (2)   average size of divisions
    (b)  Degree of divisional autonomy
        (3)   completeness of divisional profit and
             loss accounting divisional profit and
             loss accounting for all divisions (3
             points), divisional profit and loss
             accounting for some divisions (2
             points), no divisional profit and loss
             accounting (1 point)
        (4)   responsibility and authority of divi-
             sions
                  investment center (3 points),
                  profit center (2 points),
                  cost center (1 point)

    (c)  Complexity of integrative devices
        (5)   existence of group headquarters
                  exist (2 points),
                  do not exist (1 point)

APPENDIX C (cont'd)

    (6)   existence of a department that integrates interdivisional marketing activities
        exists (2 points),
        does not exist (1 point)

    (7)   existence of a department that integrates interdivisional technological activities
        exists (2 points)
        does not exist (1 point)

(d)  Degree of interdivisional coordination

    (8)   interdivisional coordination of marketing activities
        (7 point scale)

    (9)   interdivisional coordination of technological activities
        (7 point scale)

The composite score for each dimension except for the first is the average of the standardized scores of constituent indicators. Number of divisions and average size of divisions are used as the independent indicators for the first dimension. The indicators are defined also for the firms that adopt the functional form by assuming that those firms consist of one self-contained decision unit.

REFERENCES

ALLEN, S.A., 1978, "Organizational Choices and General Managerial Influence Networks in Divisionalized Company," Academy of Management Journal, 21: 341-365.

BOUWER, J.L., 1972, Managing the Resource Allocation Process, Boston: Division of Research, Harvard Business School.

BURNS, T., and G.M. STALKER, 1961, The Management of Innovation, London: Tavistock.

CHANDLER, A.D., Jr., 1962, Strategy and Structure, Cambridge, Mass.: MIT Press.

CYERT, R.M. and MARCH, J.G., 1963, A Behavioral Theory of the Firm, Englewood Cliffs, N.J.: Prentice-Hall.

DAVIS, S.M., and P.R. LAWRENCE, 1977, Matrix, Reading, Mass.: Addison-Wesley.

DILL, W.R., 1962, "The Impact of Environment on Organization Development," in S. Mailick and E.H. Van Ness (eds.) Concept and Issues in Administrative Behavior, Englewood Cliffs, N.J.: Prentice-Hall.

DUNCAN, R.B., 1972, "Characteristics of Organizational Environments and Perceived Environmental Uncertainty," Administrative Science Quarterly, 19:313-327.

DUNCAN, R.B., 1973, "Multiple Decision-Making Structures in Adapting to Environmental Uncertainty: The Impact on Organizational Effectiveness, Human Relations, 26: 273-291.

FAYERWEATHER, J., 1978, International Business Strategy and Administration, Cambridge, Mass. I: Bellinger.

GALBRAITH, J., 1977, Designing Complex Organizations, Reading, Mass.: Addison-Wesley.

GALBRAITH, J., 1977, Organization Design, Reading, Mass.: Addison-Wesley.

HAGE, J., and M. AIKEN, 1969, "Routine Technology, Social Structure and Organizational Goals," Administrative Science Quarterly, 14: 366-376.

HALL, R.H., 1977, Organization: Structure and Process 2nd edition, Englewood Cliffs, N.J.: Prentice-Hall.

HICKSON, D.J., C.R. HININGS, C.A. LEE, R.E. SCHNECK, and J.M. PENNINGS, 1971, "A Strategic Contingencies' Theory of Intraorganizational Power," Administrative Science Quarterly, 16: 216-229.

KAGONO, T., 1980, Environmental Adaption of Organizations, (in Japanese) Tokyo: Hakuto.

LAWRENCE, P.R. and J.W. LORSCH, 1967, Organization and Environment, Boston: Division Research, Harvard Business School.

LORSCH, J.W. and S.A. ALLEN, 111, 1973, Managing Diversity and Interdependence: An Organizational Study of Multi-Divisional Firms. Boston: Division of Research, Harvard Business School.

MARSCH, J.G., and H.A. SIMON, 1958, Organizations, New York: John Wiley & Sons.

NONAKA, I., 1972, Organization and Market: Exploratory Study of Centralization vs. Decentralization. Unpublished Ph.D. dissertation, Graduate School of Business Administration, University of California, Berkeley.

NONAKA, I., and F.M. NICOSIA, 1979, "Marketing Management, Its Environment and Information Processing: A Problem of Organizational Design," Journal of Business Research, Vol. 7, pp.277-300.

OUICHI, W.G., and A.M.JAEGER, "Type Z Organization: Stability in the Midst of Mobility," Academy of Management Review, 3:305-314.

PASCALE, R.T., 1978, "Communication and Decision Making Across Cultures: Japanese and American Comparison," Administrative Science Quarterly, 23: 91-110.

PERROW, C., 1961, "The Analysis of Goals in Complex Organization," American Sociological Review, 26: 854-866.

PERROW, C., 1967, "A Framework for Comparative Analysis of Organizations," American Sociological Review, 32: 194-208.

185

PERROW, C., 1970, "Departmental Power and Perspectives in Industrial Firms," in M.N. Zald (ed.), Power in Organization, Vanderbild University Press.

PUGH, D.S., D.J. HICKSON, C.R. HININGS and C. TURNER, 1969, "The Context of Organizational Structure," Administrative Science Quarterly, 14: 91-114.

STOPFORD, J.M. and L.T. WELLS, Jr., 1972, Managing the Multinational Enterprise, New York: Basic Book.

THOMPSON, J.D., 1967, Organizations in Action, New York: McGraw-Hill.

TUSHMAN, M.L., and D.A. NADLER, 1978, "Information Processing as an Integrating Concept in Organizational Design," Academy of Management Review, 3: 613-624.

URABE, K., 1965, "The Multi-divisional Organizations in Japan," The Annals of the School of Business Administration, Kobe University, 1965: 65-96.

WALKER, A.H., and P.W. LORSCH, 1968, "Organizational Choice: Product vs. Function," Harvard Business Review, November-December.

WOODWARD, J., 1965, Industrial Organization: Behavior and Control, London: Oxford University Press.

YOSHINO, M.Y., 1968, Japan's Managerial System, Cambridge, Mass.: MIT Press.

YOSHINO, M.Y., 1976, Japan's Multi-National Enterprise, Cambridge, Mass.: Harvard University Press.

# 8 C. K. Prahalad and Yves L. Doz:

# Strategic Control — The Dilemma in Headquarters-Subsidiary Relationship

In the late 1960s, the dwindling profitability of the industrial motors business of Brown Boveri & Cie (BBC) - a major international supplier of electrical equipment headquartered in Baden, Switzerland - became a source of concern to BBC's corporate management (1). The causes of the problem quickly became clear: severe price competition from Soviet and East German exporters and from efficient integrated West European manufacturers. BBC's major competitor in the motors business, Leroy Somer, was able to achieve comparable sales volume with about 3,000 employees compared to BBC's 5,000. Even though motor production was quite sensitive to economies of scale and experience, several of BBC's West European subsidiaries were manufacturing a full line of motors in small volumes. The obvious solution was to rationalize production among these subsidiaries such that each subsidiary produced only a partial range of motors for the European market but marketed the whole range. By 1971, a rationalization plan was drawn, and approved by the Management Committee by 1972. Five years later, in 1977, the plan was only partially implemented. Hopes of implementing it faded by 1977 and BBC's motor business continued to suffer.

The Industrial Vehicle Corporation (IVECO) resulted from the merger of the truck division of Deutz, Germany with the truck division of Fiat, Italy and a Fiat subsidiary in France, UNIC (2). IVECO wanted to integrate and rationalize the activities of the three national operations' subsidiaries, while maintaining

Graduate School of Business Administration
University of Michigan
Graduate School of Business Administration
Harvard University

their national identities. A year after the merger, in 1974, a Management Advisory Committee was created, consisting of the heads of the operating companies and IVECO coordinators. The economies of rationalization were evaluated by staff specialists at Fiat, Italy. The plan called for a common product line among the three companies which formed IVECO, and the avoidance of duplications in manufacturing. The plan also involved significant investments in various plants. By 1978, manufacturing rationalization had made some progress and productivity had increased. However, a series of issues remained unsolved, issues critical to the development of a strategic thrust. For example, the accounting procedures among the companies were not unified and the measurement of results was difficult. IVECO's coordinator's effort to implement a common planning and budgeting system had met with little success. Managers from operating companies were unwilling to take positions in IVECO. There were several unresolved marketing issues: Should foreign sales subsidiaries be merged? Should they promote an IVECO logo or keep separate brands? Should service and spare parts businesses be merged? In 1977, a one-week conference was organized. This resulted in a regrouping of IVECO to improve its strategic focus. Little concrete action followed.

Corning Glass Works, an internationally known glass products company, was faced with the problem of co-ordination between overseas operations and U.S. (domestic) operations during 1972 (3). Corning was a technology-driven company. Its growth, both in the U.S. and Europe, was based on high technology applications of glass - from television tubes to optical lenses, medical instrumentation and Pyrex and Corning Cookware. There were over 300 types of glass and 60,000 products in the Corning System. The UK and French subsidiaries of Corning resisted any attempt by Corning U.S. or even Corning Glass Works International to influence strategy. Corning tried several approaches to influence subsidiary strategy including the following: gaining 100% ownership, appointing product managers for specific businesses, and requiring that subsidiaries follow common accounting and reporting procedures. After 42 months of effort, the process had to be aborted. Corning asked a consulting group to initiate a comprehensive study.

Yet another MNC, let us call it XYZ Packaging, an integrated, multimaterial packaging firm, faced similar problems (4). XYZ had several subsidiaries in Europe and Latin America - some of them 100% owned and some joint ventures. One of the largest subsidiaries in Europe faced severe performance problems, and XYZ headquarters became aware of the severity of the situation in 1976. From 1976 onwards, XYZ tried to improve the situation by investing heavily in modernization. The European subsidiary was technologically mature and self-sufficient. In fact, in some aspects of manufacturing process control, they were ahead of the technology used in several U.S. plants of XYZ. There were few U.S. expatriates in managerial positions in the subsidiary. While teams of experts - manufacturing, marketing and financial - visited the subsidiary from XYZ, they could not persuade the subsidiary to change its strategy in any way. The subsidiary managers resented the intrusion of XYZ headquarters and consistently advocated alternatives to the strategy proposed by them with equally coherent reasons. The performance of the subsidiary showed no improvement as of early 1980.

The situations presented above are not in any way unique. Similar situations abound (5). They represent examples of a generic problem in headquarter subsidiary relationships - the problem of strategic control. In this paper, we will examine the concept of strategic control and develop a methodology for identifying the appropriateness of alternative methods of control. We will also outline an approach for enhancing the intervention capabilities of top management in the strategic process of subsidiaries.

## THE CONCEPT OF STRATEGIC CONTROL IN HEADQUARTERS - SUBSIDIARY RELATIONSHIPS

We may define strategic control as the extent of headquarter influence over the subsidiary in decisions that affect subsidiary strategy. Some typical decisions that affect strategy of the subsidiary are: choice of technology, product market identification, emphasis on different product lines, resource allocation, expansion and diversification of subsidiary operations, willingness to participate in a worldwide network through a regional or global control of product flows among subsidiaries and choice of key executives. The listing above is intended to be indicative of the nature of decisions that we considered in our study.

Historically, the ability of headquarters to control the decisions that affect the strategy of subsidiaries has been a matter of dependence. Implicit in the traditional concept of headquarter - subsidiary relationships is the view that subsidiaries are dependent on headquarters for sustaining their competitive advantage (6). Dependence may be predicated upon several factors; technology, access to capital, access to global marketing channels, proprietary brands, management knowhow are some of the means through which headquarters may exercise control over subsidiaries. However, we find that

a)  As subsidiaries mature and grow in size, they can afford an adequate level of internal management talent, including adequate R & D. For example, BBC subsidiaries conducted their own motors R & D and were not dependent upon Baden, Switzerland for motor technology.

b)  As the industry matures, the technological advantage that the headquarters possessed vis-a-vis the subsidiary disappears. For example, in XYZ Packaging, the European subsidiary possessed as advanced a technology as the parent.

c)  Management as a distinct skill is also becoming widespread. Further, the management skills needed by subsidiaries operating in environments dissimilar to that of the parent - like a regulated environment (e.g., Nigeria) or a highly inflationary environment (e.g., Brazil) or a low technology environment (e.g., Indonesia) - may be unavailable at headquarters.

d)  Subsidiaries with large volume, adequate technology and management develop their own overseas activities. For example, the German subsidiary of BBC established a plant in Singapore totally side-stepping BBC International.

As subsidiaries mature, the nature of dependence significantly changes. This process of shifting autonomy of the subsidiary is further facilitated by active host government involvement in the activities of subsidiaries (7). Under pressure from host governments, some subsidiaries are moving into businesses unfamiliar to headquarters. For example, Union Carbide's Indian subsidiary is involved in shrimp fishing, an unfamiliar business for the headquarters of Union Carbide. In other words, for most MNCs, headquarters influence on subsidiary strategy has to depend on mechanisms other than control over resources such as technology, capital, managerial skills, and access to markets.*

---

*Some MNC headquarters may contiue to exercise significant leadership in technology and be able to influence subsidiaries on that basis. But even in technology oriented MNC's like IBM, subsidiaries (e.g., UK, Germany) tend to be strong and possess adequate managerial and technical expertise. The technology, management and capital flows become two-way rather than one-way (from headquarters to subsidiary).

## THE NEED FOR MULTIPLE PERSPECTIVES IN STRATEGY

The problem of strategic control is further complicated by the fact that most MNCs have to be responsive to often conflicting strategic demands. For example, a subsidiary has to be responsive to host government demands (e.g., customizing products to meet local demands, manufacturing all components within the country) as well as the demands of headquarters (e.g., developing the least cost position or using a standardized technology). Similarly, the demands of diversity in local national markets (a concern of subsidiaries) must be matched with opportunities for global rationalization. BBC faced this problem. In their heavy equipment business they had to be responsive to local, national governments. In their motors business they could have been responsive to global rationalization. But in the judgement of subsidiary managers, motors business was an integral part of the heavy equipment business.

The problem of strategic control must be viewed in the context of the ever present tensions between subsidiaries and headquarters described above. These tensions cannot be wished away; neither can the MNC find a one-time resolution to the conflict. The extent to which this tension will become a major feature of the headquarters-subsidiary relationship in an MNC is determined by the nature of competition faced by the MNC and the extent of host government restrictions (8). These tensions impose the requirement that in making strategic decisions, both headquarters and subsidiary must explicitly recognize the need for incorporating multiple perspectives. One approach to achieving this capability is to institutionalize the strategic tensions inherent in the MNC environment by adopting a matrix structure which can promote and facilitate a multiple advocacy process (9).

## THE NEED FOR FOCUS

While the MNC matrix provides an opportunity for gaining multiple strategic perspectives through an advocacy process as well as flexibility in responses, it can also lead to strategic paralysis. In a headquarters-subsidiary relationship where the headquarters has no clear strategic resource edge and, if decisions are made purely on an issue-by-issue basis by a process of negotiation between two equally strong contenders, the nature of the outcomes is not predictable. The pattern of resource allocation decisions resolved on the basis of relative influence of headquarters and subsidiaries at different points in time and as issues surface is also unlikely to have a strong focus. For example, the reaction of German and Swiss national organizations of BBC in the motors business illustrates this point. While the Swiss organization followed the rationalization plan and implemented it without hesitation (the subsidiary was losing money and the motors business was an insignificant part of overall Swiss sales), the German subsidiary not only ignored the rationalization plan but went ahead and increased its capacity to $30 million in sales in 1977 from $2 million in 1972. This is a contradiction in the headquarters-subsidiary relationship, the need for gaining strategic focus while institutionalizing the process of multiple advocacy.

If the headquarters and subsidiaries have equal power to commit resources rather than equal opportunity to participate in the decision process and advocate alternative perspectives, then strategic resource commitments may not follow any predictable pattern. On the other hand, a predictable pattern of resource commitment, leading to strategic focus, may evolve if either one - headquarters or subsidiary - had relative power over the other. Relative power to commit resources may be a result of a pure accident. For example, the relative personalities of key executives may decide the focus of power. In Corning, the three product managers chosen to coordinate their business -consumer products, science and medical products, and TV - approached their tasks very differently. The product manager for consumer products wanted centralized control, power to commit resources and develop subsidiary strategies. On the other hand, the manager chosen to coordinate medical products decided to maintain a very passive role in manufacturing and let the subsidiaries develop their strategies. He was concerned with marketing coordination. In TV, the product manager thought of his role as a "conduit" between domestic and international. In all three cases the locus of relative power in the matrix was a result of the personality of the executive chosen and not a result of purposive action. On the other hand, the same task - the choice of key executives - could have resulted in providing relative power to the "appropriate arm of the matrix" and gaining strategic focus. The cases of Delta Corporation and General Motors Corporation, both discussed in the next paper, illustrate this point (10).

PROACTIVE CHANGE VS REACTIVE CHANGE

There is yet another dimension of strategic control that merits our consideration. We have assumed, implicitly, that gaining focus in resource allocation through purposive management of relative power in the matrix is a one-time task. On the contrary, top

management must have the ability to shift the locus
of power both during a crisis as well as proactively.
A continuous profit decline, for example, may provide
adequate legitimacy for such change. On the other
hand, if top managers want to shift the locus of
power, not as a reactive but proactive step, as in
General Motors, then all the constituencies involved
in the change process must recognize and accept the
legitimacy of such change.

Even in a crisis, the need for change may not be
widely accepted. For example, both in BBC and Corning
the headquarters perceived a problem - lack of competitive strength in BBC's motor business and lack of
coordination between headquarters and subsidiaries at
Corning leading to missed or underexploited opportunities. In both cases, the subsidiaries did not
fully accept either the diagnosis of the problem or
the solution. Proactive strategic change, an important part of strategic control, requires that both
headquarters and subsidiaries agree on the diagnosis
as well as the actions required to deal with the
situation.

THE STRATEGIC CONTROL DILEMMA

We can identify four elements of the strategic
control dilemma inherent in headquarters-subsidiary
relationships.

(i)   Headquarters cannot rely exclusively on the use
      of strategic resources as a basis of control,
      especially in situations where the subsidiaries
      are more or less self-sufficient in such resour-
      ces. We have to examine the process of control
      where headquarters and subsidiary relationships
      are based not on one-way dependence but recipro-
      cal dependence.

(ii)  The strategic control process must be carried
      out in a business environment with inherent
      tensions imposed by competitive and host govern-
      ment pressures. Responsiveness and flexibility
      in strategy must coexist with desires for global
      rationalization.

(iii) While the strategy must be responsive to envi-
      ronmental demands, resource commitments must be
      focused. Focus must coexist with flexibility
      and mutual rather than one-way dependence.

(iv)  The control process must be capable of purpo-
      sive, proactive changes in strategy. Further,
      changes must be perceived as legitimate.

194

The four conditions, in our view, represent the central dilemmas in strategic control of subsidiaries by headquarters.

AN APPROACH TO STRATEGIC CONTROL

The four strategic control dilemmas outlined above indicate that MNC managers should identify influence mechanisms other than the use of strategic resources, that "subtle" controls should replace more "direct and overt" controls. In our research we find that increasingly MNCs in mature businesses depend on creating an administrative context that influences the strategic thrust of subsidiaries in desired directions. Administrative context may be defined as the net effect on managerial behavior of influence mechanisms such as executive compensation, budgeting systems, and career progression patterns (11). The shift in the process of control, as businesses mature, may be represented schematically as below:

TABLE 1.  Schematic Representation of Shifts in Control in Headquarters-Subsidiary Relationships

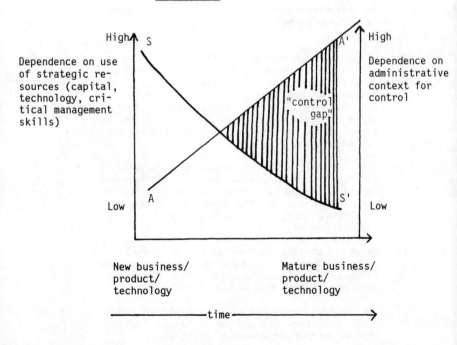

The schematic representation shows the changing nature of the control process as the business matures -
or as it moves along the product life cycle.* In
business where the headquarters controls the critical
inputs - technology, critical management skills, and
capital - headquarters managers can and often do depend on the control of these resources to influence
subsidiary strategy. We may call this approach "substantive control." But as the business matures, the
ability to use substantive control diminishes. The
nature of the linkage between maturity of a business
and the effectiveness of substantive control is represented by the line SS'. The need for the use of
administrative context increases as business matures
and is shown by line AA'. The strategic control problems experienced by Brown Boveri & Cie, Corning
International, IVECO and XYZ Packaging result from a
control gap, an inability in these organizations to
enhance their sophistication in managing the administrative context or move along line AA' as the maturity of the business pushes headquarters down SS'.

The implications of the need to shift from substantive control to administrative context are several. MNC
managers must

a) develop an analytical understanding of control through the management of administrative
mechanisms

b) recognize that as businesses mature faster
(e.g., electronics), the shift from substantive
to administrative context as an approach to control must be accomplished in a short time frame,
usually in 3 to 5 years, and

c) have high levels of sophistication in the se-
lective use of both substantive and administrative context for control in high technology,
short product life cycle business.

We will explore these issues in the rest of the paper.

-----

* It is important to recognize that while we used the
product life cycle notion to illustrate the shift in
control from "substantive" to "administrative", this
shift is by no means influenced solely by the product
life cycle of a business. The size and maturity, of
the subsidiary, and the quality of its management,
as well as the motivation of the managers, may also
influence the shift.

STRATEGIC CONTROL AND ADMINISTRATIVE CONTEXT

The ability to change the strategic direction of a
business is an important component of the concept of
strategic control. It also represents the most demanding test of the quality of control. Therefore, we
will only examine the problems of strategic change in
this paper.

The process of strategic control in a "nondependent"
headquarters - subsidiary relationship must be predicated upon a "shared concern" for change. In BBC,
for example, the concern for rationalization of the
motors business was not universal. While corporate
management was anxious, the German and French subsidiaries were not. The Swiss national organizations
did follow the corporate lead. The Italian organization could not fulfill its role. It appears that
the first task in strategic control is to ensure
that headquarters and subsidiaries share a common
information and data base and agree on a common
approach to competition. In other words, the cognitive orientation of the headquarters and subsidiary
managers as well as their strategic orientation must
coincide. Next, power to commit resources must be
aligned with the strategic orientation of the
business. This will ensure that the pattern of resource allocation is consistent with the strategic
orientation of a business. Finally, procedures and
systems must reinforce the power orientation required
in the organization. All four orientations described
above must be changed before strategic change is
effected (12).

We find in our research that most stalled strategic
moves in MNCs are a result of not fully comprehending
this process of change. In several cases, the headquarters managers did change the cognitive and strategic orientations but could not change the power
orientation. In other cases, they changed the administrative orientation without any concern for
shifting other orientations. In some others, they
shifted the power orientation prematurely. The le-
gitmacy of this shift in power was not accepted by
the subsidiaries which did not share the strategic
orientation of headquarters. But in all cases, power
orientation had to be changed before strategic
change, identified by the shifting nature of resource
allocations taking place. The only time when a change
process that was initiated with a shift in power was
seen as legitimate was when both headquarters and
subsidiaries agreed that there was a crisis, even
though they may have had disagreements on the causes
or remedies. The pattern that emerges when we look at
the approach to strategic change undertaken by the
various MNCs in our study is shown in Table 2 below:

TABLE 2.  Attempts to Change Strategy –
          Some Tentative Patterns

| Precondition | Cognitive | Strategic | Power | Administrative | Result (time horizon) |
|---|---|---|---|---|---|
| Crisis situation concern shared by H.Q. and subsidiaries | | | ① | | Strategic shift accomplished (2-3 years) |
| –Delta Corporation | ③ | ② | | ④ | |
| Noncrisis situation attempt to shift strategy proactively | | | | | Strategic shift taking roots (6-7 years) |
| –General Motors | ① | ② | ③ | ③ | |
| –IVECO | ① | ② | | | Stalled change (3-4 years) |
| Crisis diagnosis not shared by subsidiaries | | | | | |
| –BBC | ① | ② | | | Stalled change (5 years) |
| –Corning International | ② | | | ① | Stalled change (3-4 years) |

In all cases, the time horizon for evaluating the extent of strategic shift was more than 3 years. In some cases, the shift took 7 years to take hold.

The contrast between General Motors and IVECO is in how effectively the top management changed the power orientation. IVECO could not sustain its momentum, for it lacked the ability to change power orientation. In both BBC and Corning, changes were initiated very differently. But both attempts were stalled due to an inability to impact the power orientation. We could add several other cases to the list above as well as reinterpret some others. The generalizations that stand out are:

(i)  There are alternative routes that an MNC can take to achieve a strategic change, but for change to be effective, it must change all the four orientations.

(ii) Power orientation must be changed before strategic change will take place. If power orientation
is unaffected, then the attempt to change will
be stalled.

(iii)While in a "crisis situation," the change process might be initiated with a change in "power
orientation"; for proactive change to take root,
it must be seen as legitimate. This calls for a
change in cognitive and strategic orientations
before changing the power orientation.

(iv) Since strategic shifts in complex organizations
take time - at least 3-4 years in the cases we
studied - we can conclude that significant and
sustained top management interest is necessary
for change process to be effective.

THE MECHANISMS FOR CHANGE

If the task of strategic control is one of managing
the four orientations described above, how do managers change these orientations? What are the influence
mechanisms? We may identify an indicative list of
mechanisms under three categories:

(i)  People oriented mechanisms:
     Included under this category are mechanisms
     suchs as choice of key managers, career paths,
     patterns of socialization, management develop-
     ment, rewards and measurement systems.

(ii) Data management mechanisms:
     We may include under this category information
     systems, budgeting and planning systems, capital
     budgeting procedures, etc.

(iii)Conflict resolution mechanisms:
     We may include task forces, committees, new
     integrative positions, decision responsibility
     assignments, and conflict resolution systems
     such as the "contention system" at IBM.

Managers can use any combination of these to impact
on the four orientations. The important point is not
the availability of a range of mechanisms but in
picking the appropriate sequence and timing of these
mechanisms and assessing their impact on the four
orientations. In the follow-up paper, we discuss in
great detail how these mechanisms can be used. The
emerging concept of strategic control in complex MNCs
is one based on managing the four orienations through
a variety of influence mechanisms. While the concept
is relatively simple, the task is extremely complex.

## HIGH TECHNOLOGY, SHORT PRODUCT LIFE CYCLE BUSINESSES

While the concept of strategic control through the management of administrative context (rather than substantive control) was devised to explain the head-quarters-subsidiary relationships in mature busines-ses, and situations where significant local responsi-veness must coexist with economic rationalization, the concept is also useful in explaining strategic control in high technology, short product life cycle businesses (e.g., calculators, semiconductors, mini-computers). Such businesses exhibit three characte-ristics:

(i)   As the life cycle is short, the headquarters - subsidiary relationships move down the line SS' in relatively short periods of time - say 5 years.

(ii)  In order to exploit the opportunities in these businesses, the subsidiaries must have adequate technological and managerial capabilities.

(iii) The headquarters must be able to use the admini-strative context for control as well as move from substantive control to context management in relatively short periods of time.

This, in essence, means that in high technology, short product life cycle businesses, the headquar-ters-subsidiary relationships are as much dependent on context management skills as substantive control. We can characterize the substantive task in these MNCs as intense and at the same time the administra-tive system as complex. The nature of the strategic control processes may be represented as follows in Table 3.*

---

*Several examples of well-known MNCs are used to illustrate the point. Some of the data on these firms are based on the authors' interview notes.

For published data see
Brown Boveri & Cie - ICCH  9-378-115, Rev. 3/78.
Texas Instruments, Inc. in Peter Lorange & Richard F. Vancil: Strategic Planning Systems, Prentice-Hall, Inc. 1977, also ICCH 9-172-054, Rev 9/75.
Textraon (A & B), ICCH 9-373-337, Rev. 6/74.
Strategy and Structure at I.T.T., case study published by INSEAD, France.
Philips Audio (A), (B), (C), ICCH
For L.M. Ericsson see Yves Doz, Christopher A. Bartlett, C.K. Prahalad: Managing Host Govern-ment Demands in Multinationals, mimeo, Harvard Business School, 1980.

IBM - authors' interviews.
GM - authors' interviews.

TABLE 3.  The Nature of the Strategic Control Task

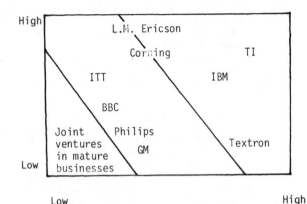

Reliance on
substantive
management
tasks

Reliance on administrative context
management for strategic control

We have focused attention in this paper on strategic
control in MNCs like BBC, GM, Corning, I.T.T. and
Philips. The problems of strategic control in MNCs
like IBM and TI (high technology, short product life
cycle) are rendered more complex due to the twin requirements of significant need and opportunities for
substantive control and at the same time a need for
administrative sophistication. This type of firm
represents a new frontier for research.

MANAGING A JOINT VENTURE IN MATURE BUSINESSES

We have argued that headquarters can use either
substantive control or context management to influence subsidiary strategy and that in high technology, short product life cycle businesses, both
approaches may be needed. The polar extreme of this
situation is the joint venture with a minority position in a mature business. The ability of headquarters to use substantive control is, by definition,
low. If the joint venture partners possess adequate
management and technical skills, substantive control
may be very difficult. At the same time, many of the
influence mechanisms, so central to creative and administrative context, may also be unavailable. The
headquarters may have to work with a few of these
mechanisms only. As a result, minority joint ventures

in mature businesses may be extremely hard to control strategically. The process of influencing these is also an underresearched area.

CONCLUSION

The ability of MNCs to use substantive control over subsidiaries is being eroded as businesses mature and as subsidiaries grow in size and sophistication. The nature of tensions imposed by the external environment also reduces the importance of substantive control as the primary tool. MNCs need to rely ever more on administrative context as a strategic control mechanism.

Creating an appropriate administrative context may be thought of as a process of managing the four orientations - cognitive, strategic, power and administrative - using several influence mechanisms. The influence mechanisms may be classified as people oriented, data management oriented and conflict resolution oriented.

Several advanced technology MNCs may be moving toward a high level of substantive control and high degree of administrative context management. In these cases the problem is not one of a tradeoff between substantive and administrative context for control purposes but of managing both at the same time. This, we believe, is a new frontier for research. The mirror image of this situation is the minority joint venture in mature businesses, equally worthy of research attention.

202

REFERENCES AND NOTES

1. Brown Boveri & Cie, ICCH 9-378-115, Rev. 3/78, case study available from International Case Clearing House, Boston, Mass. 02163.

2. IVECO, unpublished case study, Harvard Business School.

3. Corning Glass Works International (A), (B) and (C), ICCH 9-379-051, 9-379-052, 9-379-053.

4. XYZ Packaging - authors' interview notes.

5. See, for example, DAAG of Europe, ICCH 9-374-037, Rev. 11/77.

6. The concept of dependence or the need for requisite variety as a tool for control is well documented. See, for example, W. Ross Ashby: An Introduction to Cybernetics, University Paperbacks, 1956, and Eric Rhenman: Organization Theory for Long-Range Planning, John Wiley & Sons, 1973.

7. See, for example, Yves L Doz: Government Control and Multinational Strategic Management: Power Systems and Telecommunications Equipment, Praeger, 1979, and Yves L. Doz and C. K. Prahalad: How MNCs Cope with Host Government Intervention, Harvard Business Review, March-April, 1980.

8. Yves L. Doz: Strategic Management in Multinational Companies, (forthcoming) Sloan Management Review.

9. C. K. Prahalad: Strategic Choices in Diversified MNCs, Harvard Business Review, June-July, 1978. Also C. K. Prahalad and Yves L. Doz: Strategic Management of Diversified Multinational Corporations in Functioning of the Multinational Corporation: Its Internal & External Modes of Operation, A. R. Negandi (ed.), Pergamon Press, London, 1980.

10. Yves L. Doz and C. K. Prahalad: Strategic Shifts in Headquarters - Subsidiary Relationships in Multinational Corporations, paper presented at the International Research Symposium on Transnational Corporations, Institute of International Business, Stockholm School of Economics, Stockholm, Sweden, June 2-4, 1980.

11.  There is a line of research which has focused on
     the use of administrative mechanisms to influ-
     ence strategy. For a good example of this line
     of reasoning see Joseph L. Bower: <u>Managing the
     Resource Allocation Process</u>,     Division     of
     Research, Harvard Business School, 1970.

12.  For an elaboration of these concepts see C. K.
     Prahalad and Yves L. Doz: Strategic Reorienta-
     tion   in   the   Multinational   Multidimensional
     Organization,   Joint   Harvard-Michigan   working
     paper, 1979.

# 9  Laurent Leksell:

# The Design and Function of the Financial Reporting System in Multinational Companies

## INTRODUCTION

One of the major problems in the management of head-quarter-subsidiary relationships in Multinational Companies (MNC) concerns the design and management of intra-organizational communication and information systems. The geographical and cultural separation of the foreign entities and the environmental diversity and potential uncertainty facing MNC's can easily create a considerable variation in information needs. As a consequence, there are difficulties in establishing channels and procedures which meet the information needs of both headquarters and the foreign subsidiaries.

The purpose of this paper is to describe and discuss the design and primary functions of the financial reporting system in MNC's. The paper is focused on the role of the system for the management of the headquarter-subsidiary relationships. Relationships are defined herein as instruments for and processes of intra-organizational coordination and control.

## THE FINANCIAL REPORTING SYSTEM

The financial reporting system is an integral part of the international information and control system of the MNC. The flow of information provided by the financial reporting system is used for several purposes and is simultaneously part of the measurement, communication, evaluation, and decision making processes within the firm. It should be emphasized, however, that the financial reporting system is only one segment of these processes.

Institute of International Business, Stockholm School of Economics

A distinction has been made herein between the budget
and planning system and the financial reporting
system. While the first is oriented towards the
future, the latter provides information about the
past. The first system has a planning and coordina-
tive function, while the latter has a more clearly
informational and control function (cf. Östman,
1975).

The financial reporting system is defined as the formal and standardized reports, which primarily but not
exclusively are generated from and based on the
accounting system and which are submitted by the
foreign subsidiaries to headquarters. These reports
usually contain information of both qualitative and
quantitative character. The common feature of reporting systems is that they usually are standardized and
formalized in terms of content, structure, and timing.

The design of a financial reporting system is highly
dependent on company-specific factors. Any reporting
system performs different functions ranging from pure
transfer of information to being a more or less
integral part of the planning, coordination and
control processes in the firm. The design of a particular system is consequently a function of the
information needs of the firm, and the availability
and adequacy of other management systems performing
similar functions.

Although highly specific for individual companies,
designing an international financial reporting system
for foreign subsidiaries requires that certain key
issues be addressed. Among those issues, the central
question for headquarters is how to ensure a timely
flow of financial data from the foreign subsidiaries
which satisfies the needs for information, coordination and control. Once the needs for financial information as well as the primary functions to be performed by the reporting system have been determined,
some other questions remain to be answered. Just to
mention a few;

- How often should the subsidiaries report?
- How standardized should the reporting system be?
  Should it for example be differentiated for
  small and large subsidiaries?
- To whom should the subsidiaries report and who
  should receive the information generated through
  the system?
- What feedback should be given to the subsidiaries and how often should they receive it?
- How capable are the subsidiaries of generating
  and using financial reports and what resources
  do they need to handle the system?

- How to ensure that submitted information is valid and reliable?

The list can easily be made longer. By systematically investigating the design and function of the reporting system in some selected MNC's, we can hopefully clarify some of these questions. An empirically based analysis of different reporting systems, which also takes into consideration company-specific factors, ought to give valuable insights into potential determinants of any system design and function. It also allows for a better understanding of some of the requirements imposed on a system as well as the managerial problems involved.

## RESEARCH METHODOLOGY AND SAMPLE DESCRIPTION

The empriical data for this paper was generated as part of a larger research project called Management of Headquarter-Subsidiary Relationships in MNCs. This project was conducted and financed by the Institute of International Business at the Stockholm School of Economics. (See Hedlund, Leksell and Otterbeck, 1977 as well as the papers by Hedlund, Johansson et. al. and Otterbeck in this volume.)

### Sample of MNC's

The research design was based on comparison of intensive case studies. Environmental and structural variables were controlled to as large an extent as possible. In total, six Swedish multinational corporations were investigated over a three to five year period.

Table 1 describes the sample of MNC's along some summarized key dimensions. The names of the MNCs and the industries in which they operate have had to be kept anonymous.

Product diversification has been classified here according to a simplified version of Rumelt's typology, (1974). In companies I-III one single product line accounts for over 50% of total sales revenues. In company IV the product lines are related, all using a common core technology. Companies V and VI have a highly diverse and unrelated product portfolio.

Technology intensity relates to the technological level and degree of complexity of the major product lines in the MNC's. Barriers to entry are high in companies I, II and III because of capital-intensive production methods and/or the technology level. Barriers to entry exist in company IV and V primarily in the area of distribution and marketing.

TABLE 1    Summary Characteristics of the Sample of MNC's

| Company Characteristics | I | II | III | IV | V | VI |
|---|---|---|---|---|---|---|
| Degree of Diversification | Dominant | Dominant | Dominant | Related | Unrelated | Unrelated |
| Technology Intensity and level of complexity | High | High | Intermediate | Intermediate | Low | Low |
| Barriers to Entry | High | High | Large | Medium | Medium | Low |
| Industry Structure | Oligopoly | Oligopoly | Oligopoly | Oligopoly | Fragmented | Fragmented |
| Intensity and Scope of Competition | High Global | High Global | High Global | High Global | Low Local | High Local |
| Degree of Host Country and Government Influence | High | High | Medium | Medium | Low | Low |
| Total Size in terms of sales | Over USD 2 billions | Over USD 2 billions | Over USD 2 billions | Over USD 1 billion | Over USD 1 billion | Over USD 1 billion |
| Organizational Inter-dependence | High/ Reciprocal | High/ Reciprocal | High/ Reciprocal | High/ Reciprocal | Low/ Pooled | Low/ Pooled |
| Formal Organization Structure | Mother-Daughter | Mother-Daughter | Global Product Divisions | Mother-Daughter | Global Product Divisions | Global Product Divisions |
| International Experience | High/ Medium | High | High | High | High | Medium |

All companies except V and VI operate in oligopolistic markets. Competition is intense and comes primarily from other MNC's operating on a worldwide basis. In companies III and IV price and customer service are the major competitive parameters. Company III is the global price leader in its industry. Companies V and VI encounter competition primarily from local companies operating in each foreign market. In companies I and II the level of the technology and product quality are the most important competitive parameters. All companies manufacture industrial products.

Companies I and II, in particular, are exposed to considerable government influence in their operations. First, their major product lines are of strategic importance for most host countries. Secondly, national or local governments or state owned enterprises are their major customers in most countries. This creates a need to be adaptive to host country demands and has in these two firms led to fairly high subsidiary autonomy (cf. Doz, 1979; see also Hedlund above).

Companies III and IV have a customer structure dominated by a few large private enterprises. Some of their customers are MNC's which use companies III and IV as suppliers on a global basis. Companies V and VI have a fragmented customer structure and little government involvement in their operations.

In addition to the environmental characteristics facing the MNC, internal strategic and structural factors have been taken into consideration. Degree of product and market diversification, size, and organizational structure and interdependence are some of the factors which should influence the design of the financial reporting system and the information and coordination needs that exist in the organizations.

Regarding interdependence, Thompson's classification has been used (1967). Companies I, II, III, IV are faced with reciprocal interdependence while V and VI have less complex forms of interdependence, i.e. pooled. Companies I, II, III, and IV have centralized production and R&D in Sweden. This centralization is explained by substantial economies of scale in production, with a consequent need to concentrate production to a few large manufacturing facilities. From a historical perspective this manufacturing strategy has been followed by many Swedish MNC's. (cf Hedlund above.) Capital intensive production methods and a small home market have in most cases resulted in a high degree of centralization of manufacturing capacity.

The international expansion of these companies has in

general resulted in the establishment of product divisions responsible for manufacturing and R&D and foreign subsidiaries responsible for marketing and sales in their respective countries. Each division and subsidiary operates as an independent profit center reporting directly to corporate management. In general, a foreign subsidiary serves as a single sales outlet for different divisions.

Companies I, II, III and IV all have large internal flows of resources. This is a result of centralized production facilities serving global market needs. The intensity of competition coupled with high inter-dependence calls for close coordination and integration. These forces tend also to require swift communication channels.

There are also pressures for decentralization, reinforced by unstable environmental conditions, barriers to trade and increased host government pressures on and involvement in subsidiary operations. Because of these forces, and for historical reasons, companies I, II and IV have developed "mother-daughter" structures, (Franko, 1976) with independent foreign subsidiaries reporting directly to corporate management. Parallel to the subsidiaries in the hierarchy are product divisions which also report to corporate management.

Company III has developed a structure with global product divisions, where the foreign subsidiaries report to divisional management, partly as a response to competitive pressures and product rationalization. This MNC has a highly standardized and formalized production planning system which has forced the company to adopt a strong product focus at the global level.

Companies V and VI face simpler forms of interdependence; each subsidiary operates independently in its respective host country. Consequently, in these firms there is less internal trade. In fact, companies V and VI are more typical conglomerates.

All firms investigated have a long experience of operating internationally. Company II, for example, established its first foreign manufacturing subsidiary towards the end of the previous century. In all firms foreign sales account for more than 50 percent of total sales. Companies I and VI have internationalized their operations primarily during the 60's and 70's.

## Sample of subsidiaries

Within each MNC, three to five foreign affiliates were selected. Table 2 gives an overview of charac-

teristics of the sample of subsidiaries. The four
most important selection criteria were: 1) Ownership
structure (partly owned or wholly owned subsidiary);
2) Geographic location (developed and less developed
country); 3) Manufacturing subsidiary; 4) Strategic
importance of the subsidiary for the corporation as a
whole as perceived by corporate top management.

The subsidiaries were selected after discussions with
the CEO and corporate controller in each company.
These discussions were undertaken to ensure that the
selected entities were representative samples of the
subsidiaries and joint ventures within the MNC.

TABLE 2   Characteristics of sample of the MNC's foreign
establishments  (n = 27)[1]

|  | Wholly Owned | Joint Venture[2] |
|---|---|---|
| Developed Countries | Belgium, Finland Holland, Spain, United Kingdom; TOTAL: 8 | Canada, Denmark, Spain, U.S.A.; TOTAL: 6 |
| Developing Countries | Brazil only; TOTAL: 7 | Brazil, India, Iran, Venezuela; TOTAL: 6 |

[1] All establishments except Venezuela, one in Spain and
one in Brazil are engaged in manufacturing operations.

[2] The subsidiary is classified as a joint venture herein
if the MNC owns less than 90% of equity.

The primary method of securing data has been through
interviews and the study of internal company documents. All subsidiaries were visited. Research results have frequently been discussed with the respective companies in the form of management development
seminars. A more continous relationship with the
research sites has enabled the research group to
verify further the validity and reliability of the
data.

THE STRUCTURAL DESIGN OF THE INTERNATIONAL FINANCIAL
REPORTING SYSTEM

The design of a financial reporting system can be
described as to the frequency, magnitude, and content
of financial reporting, and the degree of system
standardization. (Cf. also Anthony and Reece, 1975,
and Östman, 1975, for similar classifications). Each
of these characteristics will be discussed below
utilizing the empirical data generated through the
research. As the structural design of any system is

highly dependent on situational factors, it is of particular interest to try to identify and discuss these factors in an attempt to find more generalizable determinants.

## The Purpose of Financial Reporting

The reporting system constitutes in general the major formal channel of communication within the MNC's. It is clear that the system performs several different functions. Besides those noted above, the reporting requirements imposed on foreign subsidiaries also serves as an important educational tool, forcing the subsidiaries to learn more about their business. In one of the MNC's investigated, the educational purpose is explicitly given in the reporting manual. In another firm the primary purpose of the reporting requirements, according to their reporting manual, are

> "...to keep headquarters informed, to be used for consolidation purposes, and to function as reference material about subsidiary operations."

## Frequency of Financial Reporting

As could be expected, the MNC's exhibited differences as to the magnitude of financial reporting. Table 3 shows the total number of formal standardized reporting documents and the different time intervals when they are submitted by the subsidiary to headquarters. In the table the content of the reports has not been taken into consideration.

TABLE 3    Number of Reporting Forms and Frequency ofRegular Financial Reporting by the Foreign Subsidiaries

| Reporting Frequency \ Company | I | II | III | IV | V | VI |
|---|---|---|---|---|---|---|
| Upon request only | 2 | - | - | 1 | | 1 |
| Only annually | 3 | 1 | 2 | 5 | 1 | |
| Quarterly or per tertial | 13 | 37 | 18 | 11 | 55 | 9 |
| Monthly | 1 | | 2 | 7 | 3 | 4 |
| Total numer of formal reports | 19 | 38 | 22 | 24 | 59 | 14 |

As is shown in Table 3, the reporting frequency varies considerably among the firms. The most common reporting frequency was found to be quarterly, with for example company V having their foreign subsidiar-

ies submit 55 different reporting documents each
quarter. Companies I-V require that their subsidiaries submit some reports only once a year. The figures
indicated do not include budgets. The shortest reporting period in any of the MNC's was monthly.
Monthly reports were in general telexed, while the
other reports were submitted by mail.

The magnitude of reporting gives only a partial picture of the MNC's information system. Many of the
communication requirements between headquarters and
the foreign subsidiaries are fulfilled by other
means. The total reporting requirements are also a
function of the design of the reports, how they are
produced, and in particular how they are used.

Factors such as corporate traditions and growth
history, the control philosophy and information needs
of the corporate headquarters, and group consolidation methods explain many of the differences observed
among the firms. All six MNC's consolidate their
accounts and prepare interim financial statements on
a quarterly or tertial basis. This explains why this
time interval tends to dominate the reporting frequency.

The corporate development process and control philosophy influence the design. The relatively high
magnitude of reporting in company V is explained by a
tradition in the firm of relying on formalized and
standardized reports when controlling foreign entities. Company VI on the contrary, has a tradition of
relying on more informal and personalized methods for
obtaining information about, and exercising control
of, their foreign subsidiaries.

Table 4 shows the reporting frequencies of different
items, i.e. the content of the reports. As can be noted from the table, the number of items reported regularly from the subsidiaries to headquarters is
fairly similar among the MNC's. As noted above, the
frequency is largely determined by how often the subsidiaries are requested to close their accounts and
make interim statements. Among these firms this
usually is done every third or fourth month with the
exception of company III, which does it monthly. This
explains the higher reporting frequency observed in
this company.

When interpreting the results shown in tables 3 and
4, one has to keep in mind that one MNC may provide
one type of information in several reports while in
other firms the information might be provided in only
one report. Also, overlaps may exist between different information categories.

Nevertheless, the data in table 4 provides some insights into each MNC's emphasis on different items.

TABLE 4   Reporting Frequency of Different Items

| Item \ Company | Balance Sheet | Income Statement | Specification of Cash and Credit | Inventory | Production Output | Sales per Product | Market Share in Host Country | Performance Review of Subsidiary Managers | Political and Economic Conditions in Host Country |
|---|---|---|---|---|---|---|---|---|---|
| I | 3 | 3 | 3 | 3 | 3 | 2 | 5 | 5 | 3 |
| II | 3 | 3 | 3 | 3 | 3 | 3 | 5 | 5 | 3 |
| III | 2 | 2 | 2 | 2 | 2 | 2 | 2 | 4 | 2 |
| IV | 3 | 3 | 3 | 2 | 2 | 2 | 4 | 5 | 2 |
| V | 3 | 3 | 2 | 3 | 6 | 3 | 6 | 5 | 6 |
| VI | 3 | 3 | 3 | 3 | 6 | 4 | 5 | 5 | 6 |

Key:

1 = weekly
2 = monthly
3 = quarterly or per tertial
4 = annually
5 = not at all
6 = every now and then

In companies V and VI, conditions in the host countries are not reported regularly, while in the other four MNC's this is done monthly or every third to fourth month. This is probably explained by the higher degree of host country dependence in companies I-IV and the stronger host country interest or involvement in the operations of their subsidiaries. Higher host country dependence, as well as intra-organizational interdependence, makes it important that headquarters be informed about local conditions. In the two conglomerate firms, i.e. companies V-VI, the subsidiaries operate fairly independently in their respective host countries. Lower interdependence makes these MNC's as a whole less vulnerable to changes in local conditions compared to companies I-IV.

## Standardization of the Reporting System

Most of the firms investigated have found it necessary to standardize the design of their international reporting system. There is a trade-off involved in this, as the information produced may not always be relevant for the context in which some of the subsidiaries are operating. Company VI is the only MNC which has deliberately chosen not to standardize the system, with the exception of some items required for consolidation purposes. The corporate controller in company VI commented as follows:

> "We allow each product division to develop its own planning and control system, and we request only a few items on a regular basis. We are operating in highly different businesses and it is impossible to fit a single system to the specific needs of each of these businesses. Furthermore, we are strongly committed to a decentralization of divisional operations. They should be free to develop their own systems.... Many of our foreign subsidiaries are the result of acquisitions. The integration of these is usually a long process which should primarily be managed by the divisions".

The situation in company VI illustrates that the development of the international reporting system is a complex function of the MNC's specific business needs and characteristics, and the prevailing corporate control philosophy or style.

The degree of standardization of the international reporting system with regard to format and content was found to be high in all MNC's. All firms have formalized and standardized their international reporting documents on a corporate-wide or divisional basis as to layout, measurement principles and accounting definitions.

Similarly, the reporting requirements were found to differ very little within the same MNC. Only company VI tried to differentiate the magnitude of reporting depending on the size of the subsidiary. Smaller subsidiaries were then required to report less compared to large subsidiaries.

In some of the companies the reporting requirements changed depending on the financial performance of the subsidiary. In one case, corporate headquarters imposed new requirements partly to strengthen control and increase information, but also as a way to communicate dissatisfaction with subsidiary performance. In company II the corporate controller imposed new reports as needed, claiming that these were necessary for consolidation purposes. This explanation was given in order to reduce any resistance among the subsidiaries against increases in their reporting requirements.

In earlier research it has been observed that subsidiaries consider a headquarters request for information as an infringement of their autonomy. (Brooke and Remmers, 1970, pp 53-54.) Similar observations were made in this sample, but these were more the exception than the rule. Instead, subsidiary acceptance of reporting requirements was found to be more strongly related to other factors. These are further discussed below.

Differences in reporting requirements and system standardization were observed to exist between wholly owned and partly owned subsidiaries (joint ventures). The degree of integration of standardized reporting systems in joint ventures was in general lower than in wholly owned subsidiaries. The degree of integration was found to be dependent on the overall integration of the operations of the joint venture with the operations of the MNC as a whole, while the absolute ownership share was of less importance than integration. Pressures on the joint ventures to adopt corporate-wide reporting standards tended, however, to increase if the joint venture was consolidated into group accounts. Consolidation often makes it necessary to ensure that each entity use similar accounting methods and definitions.

Some other aspects regarding standardization of control systems in MNC's have been frequently discussed in earlier research (see for example Zenoff and Zwick, 1969; and Choi and Mueller, 1978). The issue has been to what extent the reporting system used domestically should be differentiated for international operations. The major argument for using similar systems is to reduce costs. The counterargument is usually that the MNC's geographical diversification requires different types of information.

In this sample of MNC's the international reporting
system tended to be fairly similar to the domestic
systems in use. Earlier empirical findings have also
found international control systems to be identical
to domestic systems in many respects (McInnes, 1971,
Bursk et al 1971). One explanation is that the reporting system is often disciplined by the accounting
system. If the accounting system is standardized for
the Group as a whole, this often leads to a similar
standardization of the reporting system.

It cannot be excluded that standardization in terms
of content and format is undertaken by the MNC in
order to improve the information-processing capacity
of the organization. Unstructured and variable information flows can be expected to create information-
processing problems.

Galbraith (1973) has argued that the greater the
degree of environmental change and uncertainty, the
greater is the amount of information that must be
processed by the organization in order to ensure a
given level of performance. It can be hypothesized
that the MNC strives to standardize routine information flows such as those contained in the financial
reports, in order to avoid information overload.
Non-routine information needs are then processed on
an ad-hoc basis and through informal channels. The
research data partly supports this hypothesis, as the
frequency of informal communication in the MNC's was
found to be very high indeed.

The design of the reporting system also tends to be
fairly stable, changing only gradually over time. It
can be hypothesized that it takes time for the organization to identify and correct inadequacies in the
system. Abrupt changes in the design of the reports,
or in reporting frequencies, may have a negative
impact on headquarters' ability to use the subsidiary
reports, and to process, and act on the information
supplied.

One corporate controller commented for example;
(Company II)

> "Parts of our reporting system have been in
> operation since the fifties... I hesitate to
> make major changes, though, as corporate mana-
> gers by now have learned how to interpret and
> use the reports. They know the definitions and
> facts that are hidden behind the figures.."

A further indication of the degree of standardization
and uniformity of the reporting system is the heavy
reliance by subsidiaries on financial reporting
manuals. All companies have manuals describing the
reporting system, time schedules, etc. In no other

cases did the MNC's have such elaborate manuals to guide the subsidiaries as in the area of accounting and financial reporting. The explicitly stated purpose of the manuals is to create a common frame of reference and to ensure comparability between different organizational entities.

## Measurements and Comparisons in the Reports

Another design variable relates to the basis of measurements and comparisons made in the reports. As noted by Brooke and Remmers (1977 p 18), among others the financial reporting system is largely a measurement system and there has to be a basis for some form of comparisons. Measurements are primarily undertaken to evaluate subsidiary performance.

Three different standards can be used for this purpose:

- Predetermined and subsidiary-specific standards, for example subsidiary budgets and specific performance goals.
- Historical standards, for example the past actual performance of the subsidiary.
- External standards, for example comparison against the performance of other subsidiaries and comparison against corporate-wide goals such as general required rates of return and growth rates.

The MNC's investigated tended to use one or more of these bases with different emphasis on each. As an example, subsidiary quarterly reports in one company contain the following measurement standards:

- Actual results for the corresponding quarter the previous year
- Actual results for the quarter in question
- Budgeted results for the quarter in question
- Actual results for the previous quarter
- Budgeted results for the previous quarter

Besides comparisons between budgeted and actual figures, the performance of the subsidiaries is measured against some key financial variables and ratios. These variables, in turn, are compared to some extent with          corporate-wide goals or averages. In the same company as above the variables are:

- Gross profit as a percent of net sales
- Operating income with and without internal financial charges, as a percent of net sales
- Capital turnover
- Return on capital employed.

The other MNC's used similar methods for comparisons although accounting definitions for specific key variables and/or standards varied between the firms. The number of variables also differs among firms. The bases of measurements vary because of differences in corporate objectives and the nature of their specific industries. It is also related to "the prevailing corporate style of control".

## SUBSIDIARY ATTITUDES TOWARDS FINANCIAL REPORTING REQUIREMENTS

The success of any reporting system is highly dependent on the attitudes of the subsidiaries towards the system itself and the reporting requirements. The purpose of this section is to describe the attitudes observed and discuss factors which were found to influence them.

The attitude towards the international reporting system among the foreign subsidiaries were in general found to be positive. The fact that the subsidiaries are favorably inclined towards headquarter control and guidance has also been observed in earlier research (Bursk et al, 1971).

The extent to which the subsidiaries considered the reporting system to be positive or a burden was found not to be linked only to the actual magnitude of reporting (cf Brooke and Remmers, 1970, pp 53-55) but to be more dependent on, first the ease of producing the reports, and, second, on the quantity and quality of the feedback given by headquarters. Feedback can range from very simple questions regarding information contained in the reports to comments about subsidiary strategy and/or host country issues.

It can be hypothesized that the subsidiary acceptance of the reporting system, or even need for central control and guidance is primarily a function of two interrelated factors. First, as described by Hedlund (1980), the foreign subsidiaries often feel alienated from the strategy formulation process in the MNC, and lack direction about their "strategic role". Through feedback on the financial reports, and the potential intra-organizational discussion this feedback may induce, the feelings of alienation are probably lessened. The reporting system itself then becomes an instrument to facilitate headquarter-subsidiary communication.

Feedback may increase the subsidiary's feelings of affinity with the center. Many subsidiary managers use personal contacts and relationships with headquarter executives as means to solve problems and conflicts, and as a political instrument to increase their influence. The feedback given as a result of the reports and related discussions may be used to facilitate and reinforce these relationships. Headquarter feedback then also becomes an instrument to influence the future behavior of the subsidiary, i.e. as an ex ante control instrument.

Most of the subsidiaries investigated requested more feedback on their reports. In particular, requests were made for more specific and timely headquarters opinions and expectations about performance levels etc.

The research results indicate that the feedback given by headquarters is evaluated by the subsidiaries as to both content and source. If the subsidiaries consider any kind of headquarters feedback in response to the reports to be of minor importance, e.g. clarifications on accounting definitions, it tends to be regarded as "low quality" feedback. If the questions concern for example subsidiary performance, strategy or environment and similar items, it is correspondingly considered to be of "high quality". The timeliness of feedback affects "quality" too.

It was observed that subsidiary attitudes regarding feedback quality is also dependent on who gives the feedback. The more credible the source of feedback the more positively it is accepted. The hierarchical position of the executive who gives the feedback is one factor among others affecting source credibility. The research indicates that low quality feedback more often created the feeling that headquarters was intruding into subsidiary affairs.

These results have to be interpreted with some care, however, as attitudes were based on subsidiary managers' subjective comments about the reporting system as well as on their description of the type and frequency of the feedback they received.

It is not surprising, however, to find that subsidiary satisfaction or dissatisfaction with the reporting system is related to how it is used by headquarters. Most of the MNC's investigated used the information in the reports on a "management by exception" basis. Headquarters' responses are triggered by "negative" or "unexpected" information only. The specific acceptance level could vary between subsidiaries within the same MNC, over time, as well as among different headquarters executives using the reports.

Not all subsidiaries appreciated this practice. The financial manager in a subsidiary commented, for example;

> "I have never received any feedback on our reports. Still, we devote an enormous amount of time to produce them. If we don't submit the reports in time, the corporate controller calls us immediately... It's very peculiar."

Another subsidiary manager commented;

> "I don't know if they read the reports at all. As long as I don't hear anything I assume that everything is considered to be OK!"

A correlation, though not a particularly strong one, also observed between the degree of satisfaction with the system, as expressed by subsidiary managers, and the amount of effort involved in producing the reports. Relatively smaller subsidiaries, for example, found the reporting requirements to be more burdensome than did larger entities. As the degree of standardization of the system is high, all wholly owned subsidiaries are in general required to conform to uniform standards regardless of size and resources. Small entities may then not have the resources available to comply with the requirements.

The amount of effort is not necessarily related to the absolute reporting requirements e.g. measured as the number of reporting documents. The time and resources necessary to comply with the requirements are more important. These are influenced among other things by the extent to which the system is computerized.

HOW HEADQUARTERS EXECUTIVES USE SUBSIDIARY FINANCIAL REPORTS

The design and content of the reporting system establish the limits for how the system can be used by headquarters for planning and control purposes. As such it may constrain as well as direct the decision processes. The actual use of the system takes place within these limits and is process-oriented and related to other instruments of communication, coordination, and control employed by the MNC.

Several authors have made a distinction between the design and structure of the system, and the related control processes. (See Anthony Dearden, 1976, Östman 1973 and 1977). Others have noted the multiple functions of the international financial control system, and stress that the "style of control" is more important for the success of the system than its design (Bursk et al 1971 pp 5-6). Brooke and Remmers note that the financial reporting system is only one part of the total control system employed in the MNC. (Brooke and Remmers, 1970, chapter 4.)

As already noted, the subsidiaries' financial reports perform a range of different functions. Important functions are to keep headquarters informed about developments in the subsidiary, and to be used for performance evaluation purposes and as a basis for corrective action. The purpose of this section is to describe how senior headquarters executives use the subsidiary reports to perform these particular functions. Only senior headquarters executives' use of the reports has been investigated, while routine functions of the system, performed by middle- and lower level managers, have not been included.

Senior headquarters executives, e.g. top management and vice presidents in line and staff positions at both divisional and corporate levels, were asked what value they attached to information given in the reports and what types of actions were taken as a result of the reports. Similarly, as described above, subsidiary managers, i.e. subsidiary presidents, vice presidents, and financial managers, were asked about the kind and frequency of feedback they received on their financial reports from headquarters.

Headquarters response takes two major forms. The first and most frequent form is that questions are asked on specific figures and/or accounting definitions employed by the subsidiary to arrive at certain items. These types of questions are highly routine and most often asked by the corporate or divisional controllership function. The primary purpose is to clarify the specific content of the reports. No particular feedback is generally given in these situations.

More interesting are the non-routine questions and feed-back aiming at influencing subsidiary behavior and operations. The research shows, as noted above, that this type of feedback is only given in "exceptional" situations, i.e. when subsidiary operations or performance is reported to deviate from an expected pattern such as a deviation from the budget. The degree of tolerance in these cases was impossible to measure exactly but the data indicate a high degree of variability over several dimensions. The response tends not to be confined to the controllership function, but can be given by different staff or line managers at different hierarchical levels depending on the type of "exception" observed.

The finding that headquarters reacts non-routinely, on the basis of "management by exception" principles has been observed in earlier research. Brandt and Hulbert (1975) found when investigating 63 U.S., Japanese, and European subsidiaries located in Brazil that feedback given on a regular basis was not very common. While one half of the American subsidiaries received a regular response on their reports, only ten percent of the European and Japanese did.

According to the authors, the headquarters of the latter MNC's followed a management by exception policy responding only when they perceived a problem or an opportunity. This observed difference is likely to be the result of more "personalized" control systems found among European MNC's compared to a more structured and formalized approach taken by U.S. MNC's (see also Schollhammer 1971 and Franko 1976 for similar conclusions).

## Top Management Reliance on the Reports

In general, top management in all MNC's receives condensed compilations of data from the subsidiaries. These condensed summaries contained performance figures and are used by top management in several different ways. Among other things, they allow top management to ask subsidiary managers discerning questions about operations. It was also observed that questions on very specific items put pressure on the subsidiary. In one case the CEO asked questions about matters like inventory levels for a minor product, or credit terms for some customer groups etc. These very specific questions created a feeling among subsidiary managers that top management was very well informed about subsidiary operations. It can be hypothesized that these questions have a strong behavioral impact on the subsidiaries.

Most of the senior headquarters executives commented, however, that they did not rely extensively on the formal reports to extract information about subsidiary operations. Instead, informal communication channels were used, e.g. telephone conversations and personal visits. The formal reports thereby become more of a confirmation of information already known. This observation is interesting. The limited use of subsidiary reports among senior executives raises the question of how valuable these systems are for other than routine control purposes.

As intervention by senior executives into subsidiary operations is triggered by exceptional cases and non-routine matters, it can be argued that the standardized information of the type contained in the formal reports does not satisfy the information needs that arise in the exceptional situations. The finding also points at the inherent problem with standardized information systems as to their ability to satisfy the different and changing information needs that are likely to arise in highly diverse and complex organizations like MNC's.

Instead, headquarters staff and line managers create personal and informal communication links with the foreign entities in order to satisfy their information needs. The need for informal information channels can be explained partly by the lack of timeliness of the formal reports, and partly by the inadequacy of their content.

The low reliance by senior headquarters executives on the formal reports has two observed consequences. First, the role of the financial reports becomes limited and of less importance for the coordination and control process. Rather, the reports are primarily used for consolidation purposes and, e.g., for historical analyses of subsidiary operations.

Second, it was found that the increase in the flow of informal information tends readily to be accompanied by increases in the number of "sub-goals" regarding subsidiary performance. The pattern observed was that different headquarters' staff or line executives emphasized different operating areas in their communication with the subsidiaries. For example a divisional product manager may ask about sales levels, a financial manager about increases in inventory levels, and a corporate production manager about waste and material flows. The subsidiaries sometimes interpret these comments and questions as signals about headquarter goals and expectations, i.e. as those items against which subsidiary performance is measured.

As the number of "goals" increases, the likelihood of goal conflicts increases too; e.g., demands for better service and fast deliveries may conflict with demands for lower inventory levels. As a consequence, the subsidiaries easily become confused about headquarters expectations. For example, many subsidiary presidents were not able to state explicitly which performance targets or goals they were expected to fulfill, except what had been agreed upon in the budget that year, even though the corporate controller had a clear perception of the applicable goals.

An executive vice president in company IV commented on the problem as follows;

> "I am very careful in asking subsidiary presidents overly specific questions regarding their operating efficiency. If you repeat the same question too often, they start to believe that it's the most important evaluation criterion. Instead, I try to stick to their budgets and some specific performance goals".

The corporate controller in another of the MNC's commented on the use of efficiency ratios etc. in subsidiary reports;

...."They (ratios) are extremely dangerous. Managers here at the parent company use them to compare one entity with another, or to jump on the subsidiaries. At the same time, many of them don't know how the figures were computed or that comparisons cannot be made between our subsidiaries due to differences in operations and host country practices..."

## SOME DETERMINANTS OF SYSTEM ADEQUACY

Different and mixed headquarters goals and expectations were observed more frequently in companies I, II, III, and IV than in companies V and VI. Several factors seem to account for these differences. Most notable is that the need for integration and coordination is strongest in the first group of MNC's because of their high degree of interdependence, their standardized production methods and the oligopolistic industry structures in which they operate. The more complicated forms of interdependence tend to lead to more complex goal structures involving not only financial criteria but also market and production goals.

In earlier research, Berg (1969) found that conglomerates, with low interdependence among their divisions, tended to give rewards based on financial performance. Similarly, Lorsch and Allen (1973) found that performance evaluation in vertically integrated firms was more informal, often based on operating measures and less directly linked to financial performance than in highly diversified firms.

In a comprehensive study on the use of economic reports, Östman (1973) found that serious difficulties exist both in assessing user needs and in designing reporting systems which fit different needs. It can be assumed that the more complicated coordination needs in companies I-IV create larger differences between user needs, as to system design and content. Less reliance on formal reports and greater reliance on informal communication flows would consequently be expected in firms with more complex forms of interdependence. The research results support this conclusion. In the companies faced with more complex forms of interdependence, i.e. companies I-IV, the degree of informal communication and number of communication links were found to be larger than in companies V and VI.

Organizational structure may also have an impact on the adequacy of the formal reporting system. In companies III, V, and VI the product divisions have a certain freedom to design their own intradivisional systems. Each system can thereby be differentiated and better fitted, within given limits of standardi-

zation, to the environmental situation facing the
divisions. In the MNC's with mother-daughter structures, similar flexibility and adaptation cannot be
achieved with a given degree of system standardization and product diversity.

The differences in type of goals and degree of informal communication between the integrated as compared
to the highly diversified MNC's can also be explained
by advancing a slightly different though complementary hypothesis. More internal transactions as in
companies I-IV can be assumed to increase the difficulties in assessing and measuring subsidiary profitability. The internal product flows will increase
the likelihood that transfer pricing principles will
influence the measurement results and the validity of
profit figures for entities acting as profit centers.
Instead these figures are then replaced by operating
efficiency goals which are less linked to financial
performance.

The adequacy of the subsidiary reports is strongly
affected by measurement problems. Fluctuating exchange rates and different inflation rates among host
countries clearly reduce the validity of the information contained in the reports as well as the comparability among different entities. It cannot be
excluded that this also partly explains why senior
headquarter executives rely on and use the subsidiary
reports to such a small extent.

THE INTRA-ORGANIZATIONAL DISTRIBUTION OF SUBSIDIARY
FINANCIAL REPORTS

In most MNC's the corporate of divisional controller
has the primary responsibility for processing and
collecting subsidiary reports. The corporate controller in companies I, II, and IV restricted as a matter
of corporate policy the amount of subsidiary financial data which was given to the various product
divisions. The product divisions, for example, were
not allowed to receive complete financial statements
and profitability analysis of the subsidiaries.

The corporate controller in company IV commented;

> "We have decided not to give the divisions
> complete financial information about subsidiary
> performance as it would give them an upper hand
> in price and other internal negotiations. Clear-
> ly, they know fairly well the price situation
> in the different markets but to give them
> complete information could make them even
> stronger..."

The research shows that intra-company distribution of
information is or can be used to balance the relative

power between the product divisions with their global
product perspective and the foreign subsidiaries with
their geographical area emphasis. This balance, as
noted before, is particularly characteristic for the
MNC's with mother-daughter structures and extensive
intra-organizational transactions among independent
profit centers. i.e. companies I, II, and IV. Companies III, V, and VI did not follow this practice. As
these MNC's have an organizational structure where
the foreign subsidiaries report directly to product
divisions with global responsibility, they have no
need to balance the information flows.

Prahalad (1976) explored the impact of shifts in
relative power between country managers and product
divisions in an MNC with a global matrix structure.
He concluded that the locus of power influenced the
strategic orientation of the MNC. By managing, among
other things, the information flows, shifts in relative power could be achieved among staff functions,
product divisions and foreign subsidiaries in the
matrix.

In this context the corporate controller in companies
I, II, and IV, i.e. the MNC's with mother-daughter
structures, assumed the role of balancing the relative power among the units by managing their access
to information. It is interesting to note that this
function was performed as a matter of corporate
policy and thereby built into the organizational
design. In these firms, particularly companies I and
II, there are pressures for a dual organizational
focus, similar to those in a matrix. The pressures
for a dual focus are largely the result of the requirements that the firms both be adaptive to host-
country demands and rationalize production and R&D in
order to remain cost competitive. (Cf. Doz 1979).
Through limiting the internal access to information
about other entities, power is balanced and headquarters can more easily differentiate their policies and
actions among different subsidiaries.

In the case of the mother-daughter structure, the
attempts to control the intra-company flows of financial information can also be explained as a desire to
separate independent profit centers and ensure "arm's
length" intra-organizational transfers. With decentralized profit responsibility it has been argued
that negotiated transfer prices lead to greater
market orientation and responsiveness among the
trading parties (Dean 1955). The approach is assumed
to facilitate performance measurement as each party
strives to achieve the required rate of return for
his own entity.

If information about profits etc. is unevenly distri-
buted within the organization, one party can easily

obtain an advantage, e.g. in price negotiations. This is particularly true if the parties are limited in their freedom to trade with external suppliers, as is the case in companies I-IV.

## SUMMARY AND CONCLUSION

The design and functioning of an international financial reporting system is largely dependent on company specific factors. The particular information, coordination and control requirements of headquarters and the prevailing style of control influence the system, as do the existence and adequacy of other administrative systems performing similar functions. The research indicates that particularly the degree of product diversity, organizational structure and interdependence affects system design, function and use.

In more diversified firms headquarters is faced with more diverse information requirements. It then becomes difficult to satisfy information needs and to achieve a congruence between the needs of headquarters and the foreign subsidiaries if the system is standardized as to content, format etc. In this sample the most diversified firms were most inclined to differentiate the design of the reporting system and the reporting requirements among different subsidiaries.

The ability to fit a single reporting system with a given degree of standardization to different requirements is also dependent on the structure of the organization. The research shows that firms with a divisionalized structure are more able as well as more prone to differentiate the design and content of the reporting system than are the firms with a mother-daughter structure.

In an organizational structure with global product divisions, the financial reporting system can be standardized within each division and fitted to divisional needs but allowed to vary among divisions. The mother-daughter structure is less differentiated with regard to products, geographical areas, and markets - i.e., factors which influence information needs - than are divisionalized structures. Consequently, it is more difficult in the mother-daughter structure to differentiate the reporting system and at the same time achieve a given degree of standardization.

Interdependence among entities, in the form of competitive pressures and intra-organizational flows of goods, technology etc. affects system function and use. More complex forms of interdependence create more complex information, coordination and control needs. This places heavier requirements on system functioning and adequacy; a standardized reporting system is less likely to satisfy these different needs.

The research shows that the standardized reporting system satisfies user needs less well in the inter-dependent MNC's operating in oligopolistic markets, compared to the conglomerates operating in fragmented markets. This was illustrated by a tendency among headquarter executives in the more interdependent firms to rely less on the subsidiary reports, and to use them less actively, except for routine matters. As a consequence this group of firms also had more informal communication flows than did the conglo-merates.

In all MNC's there are strong pressures to standard-ize the financial reporting system. These pressures are due to several factors. First, standardized systems are less costly to design and manage than differentiated systems. Second, in all firms the reporting system is used to transmit accounting data used for consolidation of group accounts. Consolida-tion often requires standardized accounting data. Third, it can be hypothesized that the high degree of standardization observed is due to a striving by headquarters to facilitate measurements and compari-sons among subsidiaries. Standardization thereby becomes an instrument for increasing the information-processing capacity of the organization.

This hypothesis is partly supported by the .observa-tion that the design of the financial reporting system is seldom or only gradually changed over time. Changes do not occur until there is agreement that e.g. the timeliness and content of the transmitted information are obsolete. Meanwhile, headquarters executives use other, mostly informal means to satis-fy their information needs.

The research results show that senior headquarters executives primarily act on information about excep-tional or unexpected situations. Standardized systems are less able to supply adequate information of this kind. Inappropriate design and/or conflicting user needs - e.g. standardized data for consolidation purposes versus data transmitting "early warning signals" - may also explain the low system reliance among senior headquarters executives.

It was found that the extent to which the subsidiar-ies considered the reporting requirements to be a burden was not simply a consequence of the actual requirements or the resources necessary to produce the reports. Rather, subsidiary attitudes and accept-ance of the system were found to be related primarily to other factors.

First, the extent to which the subsidiaries themselves were able to use the information generated,
e.g. for their own coordination and control purposes.
If the subsidiaries perceive the information produced
by the system as being valid and relevant, they tend
to be more positive towards the system.

Second, timely and comprehensive feedback on subsidiary reports was found to be positively correlated to
subsidiary acceptance of the system. Most of the
subsidiaries investigated requested more headquarters
guidance and feedback. In particular, goal- and
performance-oriented feedback, as opposed to routine
and unfocused feedback, was requested.

Indirectly, high subsidiary acceptance is positively
correlated with the subsidiaries' own use of the
reports and thus also with the "educational" impact
of the system. In addition the role of the system as
an ex ante control instrument is improved through its
influence on subsidiary behavior.

Finally it should also be noted that the design and
functioning of a financial reporting system cannot be
analyzed, nor from a managerial viewpoint be implemented or improved, without taking into consideration
the environmental and organizational context in which
it is supposed to operate. Consequently, no single
system suits all situations equally well.

REFERENCES

ANTHONY, R.N. and DEARDEN, J., Management Control Systems. Irwin, Homewood, 1976.

ANTHONY, R.N. and REECE, J.S., Management Accounting Principles. Irwin, 3rd ed., Homewood, 1975.

BERG, N.A. What's Different about Conglomerate Management. Harvard Business Review, No. 47, Nov-Dec 1969 pp 112-120.

BRANDT, W.K. and HULBERT, J.M., Communication Problems in the Multinational Corporation: The Subsidiary Viewpoint. American Marketing Association. Combined Proceedings No 37, 1975 pp 326-330.

BROOKE, M.Z. and REMMERS, H.L., The Strategy of Multinational Enterprise. Longman, London 1970.

BROOKE, M.Z. and REMMERS, H.L. ed., The International Firm. Pitman International, London 1977.

BURSK, E.C., DEARDEN, J., HAWKINS, D.F. and LONG-STREET, V.M., Financial Control of Multinational Operations. Financial Executive Research Foundation, New York, 1971.

CHOI, F.D.S. and MUELLER, G.G., An Introduction to Multinational Accounting. Prentice-Hall, Englewood Cliffs, New Jersey, 1978.

DEAN, J., Decentralization and Intracompany Pricing. Harvard Business Review, No. 4, 1955.

DOZ, Y.L., Government Control and Multinational Strategic Management. Preager, New York, 1979.

FRANKO, L.G., The European Multinationals. Harper and Row, London, 1976.

GALBRAITH, J.R., Designing Complex Organizations. Addison-Wesley Publ. Co. Reading 1973.

HEDLUND, G., LEKSELL, L. and OTTERBECK, L., Managing Relationships Between Headquarters and Foreign Subsidiaries. Institute of International Business at the Stockholm School of Economics. RP 77/8, 1977.

HEDLUND, G., The Role of Foreign Subsidiaries in Strategic Decision-Making in Swedish Multinational Corporations. Journal of Strategic Management, Vol 1, 1980, pp 23-36.

232

LORSCH, J. and ALLEN, S.A., Managing Diversity and
Interdependence. Harvard Business School,
Division of Research, Boston 1973.

McINNES, J.M., Financial Control Systems for Multinational Operations: an Empirical Investigation. Journal of International Business
Studies, Fall 1971, pp 11-28.

PRAHALAD, C.K. Strategic Choices in Diversified
MNC's. Harvard Business Review, July-
August 1976, pp 67-78.

RUMELT, R.P., Strategy, Structure and Economic Performance. Harvard Business School, Division
of Research, Boston 1974.

SCHOLLHAMMER, H., Organizational Structures of Multinational Corporations. Academy of Management Journal, September 1971, pp
345-365.

THOMPSON, J.O., Organizations in Action. McGraw-
Hill, New York 1967.

ÖSTMAN, L., Intern Redovisning, Studentlitteratur,
Lund 1975.

ÖSTMAN, L., Utveckling av Ekonomiska Rapporter.
Ekonomiska Forskningsinstitutet vid Han-
delshögskolan i Stockholm.

ÖSTMAN, L., Styrning med Redovisningsmått. Ekonomiska Forskningsinstitutet vid Handelshög-
skolan i Stockholm, 1977.

# 10 Ulf Lindgren and Kjell Spangberg:

# Management of the Post-Acquisition Process in Diversified MNCs

## INTRODUCTION

The purpose of this paper is to explore how international diversified firms manage the post-acquisition process and to discuss the particular management problems which often arise when a foreign acquired company is integrated.

The data on which our observations are made was
collected in two large reseach projects (see Appendix), both of them conducted and financed by the
Institute of International Business at the Stockholm
School of Economics.

The reason for the choice of the topic is that during
the research it was mentioned many times that the
most crucial and difficult part of the whole acquisition process was the integration of the acquired
company into the existing systems and structure of
the acquiring company.

Acquisitions that from the point of view of portfolio
theory could be classified as excellent, have sometimes later on turned out to be failures as a result
of mistakes made during the integration phase. If
analyzed in the context of diversified firms, the
starting point would be to hypothesize that related
acquisitions need a higher degree of integration in
order for the firm to realize the potential synergy
effects that are involved in the process. This could
in its turn create more problems for the integration
work as a higher degree of diversification implies
larger changes in the existing systems, functions and
structure of the acquired company and the risks in

Institute of International Business, Stockholm School
of Economics

connection hereby that the reactions and responses
from management and personnel in the acquired company
could hinder a successful outcome of the process.

## SYSTEMS FOR MANAGING INTEGRATION

The systems for managing integration are used by
corporate managers in order to compensate for their
inadequate understanding of the marketplace. In other
words, the conditions calling for use of administrative systems in unrelated diversifed firms are more
applicable since the product/market relationships are
more complex. It was previously noted that this
additional complexity of the diversified firm historically has led to a divisionalization and also
decentralization of the decision-making. Corporate
management usually does not have first-hand information or knowledge about the marketplace and cannot
make decisions of a strategic nature involving the
business level without relying on the information
from, for example, the financial reporting system,
and hence its ability to affect the business level is
only indirect. Simon (1947) calls this indirect
influence procedural in contrast to substantive
influence. In the unrelated diversified firm, corporate management's understanding at the business
level is less than in related diversified firms, and
therefore it is not plausible that substantive influence will be exerted to the same degree. One would
also expect that corporate management relies more on
integrative devices or systems to get procedural
influence. This influence is not concerned with
substantive issues but rather with manipulation of
the decisional context, or the perceived rules of the
game. Normann expresses it in the following way:

> The systems affect behavior in the organization
> through influencing flows of information, focus
> of perception, resources for problem-solving, as
> well as individuals' and groups' ambitions and
> perceptions regarding desirable behaviors.
> (Normann, 1975, p. 153)

For similar descriptions, see Bower (1970) or Stymne
(1971). The study by Cyert and March (1963) also
supports the hypothesis that unrelated diversifed
firms need more communicating devices between different levels, since the cognitive range of managers
becomes more limited when the degree of diversity
increases.

The planning and control system is one of the means
through which corporate management controls the
business units and through which the demands on
responsible managers are communicated. In this cate-

235

gory there exist, of course, many different devices
which play a significant role in the relations
between corporate level and the management of the
acquired company. Lorsch and Allen (1973) found that
managers perceived the budgeting and budget reviews
to be among the most valuable devices for managing
diversity. Therefore it seems likely that the budget
process plays a more important role in unrleated
acquisitions.

Corporate staffs usually play an important role in
the planning procedure (Rossotti, 1968; Steiner,
1969). Since unrelated business firms usually do not
have large corporate staffs, it seems unlikely that
planning is an important tool for post-acquisition
integration in unrelated business firms.

The next system which corporate management can use to
manage the acquired company is the reward system, by
which is understood the rewards and sanctions corporate management can employ to reinforce a behavior
which is consistent with the objectives and the
prevailing values. There are many different variables
corporate management can manipulate or intervene with
in the reward system: changes in compensation policy,
prestige, status, self-esteem and external recognition. Mace and Montgomery (1962) found in their
research that poor handling of the acquired companies' executives in the integration process caused
several failures.

Salter (1973) argues that the reward system must be
tied to the strategy of the firm. Since unrelated
business firms are more likely to acquire companies
without regard to the existing portfolio of business,
and instead to focus on financial characteristics, it
is plausible that they use at least the financial
reward system more frequently as a control and integration mechanism. Berg (1965) also made this finding
in his study.

Communication systems are sometimes used to denote
the exchange of information of systems outside the
planning and control system. It seems likely that the
informal communication system is of greater importance in unrelated diversified firms since the management philosophy tends to favor informality and to
avoid bureaucratic "paper mechanisms".

Roy Ash (in Bower, 1977) said:

> We elect to manage by not managing. We have one
> rule - there is no rule. And our policy is we
> have no firm policy. What is there left for man-
> agement to do? The Management of capital. We are

decentralized, period. We grew up decentralized. We leave acquired companies alone because it is ridiculous to make everything conform to one pattern. You destroy everything that was there.

Other mechanisms for corporate mangement to integrate acquired companies are <u>task forces</u>, <u>integrating roles</u> and <u>departments,</u> <u>rules</u>, <u>direct contacts</u>, and <u>board meetings</u>.

## SOME OBSERVATIONS

There are of course several ways of analyzing and describing the post-acquisition process. (Or what is generally called the integration process.) The major issues could be summarized as how to manage integration of an acquired company into the structure, systems, climate etc. of the acquiring company, and what tools or devices are being used to succeed in this. It is possible to list several hundred such tools and devices. This is, however, not the purpose of an article of this kind. Instead, we have chosen to concentrate on a limited number of important issues that we have been able to extract from the research work and from more informal discussions with a number of Chief Executive Officers (CEOs) in large diversified companies. In the next section we will try to draw some general conclusions regarding ways of of improving post-acquisition management efficiency.

Here we will focus on some issues of major importance in the integration process. First we will discuss different <u>ways of initiating and implementing the integration process</u> in terms of magnitude of integrating devices used and the time period after which they are imposed on the acquired companies. Second, we turn to the <u>response</u> of the acquired company to the integration effort – this may differ widely from close operation to persistent resistance to all attempts at integration into the acquiring company. We then discuss effects of changes inherent in an acquisition on the existing group companies – the (possible) culture shock that could occur as a result of the mixture of organizational cultures and different management styles, the necessity of preventing key personnel from leaving the company, the danger in failure to understand the nature of the business of the acquired company, and finally, the necessity of developing an exit strategy in the case of a potential failure or disaster.

## Magnitude and time needed

A crucial part of the integration process is how the integration is managed and when it is initiated in

terms of harmonization of administrative systems,
changes in the composition of the management group
etc. By analyzing research cases we have been able to
distinguish certain patterns regarding the manner in
which the integrative work has been carried out
(described in terms of magnitude and timing of initiating and handling the integration process).

## The Blitzkrieg

Here the integration work starts immediately when the
deal is concluded - administrative routines of the
acquiring company are fully adopted by the acquired
company after a very short time. Problems have arisen
in several cases where the reception has been less
than enthusiastic in the acquired company. An example
illustrates this:

Company A bought another company in Holland. Within a
week after the deal was concluded, A's so called
"Tiger Gang" arrived at the Dutch company and started
working on adapting the acquired company to the use
of A's computerized reporting and planning systems -
this was completed within a couple of weeks' time. In
connection with the introduction of A's administrative routines, meetings and seminars were held with
the participation of relevant personnel, where they
were introduced to and trained in the use of the
systems.

In a questionnaire survey,* it turned out that in
38 % of all cases the introduction of administrative
routines has been carried out within a month's time
after the take-over. Within the category classified
as successful acquisitions the corresponding percentage was 42 %.

If one looks at the nature of the acquired company,
it is hard to find any significant difference between
those cases when the acqustion is related, dominant
or unrelated (that is the case when the acquiring
company is a conglomerate).

The Blitzkrieg seems to be equally common in all
types of acquisitions with the exception of unrelated
acquisitions. Here Blitzkrieg is more frequently used
as means of integration. When and where Blitzkrieg is
used seems to be very much the result of different
management styles and of the traditions prevailing in
the acquiring company rather than of any other
factor.

For various reasons the integration of operating
systems (production, marketing, R&D, etc.) is not

*See Appendix

likely to be carried out as fast as the introduction of new administrative routines. However, in several cases, this more complex part of the integration process has been found to be initiated shortly after the actual take-over. No difference was found between integration processes of different complexity (i.e. related-unrelated).

## The Trojan Horse

A specific case of Blitzkrieg is what we have chosen to call "the Trojan Horse" - the case when the acquiring company appoints a strong person as new managing director of the acquired company more or less immediately after the completion of the acquisition agreement. He has been assigned a certain time period to "settle down" in the new company and to prepare personnel and managers for what is to come. When this initial "honeymoon" is over, the integration is started up in full force to its full extent.

We have been able to observe serveral cases of "the Trojan Horse". One should bear in mind, however, that although a new managing director has been appointed by the acquiring company, this does not necessarily imply that he is the same person who later on initiates and manages the integration process - in many cases the responsibility lies with a Divisional Executive President or a Group Executive Vice President (president of a unit consisting of several divisions).

## Infiltration

As in the case of the Trojan Horse, the purpose of "infiltration" is to prepare the ground for a high degree integration of the acquired company. For several reasons, most often caused by a strong resistance to the purchase among one or several key persons in the acquired company, the aim of the acquiring company is to handle the process carefully, that is, not as in a Blitzkrieg, in which all potential opposition by those affected in the acquired company is ignored. This can be done in several ways:

- Either by removing people judged to be a risk. (However, there is a danger that others who are also negative to the acquisition will be "pulled along" and resign - the so called "House of Cards Effect". See page 17.)

- Or by placing the acquiror's own people in several positions in the company, either as replacements for persons judged necessary to remove (see above), or simply in newly created positions considered crucial from an integration point of view, i.e. plant manager, production manager or financial manager.

Their task often seems to be to make the policies, routines, and also the management style of the acquired company as similar as possible to those of the acquiring company.

It appears as if infiltration has been used as a tactic of integration in the cases we have studied. Infiltration is part of a well planned process as compared to the use of a Trojan Horse, where much of the influencing activity is left to the initiatives of the appointed MD.

It deserves mentioning that infiltration very rarely occurs in a pure form - in many cases this tactic is more connected with what one could classify as co-operation. Nor have we been able to find any case where infiltration has been used in an unrelated acquisition. This of course is not totally un-expected - an unrelated acquisition by definition has no need for integration in the areas of production and distribution (but does have it in finance and administration).

The use of an infiltration tactic also seems to be more frequent where the acquisition has been made in a country where the acquiring group was previously represented by a subsidiary. An example:

Company B acquired a local manufacturing company in France. The main objective for the acqusition was to create a platform for an expansion of the group's activities in Europe. No immediate action was taken, but a manager from the acquiring group was appointed vice president in the acquired subsidiary. The president, who was the former owner of the French company, was not informed of the strategic plan for the subsidiary, which implied the transfer of technology from the acquiring company and in the long run to drop the present activities (even if they were related to those of B). Half a year after the takeover, the president of the subsidiary was being informed of parts of the total strategic plan by top management in B. They let him know that his vice president was to have the responsibility for the implementation of the plan. It was now too late for the president to refuse to accept the plan, and he cooperated in gradually handing over the overall responsibility for the subsidiary to his vice president.

## Cooperation

This is the ideal case in the eyes of most managers - active cooperation by both parties aimed at achieving all potential synergetic effects as soon as possible at integrating the acquired company into the organizational structure and the administrative systems of the acquiring company. This entirely positive attitude does not usually prevail; even when it does, it is seldom used in the most effective way. One may often see tendencies for the acquiring company to try to create a cooperative climate through various actions:for example, the formation of joint merger committees and joint training programs focusing on project work, and the use of task forces.

Whether a cooperative climate will result is evidently dependent on how the acquisition has been made. If the acquisition is of a hostile nature, i.e. by making a hostile tender offer to the shareholders of the acquired company, there is good reason to expect difficulties in establishing a cooperative climate.

In certain countries, the fact that the acquisition has been made by a foreign company also creates distrust and uncertainty - this issue was often mentioned in interviews with people in the acquired companies. In some cases this had been countered with incentives and massive information to personnel in the acquired company, but it is still an obstacle to efficient and successful management of the integration process. We will return to this topic under the section "Responses".

Company C succeeded in an integration program after having acquired a relatively large US company with a large number of overseas subsidiaries. The major problem in the integration was merging the subsidiaries of C and the US company in each country where they were both represented. A starting point for the program was the principle of "equal treatment", regardless of prior company affiliation; i.e. C's own subsidiaries were not to be favored when merged with the US company subsidiaries if this was not justified for pure business reasons. By successfully communicating this principle to people in the US company, these also turned out to be very cooperative. The integration work was organized in joint committees consisting of representatives from both companies, where competence and specific knowledge determined who was appointed to the committees. During the integration work internal education programs were held for participants from both companies - the programs included comprehensive project work on future strengths and weaknesses of the merged organization, as well as a review of experiences with both

the past and ongoing merger activities to form future
acquisition guidelines for the Group.

The example shows at least two very important parts
of the post-acquisition process: first, the necessity
of communicating intentions, and second, the need for
using integrative devices in order to break down
resistance to change from persons in both companies.

## Allies

The feeling of being allied with the acquiring
company is not a frequent one, but has been identified during the research in those cases when the
acquired company itself actively has sought to be
acquired for various reasons. For example, the
company may have insufficient financial resources;
the high cost of capital may cause a drain on limited
financial means and thereby made it desirable to find
a cash-rich acquirer. Other deficiences in the acquired company may include inadequate facilities,
deficient raw material supply, obsolete technology or
marketplace problems.

The situation is different in these cases as seen
from the acquirer's point of view - if it has accepted the role of a "liberator", it is also in a position to demand much more from the target company
concerning the latter's participation in and attitudes towards the integration work.

## Do Nothing ("Leave Alone")

The most limited commitment (in reality no involvement at all) is of course the "do nothing" alternative. The acquirer has chosen to let the acquired
company continue its own life without any interference in its operations at all.

This approach is most common in unrelated acquisitions, where there is no need for integration of
operating systems. It is also used by acquiring
companies when the acquired company is a small
family-owned company, where interference in the
business could easily lead to a loss of managment,
management often consisting of one entrepreneur.

## Management of the Post-Acquisition Process

It should be noted, however, that although no integration of operating systems took place, the administrative systems of the acquired company were
altered more or less thoroughly to correspond to the
ones used in the acquiring MNC, i.e. planning and
control systems were changed or newly established in
the acquired subsidiary.

## Responses by Acquiree

We may observe different forms of introducing and
conducting the work of integration in terms of the
magnitude of integrative work and the time consumed
in undertaking the whole process; similarly, we may
note different patterns of response by the acquired
company to integration plans and integrative work. By
response is meant attitudes, which to a greater or
lesser degree are expressed in actions, and also
specific steps as a direct consequence of integrative
efforts by the acquiring company. It appears as if it
is precisely the character of these responses which
is most critical to the success or failure of integration. One CEO put it this way:

> It is really not a matter of plans or tactics;
> it is simply a problem of managing people and
> people's attitudes towards changes that we have
> judged necessary to undertake.

From the research data, we have tried to classify
different types of responses according to a scale
varying from positive receptiveness to integrative
efforts, to cases of open opposition on specific
matters.

In the questionnaire study (which is not the basis
for the special cases reported here), it was indicated that the acquisition was favorably received by
management in 95 % of the cases and by other employees in 81 % of the cases. There was no significant differences here between domestic and foreign
acquisitions.

## Liberation

As was mentioned in the section on Magnitude and
Time, an acquisition may be initiated wholly by the
company subsequently purchased, which itself is
actively seeking a buyer for various reasons. Responses to integrative efforts will then be positive.
To take the following example:

A small family-owned French company had been looking
for a buyer for over a year. One reason was that
profitability was gradually declining, mainly because
the market for the company's products in France was
stagnant. Another reason was that the owners, who had
certain financial and tax planning needs, saw more
value in selling the company than, for example, in
trying to gc public, and they realized that being
acquired was the only way for the company to obtain
the financial capital and resources needed to fund
its future growth and expansion. They approached
Company C, a diversified Swedish multinational

company that through one of its divisions had operations in the same business segment as the French
company. It was decided by C, however, to "wait and
see", and eventually offer a lower price. This also
proved to be a successful policy - after another half
year the French company was bought by C. The integration process started almost immediately with the
active involvement from the French side.

Acquisitions initiated for motives of liberation are
becoming more and more common as divestments are
becoming a more frequently used tool of actively
managing the business portfolio, also in an international company (Boddewyn, 1979; Lindgren/Spångberg,
1980); the main reason is here often financial, but
other factors may affect these decisions as well.
Often a firm will divest a profitable subsidiary that
does not fit - a strategic dimension or organizational and personal factors may play a part in the
decision.

## Cooperation

As mentioned previously, a cooperative climate is
most ideal for conducting a process of integration.
Just as the acquiring company tries to get the acquired company to cooperate in the work of integration, so can the response by the latter company be
one of actively seeking collaboration. If this is to
occur, obviously some incentive for the acquired
company must exist or be created. Steps cited in the
research as important for establishing a cooperative
climate (or avoiding a more hostile response from the
acquiree) will be discussed further in the concluding
remarks.

## The Peace Movement

In some cases one could find what could be called a
"Peace Movement" - that is, an unspoken disagreement
with the measures undertaken, but without resistance
to changes or other forms of more or less active
resistance to the process of integration. One integrative device used in many cases was a strong CEO in
the acquired company, who through actions and support
gets his subordinates to accept what has happened and
to cooperate with the acquiring company to achieve
successful integration. However, where there is a
peace movement, there is also a great danger of a so
called "house of cards" effect: if one or more key
people depart or stay on but oppose the integrative
effort, they can get others to join them and thus
cause great damage to the ongoing business.

## The Collaborators

In many cases where the overall attitude to the

acquisition is negative, there are one or several persons who perceive the acquisition as beneficial for the acquired company. They usually start exhibiting their favorable view of the acquisition to representatives of the acquiring company at an early stage, such as during negotiations or closer study of the potential acquisition by persons from the potential buyer. These so called collaborators are running a big risk, however; if the acquisition falls through, they have often played their hands and have to live on in disgrace among their colleagues whom they previously ignored (assuming they are allowed to do even this - collaborators are often fired if the acquisition does not go through).

An example:

Company D was negotiating with Company Z on the purchase of one of Z's divisions. Z had initiated the negotiations. For various reasons, however, Z soon began getting doubts about whether it really wanted to sell. Z then began proposing alternatives to a sale, such as formation of a joint venture or some form of organized cooperation in selling. But one of Z's managers (the finance director) strongly favored selling the division on the ground that the potential synergy effects were too great to be ignored. He argued for his position in opposition to that of his own CEO and in full support of the reasons given by D's representatives. After a while, Z decided at any rate to reject the purchase offer for reasons that still remain rather unclear. Six months later, D decided to make a hostile tender offer to Z's shareholders. After various happenings, success was achieved, and D assumed ownership of Z. Z's reaction was extremely negative - virtually all executives left after a while, and finally Z's former head office was closed and moved to D. One of the few Z managers left was the former finance director - he was also appointed interim president for the time required to prepare for the final integration of Z's operations into D's organizational structure.

## The Resistance Movement

More outspoken resistance than what was termed the Peace Movement can arise as a result of a Blitzkrieg or of a "do nothing" policy of the acquiring company. Resistance may be of a more or less active variety - in certain extreme cases one may even speak of <u>Guerrilla Warfare</u>. If this kind of resistance occurs, the acquisition almost always fails - the company must be resold or disposed of in some other way. It is very hard to find replacements for all the people who are unwilling to cooperate in the integration. Resistance has been observed primarily when the nature of the

acquisition was <u>hostile</u> or <u>unrelated</u> (in the latter
case when the approach to integration was Blitzkrieg
or Do Nothing in character).

## The Cinderella Syndrome

An acquisition not only affects the managers and
other employees of the acquired company - obviously,
there will also be reactions among the people in the
existing group. Particularly in companies with an
aggressive acquisition policy, there may be feelings
of insecurity and of inability to influence what
happens to one's own company within the sphere of
operations of the entire group. What we may call the
"Cinderella syndrome" may arise. (This concept was
coined by representatives of Company C during internal training programs designed to collect experience
from past acquisitions; the programs were arranged
for personnel several of the companies recently
acquired.) And there is also a risk that this syndrome could grow in significance throughout the group
as each company with the passage of time becomes a
part of the "old" group. The feeling develops that
comparisons are being made among companies in the
group. This is a new experience for the older group
companies, and there may be a widespread sense of
insecurity among employees who feel powerless to
influence the results of these comparisons.

The problem becomes particularly serious if most of
the expansion takes place within one division or
group, while other units do not expand nearly so
much.

Lack of knowledge of the overall group policy and
lack of understanding of the aims and reasons for
further expansion appear to be a contributing cause
of the Cinderella syndrome. Ways to solve this
problem include better communication of business
policies, exchanges of personnel among divisions, and
"interlocking directorates" (see Hedlund, 1979).

## The House of Cards Effect

As previously stated, there have been cases where one
or more key persons have left the acquired company,
either directly after the acquisition or after a
period of more or less open disapproval of the acquisition or of the manner in which the work of integration is conducted. In related acquisitions, there
is a great need to achieve operational synergy - this
may be done either by having integration play a
constructive role (cross fertilization) or by looking
for opportunities for cost reductions. Examples of
the latter are cutting the joint sales force, merging

administrative resources and thus avoiding dupli-
cation of procedures, using common production lines
to achieve economies of scale, etc. This often involves more or less major intrusions into the terri-
tory of other people and sometimes even the removal
of existing employees. The realization that a similar
fate is in store for them can induce many managers to
leave the company "ahead of time" and thus leave
behind a vacuum which may be difficult to fill. The
situation becomes particularly grave when these key
people also take one or more loyal subordinates with
them. The end result can be a house of cards effect,
with the acquiring company being left to manage and
run the acquired one more or less by itself. This can
be a disastrous blow to the chances for survival; it
may lead to lost customers, nondeliveries, credit
cut-offs, and many other consequences. One way successfully used by several companies to avoid a house
of cards collapse is first to try to find potential
troublemakers as soon as possible (preferably right
during the purchase negotiations) and then try to get
these people to leave voluntarily (by rewarding them
with sufficiently large severance payments). The next
step is to have a thorough talk with all the remaining managers to ensure that they stay on at least
long enough to permit replacements to be appointed
and trained.

## The Culture Shock

We have seen "culture shocks" occur for several
different reasons, but basically they all arise from
differences in management styles and in internal
company cultures between the acquirer and the acquiree. Changes in one or both styles are often
necessary; and tend to take place anyhow over time.
In many cases it is rather obvious which of the
parties will have to "step aside" - if the acquiree
is small in size compared to the acquirer, it is
rather unlikely that the latter would be severely
affected by the management style and çorporate culture prevailing in the acquiree prior to the merger.
If the acquired company is large and of major importance to the acquiring company, there seems to be a
tendency to change also at the former. (The results
referred to here are tentative - the area is, however, extremely important and interesting and is
worth more thorough studies of more sociological
character - see Pettigrew, 1977.)

One could, however, distinguish different patterns in
the cases under study. These are determined by how
and to what extent management style and company
culture have changed in the acquiring and the acquired company respectively.

## The Crushed Culture

Compay A, as mentioned earlier, has a policy of fast
and substantial integration work. They seek not only
to adapt administrative and production routines to
those of the acquirer, but at the same time to
change the existing management style to resemble A's
own, (which is characterized by a high degree of
formalization and narrowly defined areas of responsibility). And they try to do all this as fast as
possible.

In the acquisitions by A which were involved in the
study, the earlier culture has had to "give itself
up" and has been replaced entirely by A's company
culture.

A crushed culture does not necessarily have to lead
to negative effects - in many cases the companies
adapt to the new pattern, and we have even been able
to find tendencies toward actively imitating the
style of the acquiring company (Hedlund, 1977).

## The Balanced Culture

A balanced culture is not as frequent for the simple
reason mentioned earlier: it requires that the
companies be of approximately the same size so that a
change in management styles may occur on both sides -
the situation is different in pure mergers, where the
companies by definition are of the same size.

A Group Executive Vice President commented as
follows:

> The task of blending two different cultures and
> the management of resistance to necessary
> changes in the two organizations have for me
> created the two most difficult problems during
> the whole acquisition. My aim is to develop an
> "optimal" company culture, where the best parts
> of the two existing cultures together would
> create a new and better culture, and also a new
> and better management style.

## CONCLUSION

Every acquisition program is unique regarding both
acquisition motives and the implementation of the
post-acquisition process. The most important factor
when it comes to post-acquisition management seems to
be the ability of managing people rather than systems
or structure. In their answers during interviews,
CEO's in all types of firms (diversified as well as
single business firms) mention this phenomenon as the
single most important issue to bear in mind when

preparing and undertakning necessary integrative measures (Lindgren, 1978).

In research made on the management of headquarter-subsidiary relationships in MNCs, it became clear that some MNCs substituted formal administrative systems to a large extent by using a lot more of travelling, telephone calls and other communication channels. When following up this observation by comparing to what extent existing formal administrative systems were being used to integrate the new subsidiary, it turned out that the general pattern in MNCs also was followed in the integration process - i.e. a highly formalized company tended to integrate newly acquired subsidiaries by using the existing formal systems etc.

We have tried to point to some issues where this problem arises - the necessity of a careful judgement before deciding on the magnitude and timing of the integration work, how people in the acquired companies might react to the actions taken by the acquiring company, the danger of losing key personnel, the potential risk of some key persons starting a mass movement that could prove extremely difficult to stop, and also some possible outcomes of the eventual struggle that could occur as a result of mixing two different company cultures.

In analysis of the underlying explanatory factors as to why and how different effects occur, it seems likely that the degree of diversification per se does not explain, for example, the method used to integrate the new company into the existing systems and structure. We have been able to note that unrelated acquisitions tend to be integrated very rapidly. When it comes ro related acquisitions, the situation is somewhat different - here there is a need to integrate operations, which requires the use of different integrative devices, such as imposing a new production planning system, a common accounting system, etc. But on the other hand, the response by the acquired company does not necessarily become more hostile, even though the integration impact is larger in the case of integration of operations. The benefits which the acquired company believes may occur as a result of the integration process, seem to be more important than possible negative attitudes towards the fact that the company is no longer independent. Also, as has been shown in research studies (e.g. Berg, 1971), the size of the corporate office is larger in related business firms than in conglomerates, thereby allowing a more thorough effort by the acquiring company when it comes to assigning people to the job of integrating the new company - it im-

plies considerable opportunities for working with
task force committees, common project work, helping
the new company to adapt to systems that are imposed
on it etc. It should be noted, however, that excep-
tions from this rule are very common - in many cases
the situation is rather the opposite, that is, the
corporate office of the related business firm is much
smaller than the one of the conglomerate. In these
cases, however, <u>divisional</u> offices and staffs are
much larger. In related business firms having small
corporate offices, Group Executive Officers take over
a lot of the responsibilities that earlier were
carried out by the CEO himself. (On the subject of
Group Executive Officers, see Oreal, 1980.)

Another factor of great importance is the degree of
interdependence in production between the acquired
and the acquiring company - a high degree of interdependence leads to a more comprehensive integration
effort so as to achieve operating synergy from economies of scale in production, materials handling,
ware-housing, etc.

We have also noted quite a few cases where the lack
of knowledge of the acquired business has caused
severe problems when trying to manage the post-
acquisition process. This seems to evoke feelings of
uncertainty and mistrust at the acquired company. Of
course, it could also prove disastrous in the future
management of the company. A specific problem here is
the tendency of the new owners to believe they understand the business well enough to reorganize it -
without this being the case.

A general problem in all types of merger activities is
the workload assigned to managers responsible for the
acquisition. Simultaneously, working on the integration process and conducting the ongoing business
activities puts a great strain on these managers in
their attempts to allocate their time optimally (see
Lidén, 1978).

To conclude, it is hard to find any clearly distinguishable pattern in integrative processes. The
problems are unique in each case and the specific
situation may require different kinds of unique
solutions. Our purpose has been to show broadly
defined patterns that may explain some major parts of
an integration process.

MANAGERIAL IMPLICATIONS

The integration of acquired companies in a diversified firm must be guided by a carefully planned and
controlled process aiming at creating the necessary

means in order to establish a perception of legitimate changes in the structure and systems of the
acquired company.

Management must realize that in order to integrate an
acquired company, the specific characteristics of the
acquired company and the nature of the acquisition
process must be taken into account. This implies
careful planning of the integration process already
in the pre-acquisition period so as to be able to
effectuate directly after the acquisition agreement
is concluded.

An acquired company may or may not be in the same
growth stage as the acquiring company. It has been
shown that administrative systems and management
style tend to change in connection with the increasing degree of diversification of a firm - higher
degree of diversification leads to higher degree of
structural complexity and thereby creates a need for
a higher degree of complexity in the control and
administrative systems. If the acquired company has
had a lower degree of structural complexity and
thereby less complex systems, this must be recognized
when establishing how the integration should be
conducted.

Once this has been identified, arrangements must be
made in order to support the management of the post-
acquisition process which correspond to the needs of
the specific situation.

The more related an acquisition, the higher is the
degree of integration needed in order to benefit
from potential synergetic effects as a result of the
acquisition. This implies that responses from managers and personnel in the acquired company may be
more negative if the integration is not carried out
in a proper way.

If the acquired company is located in another
country, the acquiring MNC must recognize the specific circumstances arising from what one could call a
"foreigner syndrome" in the acquired company.

APPENDIX

Research Methodology and Design

The empirical data for this study was generated from two different research projects, both of them conducted and financed by the Institute of International Business at the Stockholm School of Economics.

The first research project is called Management of Strategic Changes which is an intense study of a limited number of firms (two). Selection criteria were the following: the variables involved in the work were strategic changes and their management, structural arrangements, the environment and the strategic situation of the firm. A considerable number of in-depth interviews were made at the two companies combined with a comprehensive study of written documents and other material of both external and internal nature.

The study was conducted by Kjell Spångberg and Jan-Erik Vahlne.

The second project is called International Acquisitions. The research design in this project is based on comparative case studies. Environmental and structural variables have been controlled to as large extent as possible. In total, five Swedish multinational corporations were investigated in which totally eleven acquired subsidiaries were being studied. This study was combined with a written enquiry to 25 Swedish companies which have acquired at least one company in Sweden and one abroad since 1977, when the questions were concerned with both the planning, implementation and integration of the acquired companies and relating this to contingency factors both at the acquiring company's level, as well as at the acquired company.

Project leader is Ulf Lindgren.

252

REFERENCES

BERG, N., The Allocation of Strategic Funds in Large Diversified Companies. Harvard Business School, 1965.

BERG, N., Corporate Role in Diversified Companies. Working Paper, Harvard Business School, 1971.

BIGGADIKE, R., Entry Strategy and Performance. Doctoral dissertation, Harvard Business School, 1976.

BODDEWYN, J.J., Foreign Divestment: Magnitude and Factors. Journal of International Business Studies, Vol. 10, No. 1, pp. 21-27, Spring/Summer 1979.

BOWER, J., A Note on Managing Large Diversified Firms. Harvard Business School, 1977.

CHANDLER, A., Strategy and Structure, MIT Press, 1962.

HASPELAGH, P. and BERG, N., Diversification and Mergers: Some Trends and Results. Working Paper, Harvard Business School, 1979.

HEDLUND, G., Managing Headquarter-Subsidiary Relationships as a Matter of Style. IIB Research Paper 77/9, 1977.

HEDLUND, G., The Role of Foreign Subsidiaries in Strategic Decision-Making in Swedish MNCs. IIB Research Paper 79/5, 1979.

HOVERS, J., Expansion through Acquisition. John Wiley & Sons, 1975.

LAWRENCE, P. and LORSCH, J., Organization and Environment. Division of Research, Harvard Business School, 1967.

LEKSELL, L., Financial Reporting Systems. Abstract 1980 from doctoral thesis forthcoming, Stockholm School of Economics.

LINDGREN, U. and SPÅNGBERG, K., Corporate Acquisitions and Divestments - the Strategic Decision-Making Process. Paper presented at the Third Seminar on Strategic Management, EIASM, 1980.

253

LINDGREN, U., International Human Resource Management. IIB Research Paper 78/8, 1978.

LORSCH, J. and ALLEN, S., Managing Diversity and Interdependence. Harvard Business School, 1973.

MACE, M. and MONTGOMERY, G., Management Problems of Corporate Acquisitions. Division of Research, Harvard Business School, 1972.

MADSEN, O., The Post-Acquisition Management of Diversifying Companies. Working Paper, University of Aarhus, 1979.

MEEKS, G., Disappointing Marriage: A Study of the Gains from Merger. Cambridge University Press, 1977.

NORMANN, R., Skapande Företagsledning (Creative Management). Aldus, Malmö, 1975.

OREAL, S., The Role of Group Executives in the Strategic Management of Diversified Companies. Paper presented at the Third International Seminar on Strategic Management, EIASM/ESSEC 1980.

PETTIGREW, P., The Creation of Organizational Culture. EIASM Working Paper, 1977.

SALTER, M., Tailor Incentive Compensation to Strategy. Harvard Business Review, March-April 1973.

SPERRY, R., Mergers and Acquisitions: A Comprehensive Bibliography, 1972.

SPÅNGBERG, K., Strategic Processes in Diversified Firms. Doctoral thesis, forthcoming, Stockholm School of Economics.

STEINER, G. and MINER, J., Management Policy and Strategy. MacMillan Publishing Co., 1977.

# 11  Richard H. Holton:

# Making International Joint Ventures Work

Most multinational companies do not like the joint venture vehicle. Typically they prefer to have 100% ownership of their operations abroad in order to avoid the problems raised by shared decision making. But increasingly the multinationals recognize that they must make greater use of joint ventures. A growing number of governments are either requiring that foreign direct investment must find a local partner or they are at least pressing for this approach even though it might not be legally required. Meanwhile host governments or their agencies, if they are partners in the joint venture, commonly see themselves as being exploited by the foreign partner. And local private firms also frequently feel that they are not getting a fair share of the earnings of the joint venture, or that they do not have sufficient authority over its operations.

If the prospects for the success of the international joint venture are to be maximized, both parties must recognize the causes of the difficulties which are commonly encountered in joint venture operations, and take steps to minimize those difficulties. Even under the best of circumstances, joint ventures may fail from time to time in the eyes of one partner or another. But with proper planning, negotiation and management of the joint venture agreement, perhaps the rather dismal history of international joint ventures can be improved.

Graduate School of Business Administration
University of California

This paper attempts to identify the major causes of conflict in international joint ventures and to suggest some specific means by which the experience with international joint ventures might be improved. The observations here are based on interviews with a variety of firms in the United States and Europe, and on a study of the Iranian experience with international joint ventures.

JOINT VENTURE DEFINED

The term "joint venture" will be used here to refer to what may be the most common case, i.e., one in which a multinational corporation from one of the industrialized countries has a significant share, say at least 25 percent, in an operation outside the multinational's home country, with the remainder of the equity held by a company located in the same country as the joint venture operation. This will be our "standard case," although most of what will be presented here would also apply if the two partners are both domiciled outside the country where the joint venture is based, or if there are more than two partners. I would exclude from consideration here the project joint venture, in which two or more firms form a joint venture to build a major hydroelectric project, for example, with the joint venture being dissolved on completion of the project.

TWO SETS OF REASONS FOR THE FAILURE OF JOINT VENTURES

Joint ventures will be assumed to "fail" if disagreement among the parties is such that 100% of the equity is taken over by one partner or another, or if one partner is chronically unhappy with the performance of the joint venture operation.

Joint ventures fail for two quite distinct sets of reasons. First, the multinational's operations might be such that because of the nature of the product, the production process or the nature of the market(s) served, it cannot delegate decision making to the joint venture. To the extent that the decision making is done in Tokyo or London or New York, the local joint venture partners are not true partners and they know it. If too much decision making is in the hands of the multinational, the local partner is likely to feel that his destiny is not under his control and he will want to abandon the enterprise. But the multinational recognizes that decisions made at the joint venture level can affect the rest of the multinational's operations adversely, so it insists on making or controlling those decisions in its headquarters.

The second set of reasons for the failure of joint ventures concerns disagreements over operating strategies, policies and methods. These can, and often do, arise even when the joint venture is quite self-contained and has a minimum of interaction with other units within the foreign-based multinational partner's operations. Thus differences of opinion about dividend pay-out policies, debt-equity ratios, marketing policies, quality control methods and the like can become so great that one or more of the partners either wishes to withdraw from the joint venture or at least is chronically unhappy with the operation of the enterprise.

These two sets of reasons for joint venture failure will be developed further in the following two sections.

## THE INTERDEPENDENCE PROBLEM IN THE MULTINATIONAL FIRM

In many cases the multinational company finds that it cannot delegate decision making to the joint venture in which it is participating because of the inter-dependencies which permeate the multinational's operations. The multinational may feel that it cannot let the joint venture make final decisions because these might affect adversely one or more components of the multinational firm, or because maximum economies can be achieved only if the decisions at the joint venture level are synchronized with decisions in other parts of the multinational firm.

## Illustrations

-   The Singer Company manufactured and assembled sewing machines in Brazil in its wholly-owned subsidiary there. Components were supplied in part from Singer plants in Scotland and in Italy. These components were also supplied by these two plants for other units in the Singer Company, serving other markets. Thus in designing the product line, Singer had to consider the requirements of the various markets it served, not just the markets served from the Brazilian plant. The economies of scale in the production of the components were such that product design had to be centered in New York headquarters if maximum profits were to be achieved. If Singer were to try to operate with a joint venture in Brazil, the Brazilian partner would have had to yield his authority over product design to New York. Although he might have conceivably been willing to do this, it is apparent that this could have been a major source of friction. Recognizing this point, Singer chose to avoid joint ventures in order to avoid arguments with joint venture partners about optimum product design; what is optimum for Singer as a whole might not have been optimum for the local operation.

Hewlett-Packard produces hand-held calculators in California and in a wholly-owned subsidiary in Singapore. These have high value relative to their weight and bulk, so transportation costs are low as a percentage of selling price. If the Singapore operation were a joint venture, conceivably the Singapore plant would compete with the California operation in geographic markets which could be reached economically from both plants. To avoid price competition, the pricing decision would have to be centralized at Hewlett-Packard headquarters in California. The joint venture partner in Singapore would presumably object to losing authority over the pricing decision. To avoid such arguments, Hewlett-Packard avoids joint ventures (they do operate one in Japan, under special circumstances).

The Crane Company manufactures not only plumbing fixtures but pumps and valves and similar equipment which is used in oil refineries, paper mills and many other types of installations. They sell to design engineers throughout the world; the design engineers may not be the actual buyers, but they design equipment into the plants they build and so they at least recommend the equipment to be used. In advertising to this important segment of the international market, Crane recognizes that the design engineer in Sao Paolo reads engineering journals published in the United States, Great Britain and perhaps Germany or France as well as Latin America. So Crane wants its advertising in these journals to be consistent. Therefore it does not let its foreign subsidiary conduct their own advertising without advice and clearance with New York headquarters. If they were to use joint ventures abroad, the joint venture partner would have to yield authority over advertising to New York. This could conceivably lead to discontent on the part of the local joint venture partner. In part, to avoid arguments on advertising policy, Crane avoids joint ventures.

The fundamental principle which is involved in all these cases can be instructional for negotiating joint ventures. In the cases cited, there are inter-

dependencies between the local operation and the
multinational corporation's activities elsewhere;
decisions made at the local level can affect the
costs and revenues of other parts of the multinational. When these linkages exist, the multinational
will want to centralize decision making in their
corporate headquarters. To put the matter differently, there is a sub-optimization problem in that what
is optimum for the local operation is not optimum for
the total multinational, because of these linkages.
The greater these linkages or inderdependencies, the
greater the prospect for conflict between a joint
venture partner in the local operation, on the one
hand, and the multinational corporation partner on
the other. When these interdependencies are minimal,
the joint venture is more likely to be viable.

An illustration:

-    Trailmobile Company of Cincinnati, Ohio, pro-
     duces truck trailers. It now participates in 27
     joint ventures abroad. Truck trailers do not
     move in international trade in significant
     numbers because transportation costs are high
     and, more importantly, tariffs typically serve
     to insulate the markets from each other. There-
     fore pricing can be decided at the level of the
     joint venture, because one joint venture cannot
     invade the market of another. Each joint venture
     serves its own local market, and these differ
     from each other in significant ways; hence the
     marketing policy decisions are made at the local
     level. Only a modest part of the total cost of
     manufacturing a trailer is represented by com-
     ponents bought from Trailmobile. Thus the inter-
     dependencies are limited, decision making can be
     delegated to the level of the joint venture, and
     conflicts are minimized.

One should not conclude that joint ventures are impossible if these linkages or interdependencies
exist. But the greater the interdependencies, the
greater the possibility of conflict between foreign
and local joint venture partners. These interdependencies should be identified early in the negotiating process so that they can either be dealt
with satisfactorily or recognized as constituting
such a great problem that the joint venture should
not be set up.

If the interpendencies do exist, this does not necessarily mean that a satisfactory joint venture cannot be established. But the rules for handling the
interdependencies must be negotiated so that the
local partners will know just what role they will

play in the decision making which is tempered by the multinational's own objectives regarding its total operations.

Transfer pricing on raw materials or components which are sold by the multinational to the local operation is perhaps the most obvious problem which arises because of interdependencies between the local operation and the multinational. Obviously a transfer price on a raw material which is optimal for the local operation is a low one, but the lower that price, the lower the multinational partner's profits on the sale of that raw material to the joint venture. If the multinational owns 100% of the local operation, it can be indifferent about earning $100 in the supplying unit or earning $100 in the subsidiary, exchange rate concerns and differences in taxation aside. But if they have only 40% equity in the local operation, their choice is between earning $100 in the supplying operation or earning $40 in the joint venture. They obviously will choose the higher transfer price.

Another type of interdependency which often causes conflict between the foreign partner and the local interests concerns the geographic markets to be served by the joint venture. The multinational partner in an Iranian joint venture through its other operations may sell into other countries in the Middle East, for example, and it may want to require that the Iranian joint venture limit its market to Iran. If the foreign partner sells to the rest of the Middle East through a wholly-owned subsidiary, it receives all the profits on those sales whereas it would receive only a portion of those profits if the Iranian joint venture serves all the Middle East. Agreement on this point must be reached if trouble is to be avoided later.

The problems of transfer pricing and geographic markets to be served are but two illustrations of interdependencies. Perhaps enough has been said here to make the point that these interdependencies must be identified and dealt with if the joint venture is to succeed.

## DISAGREEMENTS OVER STRATEGIES, POLICIES AND METHODS

If two local partners are engaged in a purely domestic enterprise, with no other partners foreign or domestic, they might disagree over the strategies, policies and methods which the enterprise should follow. In the same way, a foreign multinational and a local partner might disagree over these matters

even if there are no linkages or interdependencies
between the local firm and the multinational's other
operations.

These causes of disagreement might be classified into
several different categories:

1) Strategy; 2) Management style, especially regarding communication in the decision-making process;
3) Financial management; 4) Accounting and control
methods; 5) Marketing policies and practices;
6) Production policies, including technology transfer; 7) Personnel policies, including industrial
relations; 8) R & D policies; and 9) Government
and trade relations. Illustrations can suggest some
of the problems which arise in each of these categories:

-   Strategy: What strengths does each partner bring
    to the joint venture and how will these be uti-
    lized to accomplish the objectives? What markets
    are to be served and in what way, with what
    products, at what general price level? For ex-
    ample, Sears Roebuck from the U.S. and Walton's
    in Australia, abandoned a joint venture after
    about four years' operation because Walton's
    wanted a high dividend payout so the price of
    the stock would be maximized, thus permitting
    growth through acquisition of existing depart-
    ment stores on a favorable exchange-of-stock
    basis. Sears wanted a low dividend payout so
    profits could be reinvested in new stores.

-   Management style, especially regarding commu-
    nication in the decision-making process: How
    much autonomy will the local enterprise have;
    will the local representative of the foreign
    partner, for example, have to check every de-
    cision with headquarters? How frequently will
    representatives of the foreign partner come for
    board meetings? Will decision making be highly
    centralized in the hands of one or two people,
    or will more participatory management be
    practiced?

-   Financial management: What will the dividend
    payout policy be? If new financing is needed,
    which partner will provide how much, and under
    what terms, or will new debt be incurred? What
    debt-equity ratio is considered appropriate?

-   Accounting and control methods: What level of
    detail in cost accounting will be applied? How
    frequently and in what detail will accounting
    reports be submitted to the partners? Who will
    the auditors be?

- Marketing policies and practices: What product markets, geographic markets and class-of-customer markets are to be served? What should the advertising-sales ratio be? How large a sales force is anticipated? How much will be spent on training and up-dating sales personnel? What inventory levels of finished goods are to be considered satisfactory, i.e., what stock-out ratios are acceptable?

- Production policies: What will quality control standards be? What production processes will be used? From whom will technology be acquired, how, and under what terms?

- Personnel policies, including industrial relations: What will be the size and composition of the board of directors? How will the key officers of the company be selected? What will the reporting relationships be? What will be the policy about nepotism? Can one partner veto another partner's nomination for a position, and can one partner insist that an unsatisfactory executive be dismissed? What retirement and pension program will be applied? What will be the attitude toward labor unions?

- R & D policy: Will there be a budget for R & D, and if so, how big? What will be the focus of the R & D effort? What will be the source of R & D personnel?

- Government and trade relations: Will the joint venture's taxes be paid on the basis of audited profits, or will a second set of books be kept? Will government policies, e.g., re export sales objectives for the joint venture of production of new products as part of an economic development program, be pursued at the expense of profits? Regarding trade relations, will the joint venture follow a policy of independence, or will cooperation in cartel-like arrangements be acceptable?

Although this is a rather long list, anyone with experience in joint ventures can no doubt add other problems. But what has been listed above can at least provide the background for the following section on negotiating the joint venture agreement.

## NEGOTIATING THE JOINT VENTURE BUSINESS PLAN AND AGREEMENT

Even lawyers who have helped draw up joint venture agreements concede that a good joint venture agreement is only a small fraction of the totality of things which must be done right if a joint venture is to succeed. Much difficulty could be avoided if the design of the joint venture agreement were postponed until after the prospective partners had agreed on a business plan. Once the business plan is in hand, the essential elements of the plan which lend themselves to legal agreement could be extracted and included in the joint venture agreement itself. Frequently joint ventures fail because the first and only attention is on the legal agreement; only later do disagreements emerge, because no business plan was drawn up and agreed to.

It is because of the importance of starting with the business plan and only afterwards developing the joint venture agreement that this section is entitled "Negotiating the joint venture business plan and agreement" rather than just "Negotiating the joint venture agreement."

Negotiating the business plan first can have a number of advantages which should become apparent in the following discussion. In particular, this stage of the process should engender sufficient discussion among the parties so that each can learn what the expectations of the other might be. Various types of incompatibilities might come to the surface and either be solved or else recognized so the effort can be abandoned early rather than aborted painfully at a later date. And the process of putting together the business plan can be as useful in establishing rapport among the parties as can the plan itself.

### Selecting the partner

Let us first take the point of view of a firm in a less developed country which is seeking a partner from one of the developed countries. We will assume that the local firm has the support of the local development bank in this, because the local firm's plans are consistent with the country's economic development objectives.

First, would it be possible for the development bank or the local firm to ask for bids, in effect, for foreign partnership in the joint venture? Unless there is an obvious prospect whose expertise and background are such that there is no reason to look further, it might be feasible to solicit business plans from alternative prospective partners. Although these might be quite preliminary and subject to much further discussion and negotiation, they could at least suggest which prospects seem to have the best ideas for their participation in the joint venture.

Second, the prospects might be asked to spell out their own qualifications for participation in the joint venture. Financial capability, the company's market position in the product line being considered, the availability of managerial talent to assist the joint venture, the level of R & D expenditures in the product line, the willingness to divulge and share new technological developments regarding both processes and product might all be ascertained. A prospect might find such requests too demanding, especially if they come from an unknown company in an unknown market, but if the prospect chooses not to respond, that alone is useful information about the capacity if not the interest of the prospect.

Third, the credibility of the prospects might be checked by the development bank through its own personnel sent abroad to talk with banks, competing firms, customers and other industry sources. If the prospect participates in other joint ventures, conversations with their joint venture partners might be particularly revealing. If the development bank does not have the personnel for this, perhaps through banking connections, embassy personnel abroad or international consulting firms (although they are expensive and perhaps of doubtful reliability), the same objective could be achieved.

When a company from an industrialized country is seeking a partner to develop the latter's local or regional market, the criteria for selection are not quite symmetrical with those just mentioned. Financial capability is again relevant, of course. The prospective local partner's managerial performance and depth need to be assessed, as well. (One executive with much experience with joint ventures has said that one should by all means choose a strong local partner; it is a mistake, he says, to think that you can make a strong partner out of a weak one.) Knowledge of local markets and the local government structure, policies and mores is critical as well. Discussions with local banks, suppliers to and customers of the prospect and similar sources can usually yield this information.

## Negotiating the business plan

In negotiating the business plan, the parties should send their managerial and operating personnel, not their lawyers. The nine subject areas (strategy, management style, financial policies, etc.) reviewed above might provide a framework for the topics to be covered. The business plan should not be viewed as a legal document, but rather as a discussion paper, or a series of discussion papers, in which every effort would be made to bring to the surface the expectations of the parties so that any inconsistencies in those expectations can be revealed and, if possible, resolved.

Openness in these negotations is, of course, of the utmost importance. One can never be sure that the prospective partner is really being honest, of course. But one is more likely to uncover any hidden objectives of the prospective partner if the business plan is spelled out in some detail than if the business plan is skipped altogether and negotiations start immediately with the legal joint venture agreement.

It is important that the right people be involved in putting together the business plan. Too many times the step of formulating the business plan is omitted, and the multinational partner sends a lawyer, a tax man and a finance man to negotiate the joint venture agreement. They get into the agreement the things that lawyers, tax men and finance men worry about. Only after the agreement is signed do the production, marketing and control personnel get involved, and they find that countless questions which they think are important have not been resolved. If the latter types of persons are involved in putting the business plan together, such problems might be solved, or at least mimimized.

## Critical elements in the business plan

A few critical elements which must be kept in mind in the formulation of the business plan have not as yet been mentioned. These concern the over-all strategy of design, and hence have not been included above.

First, every joint venture agreement should be designed not only as a marriage contract but as a divorce contract as well. The business plan and the agreement should stipulate under what conditions, and how, the joint venture is to be broken up. Thus a partner might want to stipulate that if a certain profit target is not achieved by the third

year or the fifth year, for example, it would have
the option of seeking another party to buy out the
original local partner, or it could buy out the local party itself. Valuation of the equity to be
bought might be on the basis of the book value of
the shares; or some multiple of the average earnings
of the last three years (or some other formula based
on profits) might also be devised. The point here
is that if the divorce terms are not spelled out in
advance, the unhappy marriage might continue on in-
definitely because no one knows how to gracefully
dismantle or reorganize the joint venture.

Second, a minority shareholder can achieve control
over critical decisions through the business plan
and the joint venture agreement. It is a delusion
to think that the partner with a majority of the
ownership and therefore a majority of the board of
directors necessarily will have command over the
operation. One U.S. company which has operated
abroad successfully has used only joint ventures
and they actually prefer to have a minority interest. When disagreements arise, they say, they
prefer to be in the position of the offended minority rather than the defensive majority parties.
But they have a veto over the appointment of the
key executives; they typically have the initiating
authority in naming the controller, whom they consider to be in a critical position; they can veto
the selection of the auditing firm, and so on.
Control, they argue, is achieved primarily through
the people running the day-to-day operations, not
through the board of directors. And if the minority
partner is too unhappy with the decisions of the
majority of the board, he can threaten to activate
the divorce arrangement.

Third, discussions about the business plan should
concentrate in part on what will be done if things
do not go well and if things go better than expected.
In other words, contingency planning should be built
into the business plan. As an important part of
this, the parties should make clear to each other
what kinds of operating ratios, for example, make
them nervous. Thus an American partner typically
is accustomed to a lower debt-equity ratio than a
Japanese partner. This suggests that besides showing
the targeted debt-equity ratio year by year for the
period of the business plan, there should be at
least some general statement about how high a debt-
equity ratio is considered acceptable.

Fourth, the parties should recognize that the business plan will in all probability be changed over
time, of course. Unforeseen circumstances inevitably

develop and the parties must recognize that the
business plan will be revised at least annually.
But such revisions should be more readily and satisfactorily accomplished if the parties have come to
know one another's expectations and preferences
through the process of putting together the initial
business plan.

SUMMARY

If an international joint venture is to operate
successfully, a detailed business plan should be
agreed to by the parties involved, ideally before
the joint venture agreement itself is executed.
Strategies, policies and methods should be specified in the business plan in sufficient detail so
that the expectations and preferences of the parties
are brought to the surface and dealt with openly.
Since joint ventures are most likely to fail
when the interdependencies between the joint venture operation and the foreign partner are extensive, these interdependencies must be given particular attention. Transfer pricing, technology
transfer, market restrictions (both in terms of product and geographic markets), and R&D expenditures
are among the most common types of interdependencies
which must be addressed.

Negotiating and operating the joint venture with
a foreign partner requires time, money and talent,
and these are understandably in limited supply for
both prospective partners. But unless the planning
process itself is handled with great care, the risks
inherent in international joint ventures cannot
be minimized.

# 12  Lars Otterbeck:

# The Management of Joint Ventures

This paper - like those by Hedlund and Leksell
above - is based upon a research project conducted at
the Institute of International Business at the Stockholm School of Economics. The empirical material
comes from an in-depth study of 24 subsidiaries of
six large Swedish MNCs. The research design aimed
at varying the ownership structure (wholly owned/
minority joint venture) and location (developed
country/less developed country) in each MNC. This
succeeded almost completely. An average of ten interviews were conducted at each central headquarters
and/or appropriate division, all subsidiaries were
visited and 2-6 people interviewed, and the researchers had full access to documents, telexes, and
correspondence between HQ and the subsidiaries selected for study.

Here we take a closer look at the management of those
foreign affiliates which the parent company does not
fully own. It was hypothesized in the design of the
study that there would be differences in the way relations between headquarters and foreign affiliates
were managed that had to do with the degree to which
the parent owned the affiliate in question.

THE SAMPLE

The industries in which our six companies operate are
concentrated and technology intensive. Only a hand-
ful of relevant competitors in the world and fairly

Institute of International Business, Stockholm School
of Economics

high allocation to R&D seems to be the rule. In such industries companies may find it advantageous to enter into JVs. It is a way of reducing competition and thus increasing ones market share. It may be a way of obtaining scale economies in production, marketing or management. It may be a form for dealing with the uncertainty in large expensive new developments in high technology areas. Finally it may provide easy access to a new market.

The joint international business ventures that we study here are typically not ventures between parents of similar size or character, such as those between AGA and Air Liquide in the gas industry, IVECO in the truck industry, Renault-Peugeot-Volvo in the car industry, or KLM, Swissair, SAS and UTA in the air transport industry. All but one are between a large Swedish firm and a local firm.

Seven of the eleven joint ventures in this study were to be found in countries which did not require a foreign investor to share ownership with a local partner. Five, among them the four which required local ownership, were in developing countries. All but two were minority owned.

The character of the partner varied somewhat. Four were industrial companies. seven were conglomerates or holding companies. In a few cases some shares were also held by individual investors or by a local bank. In only two cases was the partner a government or state owned company. One partner was not a local company.

The managing director of the JV was either a local citizen whose career had been with the local partner (3 cases), a Swede from the Swedish partner (3 cases), a third country national from the Swedish parent (1) or a local outsider (4 cases). (See table 1.)

TABLE 1.  Characteristics of joint venture arrangements
and of partners

| JV No. | Share of Sw. partner | Local partner: Size | Type | Ownership | JV man dir | Country requiring local ownership |
|--------|----------------------|------|------|-----------|------------|-----------------------------------|
| 1  | 38 | med.   | congl.   | private | local partner | No |
| 2  | 30 | large  | congl.   | public  | local outsider | No |
| 3  | 50 | medium | ind.     | public  | local partner | No |
| 4  | 60 | medium | holding  | public  | TNC from Sw. partner | Yes |
| 5  | 50 | large  | industry | holding | Swede | No |
| 6  | 49 | large  | holding  | private | local outsider | No |
| 7  | 49 | large  | industry | state   | Swede | No |
| 8  | 25 | med.   | congl.   | private | local partner | Yes |
| 9  | 47 | large MNC | industry | public | local outsider | Yes |
| 10 | 24 | large  | congl.   | state   | local outsider | No |
| 11 | 51 | large  | congl.   | private | Swede | Yes |

## EXPECTATIONS ON JOINT VENTURE MANAGEMENT

Two opposing forces explain our expectation regarding the management of JVs: the drive to standardize procedures and the paralyzation of the administrative system.

### The standardization of procedures

Large, relatively mature corporations, typically in one of the later stages in a development model such as Scott's (1970) need a structure and administrative system that can function without ad hoc intervention by HQ. The depersonalization of management is necessary. Systems are introduced for coordination, performance evaluation and decision making of certain kinds.

Such systems and procedures should be easier to introduce in wholly owned subsidiaries than in partially owned. Although several studies show conflicts over organizational matters even in wholly owned subsidiaries (e.g. Garnier, Osborn, Galicia & Lecon, 1979) one should expect such conflicts to be more severe when there are two or more partners. The parents may for example employ different systems in their own organizations or they may have different management styles. We may recall Franko's (1971) findings that the more policies an MNC wanted to standardize, the more likely it was to have a high rate of JV instability and that firms at later stages in the growth pattern show a higher JV instability.

More specifically we should expect differences between how MNCs manage their foreign JVs and wholly owned subsidiaries.

The drive for control should lead the managements of both parents to try to impose its policies upon the JV. It is to be expected that the partner who controls the most critical resource, for the firms in our sample usually technology, will be the more successful. The struggle for control is expected to be conflict-ridden to a larger extent than in the "normal" struggle between HQ and the management of a foreign subsidiary.

In our sample the MNC parent is expected to dominate the management of the JV. However, this domination of management is expected to take on other forms than in a wholly owned subsidiary. The MNC parent cannot intervene into the activities of a JV as easily as in those of a wholly owned subsidiary. It is therefore expected to try to freeze to the highest extent pos-

sible the strategic decision making for the JV. In
order to be regarded as a good citizen of the host
country, it tries to leave a larger degree of autonomy in operational matters to the local board and local management.

The MNC parent is expected to try to informally influence the behavior of the JV by appointing "trust-
worthy" people in key positions. This is more important in JVs than in wholly owned subsidiaries. In order to prevent leakage of proprietary know-how the
MNC parent tries not to integrate the JV into its
systems and policies. In particular this goes for
personnel policies. Policies such as reporting are
less sensitive but may on the other hand be difficult
to impose upon the JV if the other partner does not
agree. In the finance area it is expected that both
partners try to keep the JV at arm's length and that
both would show a higher desire to "take their money
home" than they would in the case of a wholly owned
subsidiary. This would lead to a situation where the
JV as such has no autonomy at all in financial decisions. All such decision making power would rest with
the parents.

## The Paralyzed Administrative System

Administrative systems are not only formal organization structures, boxed on an organization diagram.
They include many more things. For the purpose of
this discussion let us include organization structure, systems of communication, planning-, budgeting
and reporting systems, management transfers, reward
and punishment systems and finally parent intervention characteristics.

The search for criteria that differentiate between
good and bad administrative systems has occupied several organization researchers. During the last two
decades one has become less and less certain as to
what constitutes an efficient administrative system.
"There is no one best way to organize." Researchers
have come to focus on the consistency, the fit, between the totality of the administrative system and
its environment and the consistency within the system
itself (cf. Chandler, 1962 and Lawrence & Lorsch,
1967). Several examples that constitute "a good fit"
have been suggested.

It is, however, possible that even this, admittedly
rather loose, generalization about consistency is
premature. Several authors, among them Hedlund (1978)
and Prahalad & Doz (1978) question the results of the
"consistency school". Hedlund, by analyzing very
carefully two similar corporations, concludes that

there are also several ways of establishing a good
fit. The growth history of the corporation and the
personalities of leading actors are two examples of
things that seem to affect the administrative system
profoundly and help constitute very different "good
fits" for companies.

What is a good fit?

The criteria for what constitutes a "good fit" thus
are not at all clear. Even if, after the fact, one
may be able to establish some such criteria, normative statements are difficult to make. Statements
like a turbulent environment requires an organic
structure, mature products are best managed with
mechanistic organizations, for every level of environmental turbulence there is a best level of formalization that abound are typically non-operational
and therefore of limited value as guides for management.

In JVs the totality of the administrative system is
not under management's control to the same extent as
in a wholly owned subsidiary. The partners may have
different views as to how the administrative system
should be designed. Presumably, they tend to favour
the system they use themselves. Both parents may want
to treat the JV more at an arm's length basis than a
wholly owned subsidiary. This may be for fear of
leakage of know-how, for fear of US antitrust policies or because one is uncertain about the future
relations to the partners.

Additionally, since the strategy and role of a JV may
be more difficult to change than of a wholly owned
subsidiary, it can be assumed that management in its
contractural agreement with a partner tries to freeze
more things than when a wholly owned subsidiary is
formed or acquired. In the latter case it should be
easier to change direction gradually as a response to
the performance of the company and to changes in the
environment.

Shifts of management, shifts of production or integration into a global sourcing system for wholly
owned subsidiaries are difficult enough. Compatible
reporting and evaluation systems are required. Decision making may be difficult because of concern for
the local management, for unions, for local laws and
for the changing risk profile that may be created.

If, added to these considerations, the reactions of a
partner have to be taken into account as well as
transfer pricing and technological leakage, it will
be apparent that changes in the strategic role of a
JV will be a task of considerable difficulty.

## Top people manage joint ventures

This last point also touches upon the problem of hierarchial levels. We assume that JVs tend to be managed by people of higher hierarchical levels in the organization than otherwise comparable "subsidiaries". One reason is that the impact of strategic changes for such companies may be more profound than for wholly owned subsidiaries. Another reason has to do with differences in how companies manage internal and external relations.

Several studies were made in Sweden during the late 1960s on the impact or relocations of organizations (Thorngren, 1970, Back, Dalborg & Otterbeck, 1970). The focus was on the contacts between an organizational unit and its environment. It was repeatedly shown in these studies that external contacts were dealt with at higher hierarchical levels than internal ones, given type of content. Contacts with a complex content, such as negotiations, were also taken by higher levels. Also relations with agents in the contextual environment were typically dealt with at higher organizational levels than those with the transactional environment (concepts from Emery & Trist, 1965).

During the formation of a JV the relations to the partner are dealt with at high levels: one is negotiating a business deal. Once it is formed they tend to pushed down; one is bound by a legal agreement, specifying the terms. Problems with conflicting interests, interpretation of the agreement or future relations tend to be pushed up again in the hierarchy. Issues on transfer pricing may be dealt with at somewhat lower levels.

In cases of conflict even relations with the JV as such take on some of the same characteristics as those to the partner, since they bear upon the relations to the partner. We should then expect that matters, where JVs are concerned, are dealt with at higher hierarchical levels than is the case for wholly owned subsidiaries. This would be a good illustration of a partly paralyzed administrative system.

One consequence of this, it can be hypothesized, is that decisions regarding JVs take longer than those regarding wholly owned subsidiaries. Conflicts in JVs should also upset the organization more. Top management can also be assumed to spend more time with JV management than what might be regarded as fair, given the commercial importance of the ventures in question.

276

## DATA BASE AND RESULTS

First, let us look at the sample to see how the joint
venture companies studied differed from the wholly
owned.

When interpreting these results, it must be borne in
mind that the sample is by no means randon. In fact
we tried to make the samples of wholly owned and
joint ventures as similar as possible. In discussions
with HQ management - typically the President - the
researchers asked permission to study two joint ventures and two wholly owned foreign affiliates in less
developed and developed countries. The researchers
suggested affiliates that were comparable, between
each other and in relation to the two wholly owned
subsidiaries. In most cases management accepted, in
some slight changes had to be made.

It is apparent that the sample contains affiliates
in the two categories of comparable size and operating in similar market conditions. On average the
wholly owned (WH) are somewhat larger and more capital intensive than the JVs. They also spend more on
R&D. The wholly owned subsidiaries are slightly more
complex in terms of technology and type of production.

On the financial side two interesting differences
can be seen. First, JVs have higher debt-equity ratios than wholly owned subsidiaries. This may be
interpreted as a risk averse financial policy. Both
partners tend to keep their equity as low as possible. They probably argue that any borrowing on the
part of the JV would have to be guaranteed by the
parents anyway.

TABLE 2.   Charcteristics of sample - finance and
          market data.

|                                                      | Wholly Owned n=13 | Joint Ventures n=11 |
|------------------------------------------------------|-------------------|---------------------|
| Size - turnover $m                                   | 42.6              | 38.2                |
| Assets - book value $m                               | 45.8              | 32.4                |
| Equity - $m                                          | 10.5              | 12.7                |
| Debt/Equity                                          | 4.1               | 1.8                 |
| Reported profit - $m                                 | 1.8               | 1.9                 |
| Remittances - % of reported profit                   | 28.8              | 11.0                |
| Number of employees                                  | 1315              | 1220                |
| Imports from parent - % of sales                     | 25.7              | 12.6                |
| Exports to parent - % of sales                       | 1.0               | 3.4                 |
| Exports to affiliates - % of sales                   | 3.2               | 3.7                 |
| Market share - in country of domicile %              | 39                | 32                  |
| Market concentration - % market share held by 4 largest | 87            | 79                  |
| Number of competitors                                | 6                 | 13[1]               |

[1] Very skewed distribution

Second, JVs show lower remittances as per cent of reported profits. Since equity is comparatively low,
remittances as a percentage of equity may still be of
the same magnitude as in wholly owned subsidiaries.
However, these two observations suggest that in JVs
the parents try to keep the joint financial streams
low. Instead they try to recoup their earnings in
forms that are related to inputs into the JV and that
are not shared with the partner. One would expect the
partner which provides technology and management,
usually the foreigner, to be able to get a much
higher return on its equity than the local partner.
For this sample the figures on royalty payments,
license fees, management fees etc., where available,
do not, however, indicate any differences between

what is taken home from JVs and wholly owned subsidiaries. It has not been possible to establish
whether transfer prices systematically differ between JVs and wholly owned subsidiaries.

Finally, wholly owned subsidiaries seem to be more
integrated into the parents' production system than
JVs. The proportion of sales that is imported from
the parent is much higher in wholly owned subsidiaries. We can also note that none of the two categories shows any sizeable export back to Sweden,
which is consistent with the general pattern of
foreign expansion of these firms.

In summary then, the two samples - wholly owned and
joint ventures - are very similar. Let us now turn
to the management of the two kinds of affiliates.

In the personnel area striking differences were found
(see Table 3). JVs had fewer third country nationals
and fewer expatriates or conversely more locals in
their management. It does not seem as if JVs were
closely integrated in the manpower system of the
parent either. Also the policy of "putting our man
there", i.e. a Swede, does not seem to be more
widespread in JVs than in wholly owned subsidiaries.

TABLE 3.  Differences between wholly owned subsidiaries and joint ventures in the area of human
resource management

|  | Wholly Owned n=13 | Joint Ventures n=11 |
|---|---|---|
| Number of third country nationals in management[1] | 1.9 | 0.5 |
| Number of expatriate Swedes in management | 6.1 | 3.0 |
| Number of managers sent to HQ for training | 1.1 | 1.7 |

[1] Defined as three top levels

## Autonomy of Joint Ventures

The topic of subsidiary autonomy was dealt with at
length in Hedlund's paper above. He showed that -
contrary to the expectations that guided the design
of our study - virtually no difference was found between the autonomy of wholly owned subsidiaries and

that of joint ventures. The very small difference
that can be observed, however, on all variables shows
a slightly higher autonomy for joint ventures than
for wholly owned subsidiaries and a higher spread
for joint ventures. So although the mean values are
similar, joint ventures differ among themselves.

## Conflicts with joint ventures

Relations between parent and affiliate also seem to
have been equally conflict-ridden (or conflict free)
independent of ownership share. The two variables
used, incidence of conflict as classified by sub
management and climate of interaction as classified
by the researchers, did not show any significant
differences, neither for strategic nor for operating
matters. (See Table 4).

TABLE 4. Incidence of conflict and climate of interaction between HQ and wholly owned subsidiaries vs joint ventures.
Scale 1 = low, 5 = high.

| | Wholly Owned | Joint Venture | Difference |
|---|---|---|---|
| Conflicts in strategic matters | 3.08 | 3.18 | 0.10 |
| Conflicts in operational matters | 2.08 | 2.18 | 0.10 |
| Climate of interaction - strategic matters | 2.46 | 2.63 | 0.17 |
| Climate of interaction operational matters | 2.23 | 2.27 | 0.04 |

## Formalization

Our data on formalization of management processes
show some very interesting results. It seems as if
management indeed has strived for a high degree of
formalization of the management of JVs. This formalization is relatively higher for strategic matters.
Operational matters are handled in a more ad hoc
fashion. In fact, operational matters are handled in
much more informal channels (telephone conversations,
ad hoc meetings) in JVs than in wholly owned subsidiaries, whereas strategic decisions are handled in
much more formal channels (LRP systems, board meetings) in JVs than in wholly owned subsidiaries. The
variable FODEC which is the classification of the

character of the decision making process shows a similar, but less striking difference. The budget is more important in controlling wholly subsidiaries, but the information contained in the budget is similar.

What emerges is an image of JV management where the partners try to establish the ground rules and take a decision once and for all regarding the strategic role of the joint venture. That role is not questioned or changed. Decision making is formal but personal and involves people in high positions in the corporations. This form of decision making, as will be seen in the cases that follow, is probably very flexible. When the need to change the strategic role of a joint venture arises, the positions tend to be locked, the parties will find it difficult to meet, and key people on one or both sides may have left the company or retired.

Operational matters, as they surface, are handled partially outside the established channels that are used for wholly owned subsidiaries. These matters are also dealt with in a personalized manner. They also involve people on "too high" levels. The time that top managers spend on operational problems in joint ventures seems to be way out of proportion with the economic consequences involved. Apart from the argument regarding the external nature of these matters, we might add a piece of data on the integration of the reporting systems of joint ventures into the parents' normal procedures. On a 5-point scale ranging from not integrated at all to fully integrated, the wholly owned subsidiraies in our sample averaged 4.7, whereas the joint ventures averaged 3.2. This difference is significant at the .01 % level. Since the reporting system is so loosely integrated, even operational matters have to be dealt with outside that system. There are no other ways.

This general view on how JVs relate to their multinational (Swedish) parents is in line with our expectations. As regards the differences between how strategic and operational matters are handled, it is also consistent with the findings of for example Anthony (1965) and Rhenman (1963). (See further Table 5).

TABLE 5. Differences between wholly owned subsidiaries and joint ventures in formalization of
decision making and relations to HQ in
certain other respects.
Scale 1-5, 1 = very low, 5 = very high.

|  | Wholly Owned | Joint Ventures | Diff. JV&WH | Sign. |
|---|---|---|---|---|
| Formality of channels - strategic matters | 2.69 | 3.18 | 0.49 | 0.30 |
| Formality of channels - operational | 2.54 | 2.18 | ./.0.36 | 0.53 |
| Formality of decision making - strategic | 2.00 | 3.09 | 1.09 | 0.06 |
| Formality of dicision making - operational | 2.31 | 2.55 | 0.24 | |
| Importance of budget | 3.54 | 3.00 | ./.0.46 | 0.28 |
| Informational value of budget | 3.62 | 3.64 | 0.02 | |
| Integration of reporting system | 4.69 | 3.18 | ./.1.51 | 0.01 |
| Feedback from HQ | 4.69 | 3.18 | ./.1.51 | 0.03 |
| Involvement in parent company's strategic planning | 2.15 | 1.27 | ./.0.88 | |
| Affilation to people at HQ | 3.00 | 2.82 | ./.0.18 | |

## Personal relations to HQ

Joint ventures do not seem to feel involved in the
strategic decision processes of the parent company.
Joint venture managers are significantly less involved than managers of wholly owned subsidiaries. They
do, however, feel loyal to and know people at HQ - at
least those JV managers that are Swedish. Prahalad
& Doz (1978) found that the loyalty of the local
chief executive does not depend on size of the ownership interest or the individuals nationality but on
the industry. In so called "salient industries" -
this is, industries of major significance or where
the government is the most important customer - the
primary loyalty was toward the country.

In our sample where most of the companies are in
salient industries, it seems as if degree of ownership has little influence on the loyalty of the local

management, but that his nationality has.

However, as far as local involvement in strategic decision making goes, there are business reasons why the parent should keep a joint venture at arm's length. What the parent may get from the JV is money but more unlikely any substantial amount of new knowledge in technology, management or the like. Such added assets in a JV may stay with the joint company or may go to the partner. The risk of leakage of proprietary knowledge from the parent is also there but may, according to some interviews, be overemphasized. One may argue that such technology can not easily be transferred anyway, since it rests with many people each of whom has but one piece of the total. We must also in the view of managers interviewed rely on the impact of the corporate culture on its engineers. "They just won't give our know-how away.".

SUMMARY

In summary, at this level of aggregation, the differences between how wholly owned subsidiaries and joint ventures were managed were not very great. JVs are kept at somewhat more distance than wholly owned and they seem to be given a more narrow mission. Hence the clear differences between strategic and operational matters.

JV management in process

Fuller insights into what actually happens between HQ and foreign joint ventures were provided by our analysis of JV management in process, i.e. when we looked closely at how issues were handled. A few such cases are presented below as the next step in the data analysis. They do not shed any further light on the comparison between wholly owned and joint ventures, but should help us understand better what forces are at work in foreign joint ventures.

K - the independent JV

K is 50/50 owned by the Swedish parent and a large local company. Both parents are known for their high technological standards, although they specialize in somewhat different product lines. K is unique in that it has succeeded in not complying with the strict and formalized reporting requirements used by the Swedish parent.

K was formed some 10 years ago. The then managing director of the local partner sought out the Swedish partner because of its reputation. He wanted to start a company in a new product line. The Swedish partner

had already a wholly owned sales subsidiary on the
market, a large industrial country, which did not focus on the proposed product line.

A 50/50 venture was formed. A very detailed contract
was signed by the partners. Products to be produced
and marketed were specified as well as conditions for
technical and other services, dividend policy, etc.
Both parties openly stated how they saw the new venture as part of their mission. Half the board was e-
lected by each party, the chairman was to be elected
among the local company's half and the chairman of
the shareholders' meeting was to be elected by the
Swedish partner. All major decisions specified in the
agreement required a qualified majority (two thirds)
of the board members.

In the agreement there was also a divorce clause.

> "... either party can take the initiative to
> sell his shares at a price ... named in the no-
> tice. Such offer may be accepted by the non-ini-
> tiating party or the non-initiating party may
> treat the offer as binding the initiating party
> to buy the non-initiating party's shares at the
> same price. Conversely, the initiating party
> may offer to buy the other party's shares at a
> price ... named in the notice. Such offer may be
> accepted by the non-initiating party or the non-
> initiating party may treat the offer as binding
> the initiating party to sell its shares at the
> same price. In any event, offers and acceptances
> must be for all the shares of a party."

Such agreements are not altogether uncommon in JVs.
They are sometimes referred to as "Russian roulette".
The managing director of the local company stated in
a newspaper interview:

> "This is a very happy marriage. We need one
> another equally much and we will need one
> another in the future. Therefore it is not very
> likely that we will ever use the Russian roulet-
> te."

The local partner was a listed company. A few years
after the agreement the Swedish partner bought 2% of
its shares on the market.

Back to the MD of the local partner:

> "We wanted to enter (this product line). Natu-
> rally, we could not afford to build it from
> scratch. I began to ask colleagues, clients and
> competitors for suggestions. (The Swedish compa-

ny) was near the top on everybody's list."

> "(The Swedes) had not heard of us before. They were, however, interested because their sales (of this production line in our country) did not go very well ... We could offer them a ready and functioning sales organization. It was also about 30% cheaper to produce locally rather than in Sweden and ship it, pay duties, etc."

K, which has a couple of hundred employees, was caught in between two very different management styles. It has, however, found a way of coping. Apparently it is an effective way. It strives for independence on its parents. In its country, it is often regarded as a division of the local partner which creates problems in its drive for independence.

In the first years the policy was to enter the market and gain share and volume through price-cutting. Financial results were disastrous. Both parents after 3 years stopped putting up new equity. The MD of the local partner took over as MD also of K. He, who had been the initiator of the JV, had excellent personal relations with the MD of the Swedish partner. He made several visits to Sweden, "to clear the issues" and succeeded in obtaining more recent technical knowledge and production rights.

K was unprofitable during these years. People in management positions at K as well as at the local partner had bonus systems. An exodus of managers from K back to the partner, which was profitable, resulted. K became known as the dump yard for managers.

A young engineer in the local parent company, who had taken evening classes in marketing, at this time went to the MD and suggested that the only possible cure for K was to segment the market, emphasize unique features of the product, differentiate it slightly and raise prices. He had found that in some segments K's product was one of the three leaders.

This was contrary to the high volume philosophy adhered to so far. Through personal intervention by the MD of the local partner - directly to the MD of the Swedish partner - the necessary technology was transferred and the new policy was cleared.

This was by no means easy. The culture among the Swedish engineers was totally against the idea. Sharing know-how and sharing it with a company that did not understand that volume was the oxygen of business was an alien thought.

One year later the young engineer was MD of K, the
company was a price leader, its volume had gone up
(in the midst of a recession) and the company was making money.

Success gave independence. The following exchange of
telexes regarding reporting routines from the period
illustrates the point. HQ sent a memo on corporate
reporting to K.

From K's MD by letter:

> "Your letter ... strikes us wrong ... In essence
> it dictates a rigid policy of outside and inside
> auditing ... Perhaps (you) do not realize that
> (K) is somewhat unique in (your) organization.
> The shares are not owned in a majority by (you).
> (You) do, however, as a separate matter own sha-
> res of (the local parent) ... This ... does not
> give (you) control powers ...
>
> The above is a statement of the relationship as
> we ... see them ... I do propose that (K) conti-
> nues to be cooperative..."

From HQ controller to K the same day by telex:

> "The information was sent to you by mistake ...
> We are well aware of the uniqueness of (K) ...
> it is my intention to visit your company to dis-
> cuss these questions. I think such a discussion
> will further improve our already good coopera-
> tion..."

K answers by letter two weeks later:

> "Thank you for your telex which cleares the air
> completely. We would very much welcome you to
> visit (K) in the near future..."

Internal memo in controller's department a few months
later:

> "... We should not demand (more info than he is
> prepared to give). If we want more, the same as
> required other subs, the matter must probably be
> dealt with by (the MDs of the two parents)."

Memo from Swedish parent MD to controller:

> "As agreed I talked to (K's MD) ... He had
> nothing against giving information on (K) to us.
> But he did not want to change his reporting rou-
> tines..."

K sends nine monthly reports. They do not comply with
the Swedish parent's standard reporting system.

About a year áfter this exchange a new instruction
was circulated from HQ to all manufacturing "subs".
This time it was about product standardization. The
instruction was tough and required that HQ approved
all new product decisions etc. K's MD went through it
with his production manager, sent it back to HQ with
comments and travelled to Sweden. After he had talked
with the head of production and the Swedish MD, they
all agreed that the instruction did not apply to K.
"All in good cooperative spirit" in the words of K's
MD. According to HQ he was the only one who had commented on the new instruction.

K is a very independent JV in a formalized corporate
system. In a very formalized and standardized system,
it seems as if there is no middleway. Either one
accepts the system or one has to disregard it altogether and instead take all decisions that need the
partner's approval to the top. Both partners realize
that they need one another. K is somewhat of a pet
for the then MDs of both parents. They are both on
its board and still very influential in the two corporations. K does not compete with either parent. And
overall strategy is still a matter for the board with
its strong individuals and the Russian roulette in
the background. The CEO of K is not an agressive but
a very determined manager with a proven success re-
cord.

"If it goes to hell they will blame me for lack
of control or production efficiency. I am not
sure that they understand my marketing concept."

## Company L - the no-decision joint venture

This JV was formed about 15 years ago. Two MNCs joi-
ned forces and put up share capital in proportion
2:1. Local investors were invited a few years later
to take a 25% interest, so that the two MNCs got 50
and 25% respetively.

Both founders had had sales companies in this countries since several years. When demands for local production and local participation gradually became more
strongly voiced, it was felt that a joint production
company could reduce the risk that anyway neither
party was prepared to take alone.

Company L had four divisions with profit center responsibility. These were organized around product
lines. In each division products were assembled and,
to a larger and larger extent over the years, manu-

factured locally. Import restrictions were becoming
gradually more difficult to adhere to.

The L company had very high market shares for its major products. It was therefore carefully scrutinized
by the local authorities. Licenses were required for
production rights; all new projects had to be approved by the authorities, as well as investments and
expansions of capacity. Fees for know-how, management
and licenses that went abroad had to be approved.
Normally, the authorities informed the major local
competitors about company L's plans and asked their
opinion before approval.

The partner with the lowest share of equity has far
more influence on the management of L than the partner with the larger share. In fact, L manufactures
and sells an even larger share of the latter's products than is reflected by the ownership relations,
but all the same the smaller, Swedish, partner has
control.

L is totally integrated into the Swedish parent's
reporting and budgeting systems. Its managing director is a local citizen who has had a long career in
L and before that worked for another subsidiary of a
foreign firm. He has not worked for any of the partners that own L.

The government in L's country passed a law requiring
foreign owners to limit their share to 40 % of the
local company's equity. The local managing director
after lengthy discussions with his government officials managed to get permission for the foreign
owners to keep majority ownership. One of the conditions for this was that both foreign parents guarantee that exports from L be raised to 10% of the turnover.

During these discussions the local manager had kept
the Swedish parent informed and all was done in
agreement. The other, larger parent, however, saw L
merely as an outlet for its products on the market.
They did not care much about control. Hence, they
were not interested in guaranteeing any exports from
the local market. L, from their point of view, generated a steady stream of income and was their foot-
hold on the market.

The Swedish parent now suggested that they buy the
other company's share and alone put of 51% of the
equity of L, so as to keep control. They would then
alone guarantee a 10% export share. The financial
position of this parent was so weak that they did

288

not deem it possible to take this step against the will of their partner.

The local MD was caught in the middle of the fight between the parents. He wanted a fast decision so that he could go back to business. Deliberations with the parents and with the government, all at high levels and by personal contacts, took several months. The process was personal but very formal (board meetings) and tense-ridden with severe impact on the day-to-day business of L.

Control in this JV was shared in a dysfunctional way. The largest portion of equity was held by one of the partners, who also accounted for the larger portion of its business. The smaller partner had management control, although the managing director was independent. This situation was unbalanced byt workable as long as both parents found the JV to contribute to their goal fulfilment. When the government required changes in ownership and strategy, this lack of balance became untenable.

## Company M - parent control?

M is 51% owned by the Swedish partner. The rest is held by a local conglomerate. M is fully integrated in the planning, reporting and budgeting systems of the Swedish parent. It produces products within the range of the parent's product line. Most of these are sold on the local market, but some are also exported under the brand name used by the Swedish parent.

A general strike in M occurred. A local union representative had insulted the factory manager and was suspended from work. The local union in response took some action which resulted in another 20 workers being suspended. A general strike followed.

M had no previous experience of strikes. The Swedish local MD gave the local factory manager the authority to deal with the issue and kept HQ informed all along. HQ took no initiatives.

When after two months no progress had been made, the local MD was ordered by HQ to take over the issue himself. He then started to negotiate with the union and government organizations in the country, more centrally situated than the local union. The matter was brought to court. Meanwhile the local MD - "in good Swedish tradition" - rehired all the suspended workers. The union immediately demanded that another six workers who had been suspended a few years earlier be reemployed. The local MD refused. He referred to the fact that the court had not decided on the issue.

At this point the local board, and mainly its chairman who represented the local partner, was activated by the local MD. The local chairman used his political contacts to settle the issue. Recent elections, however, had made his contacts obsolete.

Now HQ took over as things tended to drag on. A HQ official went to the country and settled things with the government. The strike was stopped four months after it started.

According to company officials, the issue was resolved in accordance with established company procedures. Local personnel relations are handled by local management. HQ is informed. Not until the matter becomes of corporate importance, in this case because of severe shortage of products and bad publicity also in other countries, does HQ take action.

The partner had no influence whatsoever, but was used at one point. The fact that the company was a JV had no impact on the resolution. It may seem, however, that the procedures in use in this company did not facilitate an efficient response. More than 60 man days of top executive time was spent and 4 months production was lost. Had the issue been identified as strategic in the first place, HQ would probably have stepped in earlier. It is also clear that the local MD, although a home country citizen from the Swedish parent, did not want HQ to "interfere". His loyalty was with M, rather than with either of the parents or the host country. The industry in which M operated might well be called salient.

## N - what price a company?

N was established about a decade ago as a joint venture between the Swedish parent and a local company. The Swedish partner has 51% and the local partner 49%. The local partner is the largest buyer on this market of the products in question.

The formation of N was from the Swedish company's point of view a way of raising barriers to competition on this market. As the partner was well aware of this, large concessions had to be made regarding ownership. Hence it was stipulated in the JV agreement that the local partner, after a certain number of years, had the right to acquire the missing 2%. If the local partner decided to do so, the Swedish partner had a right to sell also its remaining 49% to the partner at a price defined in the agreement. The Swe-

dish partner also had the right to demand that the
local partner buy its entire share at a defined
price.

The price was to be established through a formula
which took into account the net worth of the joint
venture at the time of purchase/selling, as well as
its net profit during the preceding X years.

The volume of shipments from Sweden is substantial.
The local partner has excellent relations with relevant regulatory bodies in the country. Both partners,
thus, can strongly influence profits as well as the
net worth of the joint venture. Since the Swedish
partner has management responsibility, no conflicts
over this issue have been apparent in N's day to day
operations. One may even wonder whether the Swedish
parent has at all bothered about the price, in case
an exchange of stock was proposed.

On the local board and in negotiations with the local
partner, however, it is apparent that the issue of
how profitable the partners shall allow the JV to become has been important. This may have detracted the
attention of the partners away from what from a business point of view is good for N. Consequently, N
cannot stand on its own feet, is undercapitalized and
unprofitable. The partners have created a company
which may be a good vehicle for each of their, partly
conflicting, interests, but in itself is unable to
function. This JV is "marginalized" to an extreme extent. But it may still very well fulfill its role.
The success of the JV may be totally irrelevant, as
long as the parents believe it serves its purpose.

## Company T - the chairman's pet

"This is a school-book example of how not to do it"
said the managing director of T to the interviewer.
"T was the market leader in several areas before the
joint venture was formed. Today we are hardly visible." This was, according to the MD largely due to the
joint venture agreement.

The JV was formed in the 1960s. Two local firms in
the same industry merged and in the process also the
Swedish parent stepped in with fresh capital. The
Swedish parent got a large minority share, whereas a
local holding company got 60% and a small percentage
was left with individual shareholders.

The three companies had all been competing on the local market and some neighboring markets before the
merger. For a few product lines their combined market
share had exceeded 80%. All three saw this as a logi-

cal step towards an improvement of their unsatisfactory profitability positions. They could rationalize their production as well as their marketing activities.

Products that were produced by more than one of the partners were allocated to one. The Swedish partner took care of marketing in Sweden and the local partner of marketing on the local market. Responsibility for other markets was also allocated between them. Internal exchange of know-how and R&D activities was stipulated to take place through an exchange of documents and personnel as well as study trips.

This JV is slightly less profitable than what is regarded as normal in both the parent groups. The local MD, as was stated in the beginning, sees the JV agreement as one important reason for the low profitability. The history of the JV has been unusually conflict ridden. However, the Swedish partner seems to regard the investment in T as strategically important and wants to keep it, or maybe even increase its share. The local partner does not want to sell out, apparently because of prestige, and cannot buy out the Swedish partner, who possesses the necessary technology. So both are locked into a situation of future collaboration.

The local partner has on a few occasions suggested that the agreement on production and marketing be changed. The Swedish partner has never accepted to discuss this matter. According to the MD, whose opinion in this case coincides with that of the local partner, the agreement should be changed in two respects.

1) Certain products are related and sold together. Separating the production of them, as is agreed, does not make sense, since the customer wants a package and does not care about individual products. The gain in production efficiency is too small to justify the separation.

2. T cannot control the sales force of the Swedish parent on the markets where the Swedish parent sells T's products. These markets account for about half of T's sales. The sales force of the Swedish parent gives higher priority to the parent's own products. They are evaluated and promoted by people in that organization and their careers are also within the parent's organization.

The local MD wanted T to have production <u>and</u> marketing responsibility worldwide for a smaller range of products.

Some other areas of conflict:

- An agreement was made about R&D cooperation for a new product generation. This was one of T's larger products, but one of marginal importance for the Swedish parent. The agreement allocated a large portion of the R&D work as well as production and marketing to T. The head of the product division concerned in Sweden was replaced. The new one did not honor the agreement at all, but started on a large scale to develop a competing product.

- In a similar case T agreed with the president of the Swedish parent to buy components from one of the divisions at a certain price. When the division was contacted, they had not heard about it. The chairman of the Swedish parent in subsequent board meeting at T: "Such a decision is not taken by the president but by the division."

- For three years T had discussed certain fees that one of the subsidiaries of the Swedish parent owed them. Nothing had happened. T then stopped shipping to the subsidiary. Immediately the head of the subsidiary and a vice president from the parent visited T and the money was paid.

- There is not a single Swede in T, nor anyone else who comes from the Swedish parent's organization. On the Board the Swedish parent has 2 out of 5 seats. The chairman of the Swedish parent is a member. He usually attends the board meetings in person.

- T was forced into dependence by the Swedish parent. Neither T's management, nor the local partner likes it, but there is very little they can do. T fulfills its role in the global strategy of the Swedish parent. The locals, however, want it to have a strategy of its own. They have recently embarked upon a diversification program. Several acquisitions have been made in order to obtain more independence from the Swedish parent. The latter does not like it but can do nothing.

- Support for T as a vehicle for the strategy of the Swedish parent is not widespread. Within the

Swedish company T is described as the chairman's pet.

Some of the examples above illustrate the difficulties in implementing decisions that concern T.

CONCLUDING REMARKS IN THE MANAGEMENT OF FOREIGN JOINT VENTURES

Are foreign investors best advised to avoid or accept joint ventures? Are host country governments best adviced to avoid or support the formation of joint ventures in their countries? Does it matter at all what degree of ownership the foreigner has?

The discussion that follows is limited to the types of operation that has been investigated in this project. Large scale international joint ventures such as Concorde or the Ericsson-Philips-Bell (Canada) project in Saudi Arabia thus may well merit other kinds of conclusions than those put forward here.

The joint ventures were as a whole found to be managed very much the same way as otherwise comparable wholly owned subsidiaries. Conflicts may have been more common, but they also existed in several wholly owned ones. Questions of national prestige, strong personalities or the division of responsibilities between the center and the periphery seemed at least as important in determining the incidence of conflict.

Strategic decisions are definitely more difficult to reach and to implement in JVs than in wholly owned subsidiaries. In situations of environmental uncertainty, rapidly changing market conditions or other so called turbulence the sharing of ownership may be a serious drawback. Several cases illustrate this. The result may very well be that both parties start to milk the JV when they realize that changes are too difficult to achieve.

On a similar matter several HQ executives commented that the benefits that one obtains from a JV are profits (if any) alone, but that wholly owned subsidiaries can also be used for obtaining less tangible and more long-term results as well. A JV cannot be as closely integrated into the planning, R&D, production personnel, finance or marketing systems of either parent as a wholly owned subsidiary. This is for fear of leakage and for reasons of lack of control.

Host governments should be aware of their difficulties as well. The local development effects of a JV may therefore be considerably lower than those of a wholly owned.

If large international corporations did function like the planned, administratively coordinated system they are designed to be (cf. Coase, 1937), one did not have to be concerned about the effects of joint ownership. But we have seen above that management systems are rather personal and that very often actions have to be initiated as a fast response to events on the market which are first noticed in the local company. Therefore the attitudes of the local manager and their identification do matter. It does not seem to be possible for a manager to identify to an equal extent with several parent firms.

The importance of the joint venture agreement has been stressed several times. An unbiased, clear and explicit agreement will help the parties sort out the problems as they arise and tends to diminish the incidence of negotiations in contacts between the parties. This point leads to the question what role the joint ownership really plays. If 100% ownership is required for the foreign parent to control and manage and anything less than 100% will lead to negotiations, delays and suboptimal decisions, then one alternative to full ownership that has to be considered is no ownership. The no ownership route is a purely contractual route to foreign activities. Licensing is a form for foreign production, which involves no ownership but rather a legal agreement. It gives the foreign "investor" a stream of license fees and no financial risk. The risk for technology leakage seems no greater than in a JV. Buckley & Davies (1979) give a good review of licensing as an alternative route to foreign operations. They argue that exactly the same type of ownership advantages will be required of a foreign licensor as of a foreign investor, but that the requirements for return may differ.

For the host country license agreements will probably look "cleaner" than those involving some ownership. The obvious drawback is that the country's hold on the foreign firm is much weaker. One cannot threat to nationalize or otherwise affect the property of the foreigner.

All in all, managers of TNCs should carefully consider alternatives to JVs, either full or no ownership, depending on the strength of the firm's technological leadership. Dynamic know-how would seem to be less risky to license out than static.

## REFERENCES

ANTHONY, R.N., 1965, Planning and Control Systems. A Framework for Analysis. Division of Research, Harvard Boston School, Boston, Mass.

BACK, R., DALBORG, H. and OTTERBECK, L., 1970, Lokalisering och ekonomisk strukturutveckling, EFI, Stockholm.

BUCKLEY, P.J. and DAVIES, H, 1979. The Place of Licensing in the Theory and Practice of Foreign Operations. University of Reading, Department of Economics. Discussion Paper No. 47, November.

BURNS, T. and STALKER, G.M., 1961, The Management of Innovation. London.

CHANDLER, A.D. Jr., 1962, Strategy and Structure. Chapters in the History of the American Enterprise. Cambridge, Mass.

COASE, R.H., 1937, The Nature of the Firm. Economica, Vol. 4, pp. 386-405.

EMERY, F.E. and TRIST, E.L., 1965, The causal texture of organizational environments. Human Relations, No. 18.

FRANKO, L.G., 1971, Joint Venture Survival in Multinational Corporations. Praeger, New York.

HEDLUND, G., 1978, Organization as a matter of style. European Institute for Advanced Studies in Management, Brussels. Working Paper 78/15.

OTTERBECK, L., 1979. Joint ventures på utlandsmarknader. In Otterbeck (ed) Marknadsföring och Strukturekonomi. Studentlitteratur, Stockholm, pp. 75-90.

PRALAHAD, C.K. and DOZ, Y., 1978, Strategic Management of Diversified Multinational Corporation. Paper presented at the Conference on Functioning of the Multinational Corporation. International Institute of Management, Berlin. December.

RHENMAN, E., 1973, Organization Theory for Long Range Planning. John Wiley, London.

SCOTT, B.R., 1970, Stages of Corporate Development. Harvard Business School. (mimeo)

296

STOPFORD, J. and WELLS, L.T. Jr., 1972, Managing the Multinational Enterprise. Basic Books, New York.

SWEDENBORG, B., 1980, The multinational operations of Swedish firms: An analysis of determinants and effects. Industrial Institute for Economic and Social Research. Stockholm.

THORNGREN, B., 1972, Studier i lokalisering. Regional Strukturanalys. EFI, Stockholm (Diss.).

# 13 Michael Z. Brooke and Joseph Holly:

# International Management Contracts

The management of companies abroad with minimal equity investment or none at all is an accelerating trend in international operations. The ability to control such arrangements without ownership is regarded as an important development in corporate - subsidiary relationships in this paper which describes a wide-ranging research into the phenomenon usually known as management contracts. The paper in fact brings together two important themes:

1. The relationship between the corporate headquarters and the foreign affiliate when the equity holding is small or zero.

2. The transfer of technology where, in fact, this is the main purpose of establishing or continuing the foreign operation.

These themes are traced through four disciplines and the implications worked out in terms of current research.

Among critical issues identified are the allocation of resources and the locus of authority in such ventures, as well as the policy implications for companies and governments.

## THE IMPORTANCE OF THE SUBJECT AND THE THEORETICAL BACKGROUND

"Perhaps the most important business development

---

Institute of Science & Technology
University of Manchester

of the second half of our century may prove to
be the rise of what I would call, for lack of a
better term 'corporate contract management'...
Under this new concept, the corporation does not
view itself as a direct mobilizer and allocator
of capital but as a generator and seller of management capability in the broadest sense".[1]

The provision of management services for companies
abroad under contract rather than as the result of
ownership has important implications in a number of
fields of study, these include:

1.  The theory of the firm. The deployment of sur-
    plus resources - management skill and technology
    especially - is seen to be an important reason
    for the emergence of management contracts. Other
    reasons for their increasing use in a variety of
    industrial sectors include both aggressive poli-
    cies - the search for new markets - and defen-
    sive policies, support for those which exist al-
    ready.

2.  Organization behaviour. Corporate structure is
    related to the drive for new routes abroad; and
    there are strong pressures in organizations
    against the complex power-sharing methods im-
    plied by management contracts. The mobilization
    of managerial and technical skills requires
    patterns of coordination and control different
    from those of direct investment. For instance
    there has to be a partnership with the client
    and a management system to match that partner-
    ship. This may not fit existing patterns of fi-
    nancing or marketing. Study of the organiza-
    tion's adaptation to management contracts should
    provide insights about the causes of particular
    relationships.

3.  Technology transfer. The transfer of knowledge
    is a much discussed but little understood sub-
    ject. Management contracts may be seen as a way
    of acquiring a technology while avoiding a supp-
    lier's monopolistic power over all the technolo-
    gical elements in the transfer. Some firms see
    management contracts as means of reducing the
    risks of failure in transferring a technology
    from one business environment to another. The
    mechanisms for the transmission of know-how and
    the control of technology have important impli-
    cations for both parties in a transfer.

4.  Futurology. The discussion is about a method of
    conducting international business which is not
    new, but is clearly destined to grow rapidly.

Scenarios for the next 10-15 years are likely to accord it an increasingly important place. A variety of factors - including shifting centres of production, exchange problems and controls on direct investment - will ensure this.

Each of these fields of study is explored in the research outlined below, and there is a close link between research into management contracts and other work undertaken in Manchester into organization and centralization in the international firm. The delay in developing the contractual method, in spite of many advantages, and the scepticism surrounding this development are probably related to the allure of unambiguous control to which many writers have referred[2]. It could be said that the theory of the firm explains why contracts are likely to happen (the return on investment can be very large), while an understanding of organization behaviour explains why they are not more common (the enthusiasm is limited).

The present research is concentrating especially on the transfer of technology from developed to developing nations - an important factor in the industrial policies of less developed countries. Those countries have sought various methods by which technology can be absorbed to create or strengthen the industrial infrastructure. It is recognised that technology cannot be transferred by a creeping process of diffusion, but must be transferred purposefully and more rapidly. Yet technology transfer has been uneven in its geographical impact; there is concern about a widening technology gap between the developed and the less developed countries as well as between the wealthier and the less favoured of the latter group. Despite the complex and extensive interchange of technology worldwide, the question remains why some firms and countries fail to take full advantage of the potentials offered by the transfer of technology from the developed world. Part of the answer must rest in understanding the factors which influence the application of a new technology. Not enough attention seems to have been given to this issue in the literature. Accordingly, it is necessary to move towards identifying sets of factors which are likely to influence the international transfer and application of technology. It is plausible to assume that a dominant consideration in the international transfer of technology is managerial capability. This links into the study of corporate-subsidiary relationships in general.

Because the company managed under contract is highly dependent, the relationship is a centralized one - assuming the question of ownership and ultimate responsibility is ignored. Research into management contracts has been conducted in the International Business Unit in the University of Manchester Institute of Science and Technology through a series of small-scale projects. These started in the early 1970s when the subject was identified as a priority one for research, and form the background to a major exercise funded for three years by the Leverhulme Trust. The present state of knowledge and plans for further research are described in this paper.

## THE MEANING OF MANAGEMENT CONTRACTS

An underlying assumption is that the development of managerial capability is a vital factor in successful technology transfer. Much of the literature reflects a concern with the wider problems and costs of transmitting and absorbing information. But these issues are also important at the management level. In particular they confront firms involved in technology transfer, irrespective of whether the transfer occurs domestically from one manufacturing or service facility to another, or internationally from one country to another. Success requires the transmission and absorption of a great deal of information, both technical and organizational. It is often felt that an important attribute of transnational companies is the ability to manage these functions efficiently. However, little is known about how the task is managed, the resources employed, or the costs and problems involved. The object of our study, at both the analytical and factual levels, is to increase knowledge about the international transmission of managerial, as well as technical, know-how.

The study of technology transfer has been undertaken internationally, and there now exists an extensive literature. This literature ranges from discussions of the social and macroeconomic implications of technological change to the study of specific examples. These investigations have revealed many of the practices and effects of the new technologies.

As a result governments of developing countries are adopting more sophisticated approaches to the negotiation and operation of transfer agreements[3]. Consequently international firms have been confronted with governmental policies affecting their own organization structures, policies, and investments.

301

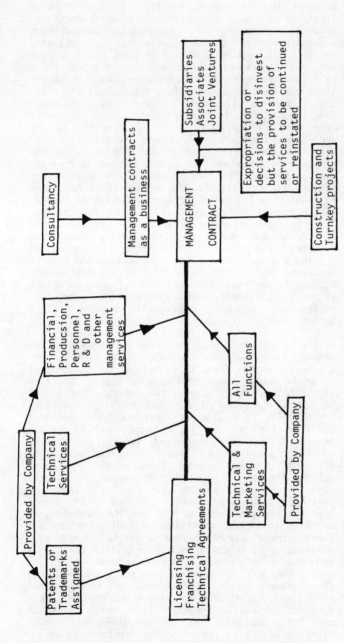

This figure is for definitional purposes. The lines do not necessarily represent historical developments.

FIGURE 1    The Management Contract

The phrase "Management Contracts" is used of agreements whereby a firm takes responsibility for one or more of the management functions of another with little or no equity interest. Such an arrangement can arise from problems with licensing agreements, from expropriation or as an appropriate and rewarding means of conducting business. Figure 1 illustrates the progenitors of management contracts and their relationships to other business methods. It emphasises the fact that there is a spectrum of undertakings along which licensing contracts shade into management contracts. This also points to the problem of definition. If a <u>pure</u> [4] licensing agreement is one where the parent company permits the use of its patents in return for payment and a <u>pure</u> management contract is one where the parent company manages all the functions of the foreign associate without ownership, most arrangements lie between those two. Some may call them licensing agreements and others management contracts. The same is true of franchising. Other arrangements such as construction contracts and turnkey projects may also develop into all-embracing packages. Indeed, with these methods of conducting foreign business, the client may well demand further services. So the ability to provide a complete managegement contract becomes part of the marketing effort. Additionally, the contract may come into existence to protect - temporarily or permanently - any of these arrangements.

As far as the developing countries are concerned, the contract can be either a negative or positive response to demands for both technology and the control of their own economic development. Indeed, the firm of the future may be seen as the one that specializes in non-equity forms of business activity: investing "principally in R & D, in international recruitment and training of skilled technical and managerial personnel, in organization of interrelated global markets.... and in the capability of engineering and starting up modern plants, farms, mines, fisheries, schools, hospitals - whatever is needed, so long as ownership is not a precondition." [5] Some of these activities, it should be noted, involve little direct transfer of technology. A hospital, for instance, is unlikely to be accompanied by a medical school although there may be educational facilities provided by a different agency. The British Council is an example of a body establishing such facilities under contract. The economic and political relationship between developing countries and international firms is changing and the management contract as a form of non-equity agreement is finding increasing use. Until Gabriel's book in 1967 there was no published research on the management contract as an al-

ternative method of business.[6] Yet Gabriel claims
that this is not a radically new concept. What he
suggests is that the system should be examined because it has proved successful before and it could be
adapted to the problems of economic development and
technology transfer which exist today.

Gabriel points to components of the contract including the commitment of intangible resources, which
are combinations of skills, techniques, knowledge,
technology, management and entrepreneurship. Although
Gabriel does not exclude contributions of capital,
his analysis concentrates on those management contracts which did not include capital investment. In a
later article Gabriel acknowledged that there were
many instances in which a firm supplying the service
or process does have an equity interest in the business or project in the host country.[7] This might be
a conventional equity interest or a negotiated
arrangement with the host government in which the
contractor is guaranteed a specific percentage return on invested capital as long as the partnership
lasts.

Gabriel also concentrated on management contracts
which operated between private companies and government-owned enterprises in the less developed countries. There are many examples of private to private,
public to private and public to public arrangements.
Research needs to be done to test whether Gabriel's
work is applicable to those arrangements as well as
testing his conclusions with a broader data-base. It
cannot be assumed, for example, that the transfer of
skills between a private and a government-owned firm
will be as feasible with a different interfirm arrangement - although preliminary results show it usually
is. There might be different legal conditions stipulated in the contract, more complications inherent in
control arrangements and division of responsibility
between firms and more complications on financing and
profit-sharing. These are a few of the possible additional problems.

For the present, research management contracts have
been defined so as to include a variety of interesting and relevant cases. Both public and private firms
are involved, but attention is focussed on the use of
management contracts in developing countries. The research seeks to define and analyse the benefits and
drawbacks from the use of such agreements both for
the country and for the firm. The focus here is on
less developed countries, but it needs to be recognised that management contracts exist and are becoming more common between industrialized countries
and between Western and Eastern enterprises.

The actual form of the contract will vary considerably from case to case, and so will the words used. For instance a particular project may be described as "for guidance and advice only" where management is also intended. The particular form of words may be for legal reasons and may not affect the activity undertaken - to avoid, for instance, liability under the Fair Contracts Terms Act. The present definition is concerned with the substance and hence covers many operations not specifically called management contracts.

THE MANCHESTER STUDIES

A pioneer survey was carried out in 1975 when representatives of fourteen British-based multinationals were interviewed by a researcher. These fourteen were virtually all the British companies known at the time to employ this method of business; some companies refused to co-operate on the grounds that, although they had management contracts abroad, they were not a multinational in the "conventional sense". This points to a definitional problem not just with the term management contract but with many social and management science terms. Five years later we find a much larger number of companies using the phrase and others recognising that they give the same activity another name such as Management Agency.

Yet even in 1975, it was possible to report about management contracts:

> "Once an anomaly in the overall international activities of the corporation, they now seem to be increasingly used as a strategic alternative to direct investment. This may be for several reasons not least of which is the increasing dislike of many countries of foreign control over sectors of their economies. One of the most important results of the current investigation has been to underline the trend towards using management contracts as a strategy in their own right. Companies can reap substantial benefits from their use especially if they set out actively to sell their stock of managerial skill and resources. The most successful companies are building an organization framework in order to exploit these opportunities; there is increasing competition amongst companies for these contracts. A further point has come out quite clearly and has serious implications for a company's policies. Although the research supports the advisability of short-term contracts it would be a mistake to see this as limiting a company's long-term opportunities in a particu-

lar country. The successful completion of a particular contract (success often being based upon
the speed of completion and withdrawal of the
company) would in many cases lead to opportunities for undertaking further contracts related
to similar ventures in the expansion or the diversification phases of the local contract enterprise. Further so competitive is the field
becoming and so few are the companies which are
experienced in operating such contracts, that
successful operations in one country have often
proved a decided advantage when opportunities
arose in others. The 'world' of management contracts operations is still sufficiently small to
be considered almost as a 'club'."

The 1975 report listed a number of factors which more
thorough research and analysis of the subject should
consider, including:

The reason for using management contracts.

A distinction was made between offensive and defensive reasons. Offensive reasons include the
employment of under-used managerial skills and
resources, as well as securing new markets or
sources of supply. The use of management contracts as a complementary part of an international strategy, as a "window" to markets where investment is possible, was considered. Defensive
reasons include support of technical know-how
agreements and joint ventures, and protection of
existing markets where the government policy was
one of indigenisation or expropriation.

The critical problems.

Notable difficulties that arise with management
contracts, and with other collaborative arrangements are:

(1)  Remuneration. Numerous methods of payment
     have been tried including a straight fee,
     a percentage of sales, a percentage of in-
     come, a share in the equity and several
     others. There are also combinations of
     straight fee and percentage and perhaps a
     small amount of equity as well. Conflict
     on incentives and on the amount and cost
     of resources contributed is expected. There
     is also a conflict of interest whose nature
     varies according to the way the remunera-
     tion issue is resolved. For instance, the
     holding of equity (which is common) gives
     rise to a conflict for the parent company

between its role as owner and its role as
consultant. The lack of equity, on the
other hand, makes other solutions to the
remuneration question more difficult.

(2) The contract itself. The document looms
large during the negotiations, but is not
always helpful in resolving conflicts; it
is normally only invoked when the business
relationship has broken down, and for this
inadequate provision is often made. Sometimes the client will have a standard form
of contract produced on all occasions. The
Algerian government, for instance, has a
document of 300 pages.

(3) Other significant problems related to the
numbers and qualifications of seconded
staff, organization and manpower planning
within the contractor firm and the distribution of control between the contractor
and client. One critical problem concerned
training and transfer, the company and the
client government often differed in their
benefits about how quickly training and the
transfer of responsibility could take
place.

The factors influencing success.

The factors influencing success in management
contracts were as much related to philosophy and
attitude as they were to skill and the ability
to overcome problems arising from conflicts of
interest. The holding of equity, in particular,
was generally held to be undesirable because of
the inherent conflict between the profit maximizing objectives of the company, and the economic
and social development objectives of the host
country.

During the intervening years, progress had been made
slowly towards the building up of a body of knowledge
suitable for launching a major research programme.
This has included interviewing companies and developing contracts overseas from which support for such a
programme has been forthcoming. The companies have
included three or four which have been attempting,
with varying degrees of success, to market management
contracts as a business in its own right. For those
companies which have had little success, the interesting question is whether their effort is running into a
blind alley, or whether they are ahead of their time.

# MANAGEMENT CONTRACTS AS A MEANS OF TECHNOLOGY TRANS-FER

One of the main concerns in the research project is to analyse the effects of various influences on functions and activities related to the production, diffusion, transfer and use of technological and managerial expertise. It is necessary to sketch roughly the conceptual relationships between management and technology, and to argue that their overlapping in many different circumstances frequently renders them indistinguishable. The research recognises that full exploitation of the transfer of technology most often takes place in the framework of interfirm co-operation. Although it is widely understood that transfer is not complete until total absorption throughout the relevant enterprise is accomplished, transfer is not fully acknowledged as requiring organizational innovation and changes in the mechanisms of control and information dissemination within the enterprise. Acknowledgement of that requirement involves recognising that technology is as much a matter of organizations and the management of organizations and their physical environment as it is of blue-prints, tools and machinery. For successful transfer there needs to be investment in management and the capability to develop a self-sustaining organization. In that process the knowledge of how to do things with both people and resources is in many ways more important than the amount and type of physical capital involved.

First and foremost, management contracts are designed so as to guarantee the continued and profitable operation of a firm and the efficient transmission of expertise. Sometimes they are also used to create a new enterprise. In those contexts technology includes organization and management as well as hardware. This definition of technology as the scientific development and application of knowledge and experience over the complete spectrum of the production process and associated services, from research to marketing. It is possible, as a consequence, to see management contracts as a form of technology transfer and to see the need for less developed countries to invest in management capability as well as technical expertise, tools and machinery.

This form of transfer, like any other, has costs for both the company and the country. These costs are hard to quantify but efforts are being made. Meanwhile most developing countries are convinced that they are paying too much for limited amounts of knowledge. The customer, in this case usually a national government, has little choice in the products

being made available and is unable to evaluate and
negotiate the best adaptations to local conditions.
It should be recognised that technology transfer may
be difficult and costly even between industrialized
countries. A study of the electronic capital goods
industry in Britain, for example, mentions that the
"process known as 'Anglicisation' that is the manufacture in Britain of American designs with some (or
all) British components, can involve a considerable
development effort. Several firms came to the conclusion that it would have been cheaper and quicker
in some cases to design a fresh product from the
start."[9] The point here is that the level of investment in the various resources for a transfer can
be high for both parties. Arrow, in a different context, points to the same conclusion: "From the case
studies.... it can be inferred that the diffusion
of information is by no means a cost free process,
even apart from artificial barriers in the form of
patents and secrecy .... considerable investment
must be made to make use of knowledge."[10]

While the transmission of some kinds of knowledge
might require trivial costs, the costs of transferring technical and managerial knowledge are
usually not trivial.[11] Aside from royalty payments,
which are in the nature of economic rents, substantial resources might have to be used not only
to transmit information, but also to ensure its
successful absorption. Only a broad outline of
technical information can be set down in patents,
formulae, and blueprints, or communicated by teaching
outside the production process or service facility itself. The implication is that when consideration is
given to both the transmittal and absorption costs,
the costs of transfer might be considerable,
especially if the ability to decode and understand
the transmitted information is not generally available. On this last point it is easy to see why a
number of management contracts have arisen from the
breakdown of licensing or franchise agreements. In
these cases the licensee has not shown sufficient
technical, marketing or financial expertise to fulfill the agreement. The licensor has had then to step
in with this expertise to carry out the agreement.
Rosenberg points to "the extent to which the transfer
of technological skills - even between two countries
so apparently 'close together' as Britain and the
United States in the mid 19th century - were dependent upon the transfer of skilled personnel."[12] The
thrust of the argument is that costs of transfer may
be considerable when the firm does not have the
necessary skills to absorb the technology. Management contracts can be seen as a way of reducing the
costs by avoiding breaks in technical and managerial

continuity, providing a period for indigenous personnel to learn the business and the technology, and avoiding expensive initial errors through inexperience.

This last point also applies to another way in which management contracts have developed, and illustrates the closeness and overlapping of the concepts of managerial and technical expertise in technology - and the overlapping is critical to our understanding of the subject. Management contracts have often been agreed after nationalization or where a government has demanded major local equity participation. Although there may be many local, technically trained people in the industry, the level of technical and managerial competence is not high enough to manage the whole organization. A management team must be brought in for a time to train locals to the required level, as well as to operate the company. In one example, in transportation, the important department was vehicle maintenance. Although the local men were mechanically competent, they had no concept of preventive maintenance as opposed to curative maintenance. As a result vehicles suffered from excessive wear-and-tear and were quickly written off. An expatriate engineer was required to re-organize the department to undertake preventive work and instil the technical and managerial concept into the working patterns of the firm.

THE SCOPE OF THE STUDY

Conceptually it is useful to distinguish between the horizontal and the vertical transfer of know-how. Vertical transfer refers to the transfer of information and expertise within the various stages of a particular, usually innovative, project. Horizontal transfer refers to the transfer of information and expertise from one project to another. Thus, the transfer of information from the experimental stage to the prototype stage of a project would be an example of vertical transfer.

The transfer from one firm to another of the expertise to manufacture a previously commercialised product would represent a horizontal transfer. Sometimes a transfer may involve transfers of information and expertise which are both vertical and horizontal, such as when a new product or process developed within one firm is first manufactured commercially within another. Nevertheless, it seems useful to retain the distinction between the two basic types because most management contracts seem to involve transfers of the horizontal kind. That is to say, the information and expertise being trans-

ferred have been tried and tested commercially elsewhere, usually with success.

A further distinction should be made between types
of horizontal technology to clarify the range of the
research still further. It is useful to distinguish
between "capital goods transfer", "technique transfer" and "capability transfer".[13] The first is
characterised by the importation of new products or
materials with no adaptation to the local environment. As already mentioned, this may not involve a
transfer of skills at all. It might also be characterised by construction projects of factories or
service facilities without responsibility for
commissioning or initial start up. In these cases,
the know-how transferred is embodied in the various
materials, products and components. The import of
embodied know-how often impedes proper understanding
of its characteristics and leads to a pseudo-trans-
ference of knowledge that, although imported, is not
understood.

The second type involves the transfer of the technical and managerial techniques to operate the factory
or service facility domestically. This will involve
the transmittal and absorption of the requisite information and skills, and may take many years as the
level of competence of indigenous personnel rises
through the organization. The third phase involves
the transfer of scientific knowledge and the capability to modify imported technology - the transferee will
use the necessary techniques to sustain and develop
the enterprise. It is during this phase that the indigenous personnel combine the different cognitive
elements of a technology and develop their own
capacity to translate different types of knowledge
into economically feasible or socially useful
processes. Both the transfer of capability and
technique can involve the employment of expatriate
managers and engineers for considerable periods of
time.

The scope of our study will be largely restricted
to horizontal transfer of the technique and capability types. The transfers occur via firms that are
international in the scope of their manufacturing or
marketing activity. Those international, mostly
British-based, firms have little or no equity
interest in the developing country's firm. Nevertheless this is an area of considerable concern,
especially to the less developed countries as im-
porters of technology.

Within the limits indicated, our study seeks to
examine the mechanics of international corporate
technology transfer as it relates to managerial
capability. It also seeks to provide evidence of
the levels and determinants of management contract
costs and benefits. The focus of the study is limited to transfers outwards from Britain, and possibly
France, to West and North Africa, and the Middle
East. The contractors are private or public companies, mostly British. The study covers a wide range
of problems arising from management contracts, with
less developed country's governments as well as its
private firms. It may also include the transfer of
managerial capability that might occur as an addition
to the export of capital goods whether by sale or
leasing. In such cases technical consultancy agreements might be incorporated into the management
contract. Purely technical consultancy agreements
would only be included for comparison or other
special reasons as being part of the basic study.

At this point there is a close connection between the
study of management contracts and of the organization
of the multinational firm. Between the determination
of some companies to retain undivided authority and
the ability of others to exercise their normal control system even where their ownership is less than
half of the equity, much experimentation is taking
place. An understanding of this invokes a consideration on the boundaries of organization. The influence
of the parent company can be pervasive for an
affiliate where ownership does not exist, while a
wholly owned subsidiary can pursue completely independent policies. The control of collaborative
arrangements - such as agencies, licences or management contracts - can vary in most of the ways that
control of subsidiaries does. They can be treated at
arm's length or effectively incorporated into the
parent organization.

METHODOLOGY

The preliminary surveys have relied on interviews
with company executives as well as the limited
existing literature. The main thrust of the forthcoming research will be on interviews. It is planned
to concentrate on government policy-makers and
company executives in Britain, West and North Africa
and the Middle East. Over 200 firms have been contacted, covering a wide range of industries. The
contact list is being expanded as more information
is forthcoming. Fifty companies have already been
interviewed. Most of these have agreed to further
interviews and co-operation. This will ensure that
useful and comparable data can be obtained from
each.

The companies which did not provide data claimed that they did not operate management contracts, or that the information was proprietary and could not be made available. Nevertheless, some of those which could not provide relevant data have often been willing to discuss their experiences with related forms of business, and this information will be useful for developing hypotheses and models of the structure and operation of management contracts.

Abroad, similar interviews will be conducted in order to assess the working of management contracts from as objective a standpoint as possible. Management contracts have partly arisen from restrictions placed on international companies by less developed countries. It is therefore necessary to know what the latter think of management contracts, their development, their operation and their future. The actions of less developed countries based on their views of management contracts are of increasing importance in equity and non-equity forms of business. Moreover, since accounting, control and technical systems are not generally designed to supply data in the form wanted, the available data will have to be adjusted. This can only be done with the full assistance from individuals in firms who have intensive experience of operating management contracts and from other experts knowledgeable in the various industries, technologies and countries.

Our research will only improve on the quality of explanation and understanding already available if considerable care is taken to clarify the methods and assumptions of the inquiry. Decisions as to which agreements, organizations and types of behaviour are to count and how they should be grouped for investigation have far-reaching implications for the adequacy of the subsequent analyses. This is especially the case with a complex subject which includes technology transfer, economic development and organization behaviour. It is necessary to develop modes of classification which do justice to the rich variety of contractual relationships. The problem may be perceived to be that of delineation of the field, but the real danger is over-exclusion. It is only by comparing the types of companies, industries, techniques and practices of paradigm cases of management contracts with commercial arrangements on the periphery of the category that a social scientific approach can succeed in its major objective: that of providing a critical understanding of the behaviour of organizations (public and private), of the economic and political processes by which their contracts have arisen and sustained, of the processes of technology transfer and of the significance of their practices and outcome for continuing and growing international trade.

A study of management contracts needs to be wide-ranging. The study will include theories and techniques ranging from economics to social psychology, as well as from politics and social geography. The problems of such an enterprise are well-known, but it is hoped that the investigation will show how an inter-disciplinary approach is capable of resulting in much that is genuinely analytical, and potentially beneficial. The view of the research group is that few social scientists have yet addressed themselves to the issues raised by management contracts, the present approach is best suited to the problem, and it is appropriate initially to delineate the subject of study in broad terms.

RESEARCH ISSUES AND PRELIMINARY INDICATIONS

The initial interviews with British-based companies have provided preliminary indications for further progress in the research. Several industries have been approached and six roughly distinguishable groups of companies are providing a basis for further research.

1.  The first group is made up of state-owned industries which undertake management contract work to use excess management resources and as part of a deliberate policy to act as spearheads for British manufacturers exporting to particular markets. A number of these industries have undertaken management contracts in their own right for many years and provide a fertile source of long-term agreements with no equity. These same industries have often formed consortia with private companies for particular projects in turnkey-like operations. There has, however, been an increasing willingness to take on the operation of an enterprise after commissioning with a management contract.

2.  The second group comprises service industries which have long experience with management contracts in the Middle East and Africa. These have taken on management contracts as an alternative to investing risk capital rather than as a result of government policy, in less developed countries. Management contracts in the hotel business are the prime example and there is a body of literature available to assist our research. Other service industries in this area are those in health and transportation, although their histories are different.

3.  The agricultural processing industries provide
    the third area of research which most closely
    accords with our aim of studying management con-
    tracts as income providers rather than equity
    protectors. Agricultural projects in the Third
    World would seem to offer the best long-term
    prospect of management contracts as the world
    demand for their products is high and will con-
    tinue to rise. The agricultural industry covers
    a wide range of activities including livestock
    rearing, irrigation schemes, plantations and
    outcropping as well as the processing and refin-
    ing of products.

4.  The fourth area is that of the extractive in-
    dustries of non-fuel minerals and timber. The
    governments of LDCs have been most active in
    this area as nationalist attitudes demand con-
    trol of a country's natural resources. Unlike
    the other areas of research, substantial - al-
    though still minority - equity may be involved.
    Research has already been done in the nationali-
    zation of mining which has led to management
    contracts. It provides an interesting demonstra-
    tion of the political conflicts arising from
    multinational companies and governments seeking
    to control resources available to world markets.
    The cases of the copper mines of Zambia and Chi-
    le are the best known and provide interesting
    parallels and comparisons for our work in other
    parts of the world.

5.  The fifth area of research is receiving large-
    scale consideration from many quarters and many
    standpoints. The general area is petrochemical
    and chemical industries in which exists a com-
    plex network of agreements on technology, natur-
    al resources and expertise. Problems of the
    relationships of ownership and control are
    important politically in this area. The research
    includes the Middle East and North Africa, and
    there is a fund of information to be made avail-
    able. However, it is also a politically sensi-
    tive area and companies have been unwilling to
    respond, although there are many activities
    undertaken in these sectors.

6.  The sixth group is the least well-defined. It
    contains many manufacturing industries which
    are oriented predominantly to direct investment
    or the sale of equipment. The allure of undi-
    vided authority in direct investment, mentioned
    above, makes many unwilling to enter collabora-
    tive ventures while their market power and
    technical capability make it unnecessary. When

for political reasons they are forced to accept
nonmajority shares, management contracts are used
as a means of equity protection rather than as
income producers. The principal aim is control,
to such an extent in some cases that a management
contract is operated with a nominal fee or none
at all. However the increasingly competitive
environment can be expected to enforce changes
in strategy. In the case of equipment manufacturers, the aim of a management contract is to
create or expand a market which requires more
equipment. The object is to sell equipment
manufactured at home, and the management contract
ensures sales by transferring knowledge of how
to use the equipment.

Across the six groups there is a mixture of motiva-
tions. There are also common issues that arise with
regard to national development plans, business
strategies and technology transfer. Development plans
need to include the import of managerial know-how
and the creation of indigenous managerial skills.
Management contracts need to be examined in order to
ascertain whether they are an economic and effective
way of ensuring technology transfer so vital to the
developing world.

The economic and political costs and benefits of
management contracts in comparison to other possible
corporate strategies such as licensing, franchising
and direct investment need to be investigated. Issues
of financial and personnel commitment and conditions
arise as soon as any business venture is contemplated,
but the problem for management contracts is that
there are few research-based criteria on which to
make decisions. Moreover, the criteria of acceptance
and success will vary if the industry is resource-
based, technology-based or service-based. In each
case, problems of resource allocation, legal obliga-
tions and responsibilities, and control have been
dealt with by firms and countries on an ad hoc
basis. At this stage, the issues can only be indicated and questions posed about the success and failure
of management contracts. The research is designed to
bring more clarity to the factors important to the
negotiation and operation of a mode of commercial
activity which is being adapted to changing
conditions in both companies and countries.

316

NOTES AND REFERENCES

GABRIEL, Peter P. (1970) "New Concepts in Overseas Investment" in MANN, R. The Arts of Top
Management, McGraw-Hill, London p. 106.

2.    See, for example, BROOKE M.Z. and REMMERS, H.L.
(1978) The Strategy of Multinational Enterprise,
2nd Edition. Pitman, Chapter 3.
and
STOPFORD, J.M. and WELLS, L.T. (1972) Managing
the Multinational Enterprise, Basic Books, Chapter 8.

3.    Under the Andean Pact agreement much discussion
of "unpackaging technology" has taken place. See
JUNTA    DEL    ACUERDO    DE    CARTAGENA    (1976).
"Technology Policy and Economic Development"
International    Development    Research    Centre,
Ottawa.

A useful introduction to the literature of technology transfer is to be found in SPIEGEL-
ROSING, I. and DE SOLLA PRICE, D. (1978) Science,
Technology and Society. Sage, London, Chapters
14 and 15.

4.    The phrases used in most accounts of multinational companies are used here of those with management contracts. Thus, parent company and head
office are used of the company that provides the
management services, while home country is the
country of origin of that company. Host country
is used of the native country of the firm in
which the contract is exercised which may be
called an affiliate or subsidiary or associate
according to its status.

5.    ROBINSON, Richard in BROWN C.C. ed. (1970)
World Business: Promise and Problems. New York:
Macmillan, p. 276.
See also GALLOWAY. J. (1970) "World-Wide Corpo-
rations and International Integration: the case
of Intelsat"
International Organization, 24. Autumn, pp. 503-
519.

6.    GABRIEL, Peter P. (1967) The International
Transfer of Corporate Skills: Management Contracts in Less Developed Countries. Harvard, pp.
38-55.

7.    See GABRIEL, P.P. (1972) "Adaptation; the name
of the MNC's game" Columbia Journal of World
Business, 7.6, Nov-Dec, pp. 7-14.

317

Also GABRIEL P.P. (1972) "Multinationals in the Third World: Is Conflict Unavoidable?" Harvard Business Review, 50, July-August, pp. 93-102.

8. The report has been summarised in BROOKE, M.Z. and REMMERS, H.L. (1977) The International Firm Pitman, p.p. 25-32.
See also, ELLISON, R.J.T. (1976) "Management Contracts"
Multinational Business. March p.p. 19-28.

9. FREEMAN, C.L. (1965) "Research and Development in Electronic Capital Goods" National Institute Economic Review 34, Nov. p. 63.

10. ARROW, K. (1962) "Comment" in The Rate and Direction of Inventive Activity. Princeton University Press, p. 354.

11. For a study of the costs of technology transfer, see:
TEECE, D.J. (1976) The Multinational Corporation and the Resource Cost of International Technology Transfer.
Cambridge, Mass.: Ballinger.

12. ROSENBERG, N. (1976) Perspectives on Technology Cambridge University Press. p. 154.

13. Similar phases are distinguished by TEECE, D.J. (as note 11 above) p. 7. Extensive use of Teece has been made throughout the discussion without the use of quotation marks.

# 14 David H. Blake:

# Headquarters and Subsidiary Roles in Managing International Public Affairs — A Preliminary Investigation

In the management of international public affairs, what should the responsibilities of subsidiary managers be? What role should headquarters managers have? How should they relate to one another? These questions are answered quite differently by different transnational corporations. Some international firms insist that there is a high degree of decentralization in the function with subsidiary managers shouldering most of the burden for maintaining effective relations with the host country environment. Others exhibit a more highly centralized organizational structure. For some, the function is quite unimportant, but for many multinationals, the pattern that has emerged is a mixture of responsibilities at both levels that has often evolved over time without a well-founded guiding principle. Few companies have been as self-conscious in this effort as Caterpillar Tractor which has developed the concept whereby headquarters and subsidiary managers are <u>separately responsible</u> for the management of international public affairs.

* This research was partially funded by the Fund for Multinational Management Education of New York and by the Graduate School of Business at the University of Pittsburgh. Coral Snodgrass and Robert Stephens were instrumental in all phases of the project.

University of Pittsburgh

For several reasons, the nature of the respective roles of headquarters and subsidiary managers in international public affairs is an important and largely unresolved issue. First, few firms have been able to allocate precisely various public affairs tasks since the tasks themselves are still being defined, and the skills, tools, and techniques of public affairs management are still being developed. Second, since many subsidiary managers of public affairs report to local operating managers, the relationship with the headquarters public affairs professionals is often indirect and complex. Further, in many subsidiaries the responsibility for public affairs is assigned to a manager with other duties such as marketing or personnel, further complicating the issues of authority, responsibility, and reporting both within the subsidiary and with the headquarters. Third, because it is difficult to measure the value or success of public affairs efforts, reporting relationships between headquarters and subsidiaries rarely involve the filing of reports which readily indicate public affairs accomplishments as opposed to public affairs activities. Thus, a simple monitoring of performance and results, which allows for a clear definition of responsibilities, is not often achieved. Fourth, the ease with which actions and events in one country can cross borders to create problems for subsidiaries in other countries has required shared responsibility for the management of international public affairs in individual countries and on a regional or corporate-wide basis.

These difficulties take place within the context of a growing recognition by top management of the importance of national and international public affairs activity. However, as more resources are committed to international public affairs and as the costs of ineffective relationships with segments of the environment become more apparent, high level executives are insisting that public affairs efforts produce results. In some companies, the function no longer operates in the backwater of company attention and resource commitments, but along with this greater attention comes closer scrutiny of methods and outcomes. Consequently, the management of the public affairs function at headquarters and subsidiaries requires more coordination and control than when the function was essentially ignored.

In the light of these developments and characteristics, the roles of subsidiary and headquarters executives in the management of public affairs is an important subject for corporate policy analysis and academic study. Research on the topic is essentially

321

non-existent and fraught with significant problems.*
To begin with the systematic and conscious management of international public affairs is highly
underdeveloped. A few firms have made great strides
in this field, but most are just beginning to recognize its importance and have a long way to go before
developing and implementing an overall strategy.
Indeed, in practice, there is substantial disagreement about the substance of international public
affairs varying from press and community relations
to the preparation of publications to sophisticated
issue management and environmental scanning techniques and responsibilities. Secondly, international
public affairs practice differs widely among various
transnational corporations. In addition, for many of
the larger and more complex firms, there is great
variation in practice among the company's foreign
subsidiaries. Thus, meaningful generalizations cannot be made with a high degree of confidence. Thirdly, given the underdeveloped state of the field,
research on these issues is dependent upon the good-
will and forebearance of corporate managers in
responding to the questions of probing academics who
implicitly or explicitly try to impose a structure
or degree of rigor which is often not compatible
with corporate practice. In spite of these and other
serious problems, an exploratory attempt has been
made to gather information about headquarters and
subsidiary roles in the management of public affairs
at the foreign locations of transnational corporations.

This paper reports on the results of this investigation. While the limitations of the study and the
data collected are severe, it is hoped that the
"findings" will enable subsequent research to define
more clearly the questions to be asked and to develop a more effective research methodology.

The next section of the paper explains the research
approach used and its limitations. Then the results
of the research follow. The final section restates
some of the unanswered questions and discusses
directions for further research.

* A list of books and articles on the management
of international public affairs is appended to this
paper. To varying degrees, some of these address the
issue of headquarters-subsidiary relationships.

METHODOLOGY

The purpose of the research was to obtain information about the roles of headquarters and subsidiary
managers in the management of international public
affairs. Specifically, the research focused on the
degree of involvement of headquarters and subsidiary
personnel in various elements of this managerial
function. We were not concerned with some arbitrary
measure of centralization or decentralization of
activity and responsibility; instead an investigation into the depth and nature of the involvement of
each level was intended. In addition, the importance
of company characteristics like overall sales, percentage of income from subsidiaries in developing
countries, degree of integration, type of business,
and other similar factors were analyzed in terms of
their relationship to the degree of headquarters and
subsidiary involvement.

A questionnaire was developed and sent to headquarters public affairs officers at 159 multinationals
based in the United States. Unfortunately, a disappointing 30 useable responses were received, far
too few for any meaningful results. Interviews were
conducted with twelve firms to supplement the
questionnaire. The companies and managers were
obtained from lists of people who had evidenced
interest in the subject by participation in various
meetings on the subject of international public
affairs management.

There were several parts of the questionnaire. One
asked for background information about the company
and the respondent's views on matters like the
degree of integration of operations, the likelihood
of expansion, and the amount of top management
support. The second part of the questionnaire asked
the responding managers to indicate on a five point
scale from no involvement (1) to deep involvement
(5) the degree to which headquarters and subsidiary
managers were involved in 18 different aspects of
public affairs management printed below. These 18
tasks were grouped into three basic functions,
formulation of international public affairs policies, implementation of international public affairs
policies, and evaluation of international public
affairs policies.

Formulation of International Public Affairs Policies

1.  Identification of public affairs issues
2.  Gathering information about public affairs
    issues
3.  Setting objectives for public affairs efforts

4. Devising strategies for dealing with public affairs issues
5. Establishing general procedures for managing public affairs activities

## Implementation of International Public Affairs Policies

1. Developing tactics for dealing with specific public affairs issues
2. Execution of public affairs policies and tactics
3. Determination of budget for subsidiary public affairs efforts
4. Integrating public affairs concerns and efforts with the planning process
5. Organizing and coordinating public affairs efforts and concerns with operating functions
6. Involvement in selection of personnel (staff or line) with public affairs responsibilities
7. Training personnel to be more effective with public affairs issues

## Evaluation of International Public Affairs Policies

1. Obtaining feedback on effectiveness of public affairs efforts
2. Evaluating personnel (staff or line) with regard to public affairs effectiveness
3. Determination of reward structure for personnel with public affairs responsibilities
4. Dissemination of information about public affairs efforts

In the third part of the questionnaire, the headquarters public affairs managers were asked to indicate the degree of headquarters and subsidiary involvement in each of these 18 tasks on 12 different international public affairs activities, the thought being that the nature of involvement would vary by issue. Unfortunately, this part of the questionnaire was viewed as being too long and complex to obtain reliable results. Nonetheless, results from the first two parts of the questionnaire show that among the companies responding subsidiary and headquarters managers do have somewhat different roles in the management of international public affairs. A fourth part of the questionnaire asked the respondents to indicate the degree of importance of these 12 international public affairs tasks to their companies.

Because of the low response rate and the lack of general acceptance of a precise definition of public affairs activities, the data gathered are only suggestive, not definitive. In addition, the questionnaire sought the perceptions of headquarters public affairs officers about the degree of involvement of both headquarters and subsidiary. Unfortunately, we were not able to obtain the views of subsidiary managers on the same issues. Nor were we able to obtain independent verification of the results using non-reactive research techniques. In sum the nature of the issues and the inadequacies of the questionnaire methodology have provided data which are not appropriately subjected to sophisticated statistical techniques. Even use of the chi square test seemed unwarranted, and therefore the data have been analyzed in the most simple way. Differences and magnitudes are stated in percentages, for we did not want to mislead the reader into thinking that there should be great confidence in the data.

RESULTS

The data about the level of headquarters and subsidiary involvement in international public affairs were analyzed in two ways, each yielding somewhat different results. Using one method, an average score on the five point scale for all respondents was computed, and these aggregate figures of headquarters and subsidiary scores compared for the major categories of formulation, implementation, and evaluation. As reported in Table 1, headquarters are slightly more involved than subsidiaries in the formulation of international public affairs policies, less involved in implementation of international public affairs and slightly more involved in evaluation.

TABLE 1. Aggregate Average Score on Level of Involvement
(on a 5 point scale) n = 30

|  | Headquarters | Subsidiary |
| --- | --- | --- |
| Formulation | 3.1 | 2.88 |
| Implementation | 2.69 | 2.89 |
| Evaluation | 2.65 | 2.53 |

However, this table indicates that based on headquarters managers' perceptions on the average neither headquarters nor subsidiary managers are very involved in international public affairs. The highest average score is 3.1 for headquarters involvement in formulation efforts and that is just slightly above "some involvement", the mid-point on the scale. This finding suggests that international public affairs is still a new function and not re-

325

ceiving the attention it should at either headquarters or subsidiary levels.

A second important result is that the function of evaluating international public affairs policies does not command much attention at either headquarters or subsidiaries. For both, the degree of involvement is aproximately mid-way between "little involvement" and "some involvement" on the scale. An implication is that managers of international public affairs need to develop and use mechanisms which will help them and other corporate managers to evaluate the effectiveness of public affairs efforts. Supplementary interviews have also indicated that few companies have attempted to establish techniques to measure or at least assess the performance of individual operating and staff managers on public affairs.

In sum, according to the perceptions of the respondents, headquarters managers are somewhat involved in the formulation of international public affairs policies; they are more likely to leave implementation to subsidiary managers; but then they do not follow through very energetically with procedures to determine whether the public affairs efforts have been successful. Subsidiary managers are also relatively inactive in the evaluation of their public affairs efforts. This lack of effective control measures at headquarters is of particular concern given the importance of environmental relations to successful operations and the ease with which public issues and company policy travel from subsidiary to subsidiary. Top management is beginning to demand results from the resources expended on international public affairs, for they are increasingly aware of the importance of developments in the environment to the successful operations of the subsidiary. Thus, the public affairs function needs effective control mechanisms which must be built upon the ability to evaluate the success of public affairs efforts and assess managerial performance.

A second method of analyzing the data sheds further light on the respective roles of headquarters and subsidiary managers in the management of international public affairs. In this method, average scores for each company respondent were computed for the major categories of formulation, implementation, and evaluation, and then headquarters and subsidiary averages compared by company. As shown in Table 2, this company-by-company comparison (as opposed to the aggregate comparison reported in Table 1) shows that headquarters managers are more deeply involved in the formulation process and somewhat more involved in evaluation than subsidiary managers. Subsidiaries are more active in the implementation of international public affairs.

TABLE 2. Company-by-Company Comparison of Degree of Involvement of Headquarters and Subsidiary Managers
(No. of Companies is the Unit) n = 30

|  | Greater Headquarters Involvement (by at least ½ point on scale | Approximately Equal Involvement | Greater Subsidiary Involvement (by at least ½ point on scale |
|---|---|---|---|
| Formulation | 13 | 9 | 8 |
| Implementation | 10 | 7 | 13 |
| Evaluation | 13 | 7 | 10 |

Further analysis of the data was accomplished by dividing the responding companies into thirds according to the average scores on the degree-of-involvement scale by headquarters and then by subsidiaries in international public affairs activities. This allowed a comparison of the most headquarters-involved companies with the least-involved ones on a number of different dimensions characteristic of the companies responding. Similarly, the top third of the most subsidiary-involved companies were compared with the bottom third on this dimension. The data for both types of analysis are reproduced in Table 3. In the dicussion that follows we will examine first the comparison between the most and least headquarters-involved companies.

Several of the corporate characteristic variables made little difference in the comparison of the most headquarters-involved companies with the least involved. The percent of corporate income from foreign operations was approximately the same for the top and bottom groups of companies. Similarly, overall size of companies as measured by corporate sales made little difference among the companies. In addition all respondents felt that moderate or substantial expansion overseas was likely for their firms, and there was no correlation with the most or least headquarters-involved companies. Incidentally, and perhaps surprisingly, none of the respondents felt that there would be contraction or even no expansion in overseas business operations. Also, there was no difference between the top third and bottom third of headquarters-involved corporations in terms of the acceptance of joint venture arrangements.

Contrary to intuition, the top third of the companies in terms of headquarters involvement earned on
the average only 18% of their foreign income from
the developing countries while for the bottom third,
on the average 34% of foreign income came from developing countries. It was thought that headquarters
would have a larger role to play where developing
country business was a more important part of the
total foreign activity because of the sensitivity of
many of these countries to foreign investment and
the volatile investment climates often associated
with these countries.

Although the average score on the degree of integration was approximately equal for the most- and least-
involved headquarters companies, 33% of the headquarters-involved companies were classified as
having a high degree of integration of foreign operations; only 8% of the least headquarters-active
companies were highly integrated. Highly integrated
multinational firms may be more vulnerable to problems in individual states and, therefore, greater
headquarters efforts may be necessary to ensure that
subsidiary public affairs activities contribute to
smooth and reliable operations.

Not surprisingly, respondents from the top third of
headquarters-involved firms felt that there was substantially more top management support for the international public affairs function (3.8 on a five
point scale) than the least headquarters-active
firm (2.8). This finding reinforces the belief of
many public affairs professionals that the commitment of top management is necessary for an active
international public affairs effort.

Similarly, the respondents at the most-involved
headquarters companies feel that international public affairs is slightly more centralized at their
companies than the traditional business activities
like marketing and production (1.75 on a three point
scale). In the least headquarters-involved companies, the score was 2.8, close to a unanimous opinion that international public affairs is less
centralized than the traditional functions.

Finally, the respondents were categorized according
to the type of business in which their companies were
engaged, and there were some striking differences in
comparing the top third of headquarters-active companies with the bottom third. Sixty-six percent of
the former were in consumer and service businesses;
only 50% of the bottom third were in these kinds of
businesses. Thirty-three percent of the former
characterized their businesses as being in high

technology; 67% of the least headquarters-active companies were in this category. None of the top third were in the extractive business, while 42% of the bottom third were. Given the nature of the sample, it is inappropriate to make definitive statements about this finding, but it is not surprising that firms which are consumer or service oriented would have more headquarters involvement in public affairs. In the first place, they are likely to be more marketing oriented, a function closely related to public affairs. Secondly, adoption of a low-profile strategy is not possible given their consumer and service-oriented characteristics. Thirdly, consumer and service firms generally face stiffer competition from local enterprises and are less welcome as foreign investors than either extractive or high-technology firms. These factors may require the consumer and service firms to adopt a more aggressive public affairs posture under the leadership of headquarters than firms in other lines of endeavor.

A similar analysis for the level of subsidiary involvement in international public affairs activities was also performed. Table 3 presents the results of this analysis and allows ready comparison with the level of headquarters involvement. While the most subsidiary-involved companies are substantially larger in terms of overall sales than the bottom third, not much significance should be ascribed to this. The fact that there are only 10 companies in each group means a very large or rather small company in terms of sales will greatly skew the results. Secondly, since this figure represents total world-wide sales including domestic U.S. acitivity, the theoretical relevance to international public affairs is not clear.

The top third of subsidiary-involved companies obtain on the average 37% of their income from foreign operations, the bottom third only 27%. This difference is in the direction expected, that is the more dependent a firm is on international earnings the higher the involvement level will be, but this is not substantiated by the headquarters-involvement analysis. The most involved subsidiary companies obtain a greater percentage of their earnings (79%) from advanced industrial states as opposed to developing countries than do the least involved subsidiary companies (68%). One interpretation of this is that subsidiaries in developed countries are more likely to be active in international public affairs because of the more highly developed social and political groups and systems which exhibit and convey concern about private enterprises to governments.

TABLE 3. Company Characteristics and Perceptions of Headquarters and Subsidiary Involvement in International Public Affairs

| | Level of Headquarters Involvement | | Level of Subsidiary Involvement | |
|---|---|---|---|---|
| | Top Third* | Bottom Third* | Top Third* | Bottom Third* |
| Average Company sales in billions | 5.8 | 7 | 13 | 4.3 |
| Average % of sales from foreign operations | 32 % | 30 % | 37 % | 27 % |
| Average of countries with subsidiaries | 39 | 29 | 34 | 35 |
| Average % of foreign income from LDCs | 18.4 % | 34 % | 21 % | 32 % |
| % of companies accepting of joint ventures | 77 % | 75 % | 80 % | 70 % |
| % of companies which are highly integrated | 33 % | 8 % | 40 % | 30 % |
| Average score on degree of expansion (5=substantial expansion; 1=substantial contraction) | 4.3 | 4.4 | 4.3 | 4.3 |
| Average score on top management support for international public affairs (5 = great deal of support; 1 = no support) | 3.8 | 2.8 | 4.1 | 2.9 |
| Average score on whether international (n = 27) public affairs is more or less centralized than other functions (1 = centralized; 3 = less centralized) | 1.75 | 2.8 | 2.4 | 2.0 |
| % of companies in extractive business | 0 % | 42 % | 30 % | 30 % |
| % of companies in capital goods manufacturing | 0 % | 17 % | 20 % | 20 % |
| % of companies in high technology | 33 % | 67 % | 60 % | 40 % |
| % of companies in intermediate goods manufacturing | 33 % | 50 % | 50 % | 50 % |
| % of companies in consumer goods manufacturing | 44 % | 33 % | 40 % | 20 % |
| % of companies in service industry | 22 % | 17 % | 20 % | 30 % |

* Because of tied rankings, the thirds are not equally divied into groups of 10.

Moreover, skilled public affairs professionals are more likely to be found in the advanced industrial states than in the developing countries.

While the difference is not nearly as dramatic, more of the top third countries are highly integrated (40%) than the bottom third (30%). Supporting this is the finding that none of the most-subsidiary involved companies were described as having little or no integration whereas 40% of the least involved companies had little or no integration. Again, highly integrated firms may require a more active posture in international public affairs in order to ensure that the company's inter-related functions are not disrupted by problems in any one of the component processes.

As in the headquarters-involvement analysis, the respondents for the top third of subsidiary-involved countries feel that international public affairs activities have much more support (4.1) from the higher echelons of management than do those working for the bottom third of the companies (2.9). Other corporate characteristics seem not to be particularly important in differentiating between the most and least subsidiary involved companies.

The analysis of the top and bottom thirds of subsidiary involved companies by industry types did not produce the same differences found in the headquarters involvement data. Particularly noteworthy is the fact that extractive companies were much more well-represented in the most active subsidiary category whereas no extractive companies appeared in the top echelon of headquarters involved companies. Again in distinction to the earlier analysis, there was a greater percentage of high technology companies in the top third group of subsidiary involved companies than in the bottom third. In addition, 60% of the top third companies were in the consumer and service industries, 50% in the bottom third. Because of the small numbers involved, it is risky to read too much into these data, but they do suggest a number of issues for future research.

One final set of data collected concerns the degree of importance of various international public affairs acitivites to the respondents' companies. Table 4 lists the issues in order of decending importance with their scores on a five point scale from not important (1) to very important (5).* This

---

* This list of international public affairs activities was developed from comments submitted by business executives and academics who are particularly active in the field.

TABLE 4.  Rank Ordering of International Public Af-
          fairs Activities According to Importance
          to Company

                              Average score on
                              5 point scale
                              from not impor-
                              tant (1) to very
                              important (5)

1. General maintenance of government relations including monitoring of legislative and regulatory developments                    4.0

2. Tracking, understanding, and
   developing responses to major
   social, political, and economic
   trends and changes                      4.0

3. Developing and promoting public
   affairs consciousness and skills
   among subsidiary managers               3.83

4. Re-negotiations with host government on terms of investment such as
   remittances, export/import matters,
   transfer of technology, etc.            3.77

5. Negotiations with host government
   for investment expansion, investment reduction, or divestment           3.73

6. Re-negotiations with host government
   regarding local participation in
   ownership                               3.67

7. Maintenance of relations with critical interest groups, political parties, universities, etc.                3.47

8. Maintenance of relations with media    3.37

9. Measuring and communicating about
   company contributions to host state     3.23

10. Labor contract negotiations            3.13

11. Maintenance of relations with inter-
    national and regional organizations
    like U.N., OECD, etc.                  2.93

12. Development of corporate posture
    during and after election or change
    in government                          2.90

information is not directly relevant to the question of headquarters subsidiary relationships, but it does indicate what headquarters public affairs officers think are critical public affairs activities. Their responses to this list exhibit a surprisingly high degree of importance with only two items being slightly below the mid point of "important".

It is noteworthy that items 2 and 3 are somewhat more process or managerially oriented than most of the other "more important" items on the list which tend to be more substantive in nature. The broadguaged tracking function, item 2, is ranked at the top along with government relations. This is encouraging, for this suggests that the professionals who responded to the questionnaire see themselves as having a long range managerial function, not just solely a reactive role relating to the environment.

Even more surprising and encouraging is the high ranking given to item 3, developing and promoting public affairs consciousness and skills among subsidiary managers. This activity is an internal managerial function which suggests recognition of the need for the public affairs professional to work with his or her own operating managers to increase their public affairs effectiveness. Effective public affairs must include the operating managers at subsidiaries, and the high degree of importance ascribed to this function provides evidence that the profession is viewing itself as having a critical internal managerial role in addition to its traditional external orientation.

CONCLUSION

This preliminary investigation points to a number of areas for further corporate analysis and policy-oriented research. The major findings are that generally headquarters and subsidiary involvement in international public affairs is only moderate. Even more striking is the relatively low level of involvement in the evaluation function of international public affairs managment as both top management and host country officials demand more effective relationships between corporation and country. Moreover, as subsidiaries are given the responsibility for implementing public affairs efforts, mechanisms for assessing their managers and their programs will become increasingly important.

The research suggests that the most deeply involved companies at either the headquarters or subsidiary level obtain a higher percentage of their income from developed countries than from developing countries. On the one hand one would think that more attention would have to be paid to the more volatile developing country environments, but perhaps this finding reflects the more highly developed interest representation systems in advanced industrial states, the generally larger investment in developed countries, or the more advanced stage of public affairs management in the developed world.

The degree of transnational corporation integration seems to be a potentially important factor in the level of headquarters and subsidiary involvement in the management of international public affairs. However, the importance of corporate characteristics like size of company, percent of sales from foreign operations, and number of countries where subsidiaries are located is not clear. The nature of company activity seems also to have the potential to affect the level of involvement in international public affairs management, but the sample was too small to allow for definitive relationships to emerge. Nonetheless, consumer and service oriented companies may be more active in public affairs management at headquarters, at least, than extractive companies. Industry comparison studies would be helpful in investigating these relationships more effectively.

While it may appear to be tautological, the data do suggest that top management support for international public affairs activities is an important ingredient in bringing about greater headquarters and subsidiary involvement in the management of international public affairs. One implication of this is that given the appropriate encouragement (and resources one would expect) managers can undertake to develop and maintain effective relations with the company's environment.

Elsewhere I have addressed at length the issue of how transnational corporations can manage the international public affairs function, and this publication is not the appropriate place to examine the components of effective management in greater depth.* However, the function is important, and a few academics and especially corporate managers are creatively pursuing the task of developing a managerial orientation to external affairs. An important part of such efforts is the allocation of responsibilities and tasks between headquarters and subsidiary managers.

---

*   David H. Blake, Managing the external Relations of Multinational Corporations (New York: Fund for Multinational Management Education, 1977).

The findings reported above are based on the views of international public affairs officers at the headquarters of thirty U.S.-based transnational corporations. The sample is small, diverse in terms of company characteristics, and reflects the bias of headquarters managers. Thus the results can only indicate general trends and provide suggestions for further research. However, future studies will also be hindered by the developing nature of the field, meaning that the rapid rate of change and the lack of agreed upon structure and even definition of terms will raise questions about the reliability and validity of any results.

Moreover, as new public affairs issues arise, as corporate managers are able to develop more sophisticated approaches to the management of external affairs, and as there is greater acceptance of the function, the practice of international public affairs management will change dramatically. The relative roles of headquarters and subsidiary personnel will also change. In spite of these changes and the difficulty of conducting rigorous research studies in such a rapidly developing area, the management of public affairs in transnational corporations is too important for the corporations and for the host countries to shy away from efforts to understand this critical managerial function.

REFERENCES

APTER, David E. and GOODMAN, Louis Wolf, eds. The
     Multinational Corporation and Social
     Change. New York Praeger Publishers, 1976.

BLACK, Robert; BLANK, Stephen and HANSON, Elizabeth
     C., Multinationals in Contention: Responses
     at Governmental and International Levels.
     New York: The Conference Board, 1978.

BLAKE, David H., International Public Affairs Pro-
     grams for the 1980's. Washington: Founda-
     tion for Public Affairs, 1978.

BLAKE, David H., Managing the External Relations of
     Multinational Corporations. New York: Fund
     for Multinational Management Education,
     1977.

BLAKE, David H. and DRISCOLL, Robert E., The Social
     and Economic Impacts of Transnational
     Corporations: Case Studies of the U.S.
     Paper Industry in Brazil. New York: Fund
     for Multinational Management Education,
     1977.

BOARMAN, Patrick M. and SCHOLLHAMMER, Hans., Multi-
     national Corporations and Governments:
     Business-Government Relations in an Inter-
     national Context. New York: Praeger Pub-
     lishers, 1975.

Business International S.A. Corporate External
     Affairs: Blueprint for Survival. Switzer-
     land, 1975.

DOZ, Yves L. and PRAHALAD, C.K., "How MNCs Cope with
     Host Government Intervention." Harvard
     Business Review, 58 (March-April, 1980).

DUNN, S. Watson, CAHILL, Martin F. and BODDEWYN,
     Jean J., How Fifteen Transnational Corpora-
     tions Manage Public Affairs. Chicago: Crain
     Books, 1979.

FAYERWEATHER, John., International Business-Govern-
     ment Affairs: Toward an Era of Accommoda-
     tion. Cambridge, Mass.: Ballinger, 1973.

FAYERWEATHER, John and KAPOOR, Ashok., Strategy and
     Negotiation for the International Corpora-
     tion. Cambridge, Mass.: Ballinger, 1976.

HARGREAVES, John and DAUMAN, Jan., Business Survival and Social Change: A Practical Guide to Responsibility and Partnership. New York: Halsted Press, 1975.

HUMBLE, John., The Responsible Multinational Enterprise. London: Foundation for Business Responsibilities, 1975.

HUTZEL, John M., Strategy Formulation in the Multinational Business Environment:A Guide to International Political Forecasting. San Jose, Calif.: Institute for Business and Economic Research, 1976.

LaPALOMBARA, Joseph and BLANK, Stephen., Multinational Corporations and National Elites: A Study in Tensions. New York: The Conference Board, Inc., 1976.

LaPALOMBARA, Joseph and BLANK, Stephen., Multinational Corporations in Comparative Perspective. New York: The Conference Board, Inc., 1977.

THUNELL, Lars H., Political Risks in International Business: Investment Behavior of Multinational Corporations. New York: Praeger Publishers, 1977.

TRUITT, Nancy S. and BLAKE, David H., Opinion Leaders and Private Investment: An Attitude Survey in Chile and Venezuela. New York: Fund for MultinaionalManagement Education, 1976.

United Nations. Centre on Transnational Corporations. Survey of Research on Transnational Corporations. ST/CTC/3) (1977).

WALTER, Ingo and GLADWIN, Thomas N., Multinationals Under Fire: Lessons in the Management of Conflict. New York: John Wiley and Sons, 1980 (forthcoming).

# 15 Lars Otterbeck:

Book Title

## : Concluding Remarks
## — And a Review of
## Subsidiary Autonomy

CULTURAL BIAS

In the introductory chapter I ventured to say that
this volume introduces other biases than the most
prevalent American bias in analyzing MNCs. The obser-
vant reader may, however, have noticed that although
several authors were not Americans and a large part
of the empirical data stemmed from European and
Japanese firms, the American influence is great. It
can be seen in the lists of references and it can be
deducted from the frameworks utilized. It also reflects the fact that the object under study, i.e.
MNCs from any country, is strongly influenced by how
US firms are organized. The profound impact on the
market for management consulting and advice that is
derived from reference objects of a large and dominant home market cannot be neglected. Success of
course is not to be forgotten.

There are, however, important cultural biases that,
probably unconsciously, are introduced when recommendations from American or American-influenced consultants are implemented.

One way to gain further insight into this is by going
back to the collective data base, parts of which were
used in the articles above by Hedlund, Welge, Negandhi & Baliga, Leksell, and Otterbeck. It will be re-
called that an identical questionnaire was used in
interviews with headquarter managers as well as subsidiary managers of MNCs from the US, Japan, Germany,
the UK, and Sweden. The total sample is described in
table 1. All the companies are large industrial firms.
They are spread over several industries, with a similar pattern for all countries. They show a mixture of
organizational forms, ranging from mother-daughter
structures through various forms of divisional ar-

Institute of International Business, Stockholm School
of Economics

rangements, with or without international divisions, to formal matrices. There is no clear country pattern here either.

TABLE 1.    Sample Characteristics

|          | ≠ SUB's | ≠ MNC's | ≠ Countries |
|----------|---------|---------|-------------|
| Overall  | 158     | 39      | 16          |
| U.S.     | 34      | 9       | 7           |
| Japan    | 41      | 14      | 6           |
| Germany  | 45      | 6       | 7           |
| U.K.     | 14      | 4       | 10          |
| Sweden   | 24      | 6       | 10          |

So, although not entirely justified, let us assume that the only difference between the 39 firms and their 158 foreign subsidiaries (some of which are partly owned) is their home country. Any differences in their way of managing their HQ-subsidiary relations would then be attributable to their home country origin.

Table 2 summarizes how much influence the subsidiary has on fifteen sets of decisions. The issue of subsidiary autonomy is particularly well suited for this kind of intercountry comparison. It is not a decision variable like organization structure, formal reporting requirements or nationality of the subsidiary managing director. MNC managements do not sit down and decide on how much autonomy they shall grant their foreign subsidiaries. They decide on other things. These decisions and some other characteristics of the way the day-to-day relationships are handled together form a pattern which we may call autonomy. Therefore we may see subsidiary autonomy as one reflection of certain, as yet not well defined, country characteristics.

Table 3 shows a condensed version of Table 2. Here also the influence of HQ is shown. From this table it is very clear that the American companies are extreme in that they grant their subsidiaries very little autonomy. All other home countries seem fairly similar, with Sweden taking the other extreme position.

The way influence is measured here does not presuppose a "zero-sum" game between HQ and subsidiaries (cf. chapters 1 and 2). They may both perceive they have high influence. The UK firms would be the ones that have best mastered the task of maximizing total influence, if the sum of HQ influence and subsidiary influence could be taken as an indication. Be that as

TABLE 2. <u>The 15 Autonomy Items</u>: "How much influence does your subsidiary management have on the following sets of decisions:..."*)

| Item | Code | Overall | Mean Scores U.S. | Japan | Germany | Sweden | U.K. |
|---|---|---|---|---|---|---|---|
| Personnel training program for your subsidiary | SUBTRAIN | 4.4 | 3.8 | 4.6 | 4.5 | 4.3 | 4.6 |
| Layoffs of operating personnel | SUBFIRE | 4.6 | 4.4 | 4.9 | 4.4 | 4.6 | 4.8 |
| Use of expatriate personnel from headquarters | SUBEXP | 3.2 | 2.7 | 3.6 | 2.4 | 3.7 | 4.3 |
| Appointment of chief executive of your sub. | SUBCEO | 2.3 | 1.5 | 2.8 | 1.7 | 3.2 | 2.9 |
| Maintenance of production facilities at subsidiary | SUBMAIN | 4.2 | 3.3 | 4.3 | 4.8 | 4.5 | 4.1 |
| Determining aggregate production schedule | SUBPROD | 4.0 | 3.2 | 4.2 | 4.3 | 4.1 | 4.5 |
| Expansion of your production capacity | SUBCAP | 3.1 | 2.5 | 3.5 | 2.7 | 3.4 | 4.5 |
| Use of local advertising agency | SUBAD | 4.5 | 3.9 | 4.7 | 4.5 | 5.0 | 4.2 |
| Servicing of products sold | SUBSERV | 4.7 | 4.4 | 4.7 | 4.7 | 4.6 | 5.0 |
| Pricing on products sold on your local market | SUBPRICE | 4.0 | 3.0 | 4.5 | 4.0 | 4.1 | 4.9 |
| Introduction of a new product on your local market | SUBNEW | 3.5 | 2.6 | 4.1 | 3.1 | 3.8 | 4.4 |
| Choice of public accountant | SUBCPA | 3.7 | 2.7 | 4.6 | 4.4 | 3.0 | 3.5 |
| Extension of your credit to one of your major customers | SUBCRED | 4.3 | 3.7 | 4.5 | 4.3 | 4.6 | 4.7 |
| Use of cash flow in your subsidiary | SUBCASH | 3.8 | 3.2 | 4.2 | 3.4 | 4.5 | 4.5 |
| Your borrowing from local banks or financial inst's | SUBBANK | 3.6 | 3.2 | 3.6 | 3.4 | 4.5 | 4.1 |
| Average (means) | | 3.86 | 3.21 | 4.19 | 3.77 | 4.13 | 4.33 |

*/ The responses were pre-coded from "1" for "Very little or no influence" to "5" for "Very high influence".

TABLE 3. Relative Influence over Decision Areas: Averages*/

| Country of HQ | Subsidiary Influence | HQ Influence | Difference |
|---|---|---|---|
| Overall | 3.86 | 2.81 | 1.05 |
| U.S. | 3.21 | 3.10 | .11 |
| Japan | 4.19 | 2.69 | 1.50 |
| Germany | 3.77 | 2.75 | 1.02 |
| Sweden | 4.13 | 2.52 | 1.61 |
| U.K. | 4.33 | 2.98 | 1.35 |

*/ The figures in the Table represent mean values across the 15 decision areas identified in Table 2. As in Table 2 a value of "1" indicates "Very little or no influence", while a value of "5" stands for "Very high influence".

it may, the fact remains that managements of non-US MNCs seem to grant their subsidiaries higher autonomy than those of US MNCs and still they are heavily influenced by American management theory and management education, in absence of any acceptable alternative. All so called international business schools teach American management.

Taking our analysis one step further we might look at Table 4. Here correlation coefficients between the mean levels of autonomy for the fifteen decision areas are shown.

The table indicates quite clearly that US management practices are indeed the norm (correlation coefficient between the overall sample and the US being the highest of them all or .95). Each of the individual countries also correlates quite strongly with the US. That is, although the US mean level of autonomy is far from any other country's, the pattern of HQ-subsidiary relations, as measured here, for every home-country closely resembles that of the US. I see this as a very strong indication of the existence of one worldwide norm for managing MNCs, accepted and used by "all", but with strong national biases.

Germany and Japan also closely resemble the general pattern and, even more, resemble one another. The two most dissimilar home countries are Germany and the UK, whereas Sweden shows very little similarity with Japan. Turning back to the previous level we find, however, that Sweden and Japan are the two countries that give their subsidiaries the highest autonomy.

Whether one would explain these findings by focusing on the role of the language ("everybody" speaks

English, "nobody" Japanese or Swedish), the remaining
traditions from old Caesarian times (Germany and
Japan) or codetermination movements (Sweden) and
strong unions (Sweden and the UK) shall not be dwelt
upon here. A fuller treatment of these subjects is
given elsewhere[1]. The point to be made here was only
the strong US impact which is given nationally biased
interpretation and that one must look rather closely,
i.e. beyond organization charts and policy statements
to find the reality of HQ-subsidiary relations.

TABLE 4. Correlation Coefficents between mean levels of autonomy*/
for different countries

|  | Overall | U.S. | Japan | Germany | Sweden | U.K. |
|---|---|---|---|---|---|---|
| Overall | 1.0 (0) S=0.001 | 0.95 (15) S=0.001 | 0.93 (15) S=0.001 | 0.92 (15) S=0.001 | 0.77 (15) S=0.001 | 0.69 (15) S=0.002 |
| U.S. | 0.95 (15) S=0.001 | 1.0 (0) S=0.001 | 0.82 (15) S=0.001 | 0.80 (15) S=0.001 | 0.82 (15) S=0.001 | 0.71 (15) S=0.001 |
| Japan | 0.93 (15) S=0.001 | 0.82 (15) S=0.001 | 1.0 (0) S=0.001 | 0.90 (15) S=0.001 | 0.56 (15) S=0.015 | 0.60 (15) S=0.008 |
| Germany | 0.92 (15) S=0.001 | 0.80 (15) S=0.001 | 0.90 (15) S=0.001 | 1.0 (0) S=0.001 | 0.59 (15) S=0.009 | 0.48 (15) S=0.034 |
| Sweden | 0.77 (15) S=0.001 | 0.82 (15) S=0.001 | 0.56 (15) S=0.015 | 0.59 (15) S=0.009 | 1.0 (0) S=0.001 | 0.59 (15) S=0.010 |
| U.K. | 0.69 (15) S=0.002 | 0.71 (15) S=0.001 | 0.60 (15) S=0.008 | 0.48 (15) S=0.034 | 0.59 (15) S=0.010 | 1.0 (0) S=0.001 |

(coefficient/(cases)/significance)

*/ Given in Table 2.

1/ Hedlund G., Johansson, J.K. and Otterbeck, L.
with the collaboration of Edström, A., Negandhi,
A.N. and Welge, M.K., "Autonomy of subsidiaries
in multinational companies". Research paper IIB,
submitted for publication.

- All tables here and part of the analysis are
taken from this paper.

## MANAGING MATRIX BUSINESSES

The most difficult administrative challenge to the
MNC seems to be the need for a multiple focus. By
definition an MNC operates in several countries. Most
of them are also active within more than one product
line, some in several. In a way all the articles in
this book have been concerned with corporations with
a need for multiple focus. Some have specifically
addressed the organizational structural problems in
such companies, namely Bartlett, Kagono, and Prahalad
& Doz. I think we may now begin to see some emerging
normative implications from these and other studies
on MNC structures.

First, beware of formal matrices. Most managers find
it frustrating and confusing to have two bosses.
Probably only very large (because of the costs involved) and very formalistic companies would be well
adviced to try it or even to keep it. One might argue
that also the least formalistic ones would find it
easy to operate in a matrix structure. But, then, what
would a matrix be in an informal structure? Everybody
is used to confusion, or organic structures, as the
term might be. The skill to operate in the matrix
mode was mentioned earlier. A firm where people have
this capacity may function quite well with almost any
structure (cf. Bartlett's article). How one develops
that skill is not finally answered. Kagono suggests
that there may be something in the Japanese management tradition that helps. Proponents of codetermination in Germany or Sweden might say that true codetermination gives employees the insight, feel for
responsibility and capacity to see further than the
immediate consequences of actions and decisions
needed for operating in the matrix mode. I would say
that only education can give employees this capacity,
unless, which is a fascinating thought, some countries have it embedded in their culture. But for the
rest of us education, meaning not only lectures or
courses but also mixed careers, giving the employee
the chance to see new perspectives, and on-the-job-
training in projects, working teams etc outside the
current position would be needed.

Second, some strategies are simply too complex for a
firm to effectively manage. One might be able to
create immensely complex, but logical, systems to
manage immensely complex and maybe logical strategies. But people who are put to manage these super-
systems cannot effectively handle the complexities.
Interestingly the current trend seems to be away from
the conglomerates of the 1960's. Instead one often
tries to create firms with rather simple strategies.
Alternatively, if there is a strong financial link or
ownership link, it seems as if only financial control
is left to the corporate central body and very auto-

nomous divisions are formed which are left to form
their own business strategies. Indeed the portfolio
theory of corporate strategy, so much en vogue in the
late 1970's suggests precisely that.

Third, HQ's capacity to control its subsidiaries is
to a large extent a function of what HQ has to offer.
Typically, early in a product's life cycle, HQ possesses all the relevant knowledge and effectively controls everything. The more mature a product becomes,
the more HQ will have to rely on administered systems
for control, now deriving from the implied right the
owner has rather than from HQ's superior relevant
knowledge. Hence, the norm would be to also secure
control through administrative mechanisms early on.
Sooner or later, subsidiaries, not to talk about host
countries, will not accept such efforts. Another
implication is, of course, that as long as HQ does
possess unique and demanded knowledge (usually technology), control from the center can be achieved.
And, when HQ does not possess such technology, control
from the center is no longer necessary.

OWNERSHIP POLICIES

I have not got much to add here since most of it was
said already in the previous chapter. Let me only re-
peat that it seems to be clear that shared ownership
and shared control over productive resources seem to
become inevitable in the years to come. Not because
it secures effective management. I believe it does
not. But because the tensions between the industrial,
efficiency-oriented culture of a well-run MNC and the
self-reliant, tradition-conscious culture of a well-
run nation so far seem to lead to a demand from the
latter for shared ownership. How that is to be managed to avoid inefficiencies was the subject of a few
articles, as well as alternative strategies on the
part of the MNC in the light of such demands. (Holton, Otterbeck, Brooke & Holly.)

Finally, it needs to be said again, the world will
need effective multinational production and distribution systems that need some form of central coordination and control. The world also needs safe, stable
and ethnically aware nation states where people find
that life is dignified and their national heritage is
respected. I refuse to see these tensions as simple
zero-sum games. There are ways of managing the tensions to the benefit of both parties. An indepth
understanding of how MNCs actually function is a
necessary ingredient in the search for these ways of
managing.